Principles of Retirement Planning
Editor's Update

W9-BHT-041

In late August, 1996, a number of new bills were signed into law that amended several Internal Revenue Code provisions related to health insurance and qualified retirement plans. These changes are noted in the booklet that accompanies this text. In addition, the following changes have taken place since this text was published:

Chapter 4: Social Security

For 1997, the *earnings limitation* (i.e., the amount one can earn before Social Security benefits are reduced) has increased to $8,640 for those under age 65 and $13,500 for those between the ages of 65 and 69.

Chapter 7: Corporate Qualified Plans

The *defined benefit dollar limit* has increased to $125,000, effective 1997. The *defined contribution limit* remains at $30,000/25 percent of compensation.

The annual limit on *elective employee deferrals* to 401(k) plans is now $9,500, and will remain so through 1997.

Chapter 8: Individual Retirement Plans

The *minimum annual compensation limit* for participation in a SEP is $400, and will remain so through 1997.

Annual deferrals to TSA plans are limited to $9,500, at least through 1997.

Chapter 11: Health Care and Health Insurance

In 1997, the Medicare Part A deductible increased to $760. The co-payment amounts increased to $190 per day (for the 61st to 90th day) and $380 per day (for the 91st to 150th day). The daily co-payment for skilled nursing facility benefits after 20 days is $95.

For 1997, the Medicare Part B deductible remains at $100.

> *Note: If you are taking this course through our Supervised Study program for continuing education or other credit, you will not be tested on this new information.*

December 2, 1996

PRINCIPLES OF
RETIREMENT PLANNING

Dearborn
R&R Newkirk
a division of Dearborn Financial Publishing, Inc.

This publication is designed to provide accurate and authoritative information in regard to the subject matter covered. It is sold with the understanding that the publisher is not engaged in rendering legal, accounting, or other professional service. If legal advice or other expert assistance is required, the services of a competent professional person should be sought.

This text is updated periodically to reflect changes in laws and regulations. To verify that you have the most recent update, you may call Dearborn•R&R Newkirk at 1-800-423-4723.

Project Editor: Debra M. Hall
Interior Design: Lucy Jenkins
Cover Design: Tessing Designs, Inc.

Published by Dearborn•R&R Newkirk,
a division of Dearborn Financial Publishing, Inc.

Printed in the United States of America.

Seventh printing, December 1996

Library of Congress Cataloging-in-Publication Data

Principles of retirement planning.
     p.   cm.
   ISBN 0-7931-1176-5
   1. Retirement—United States—Planning.   2. Retirement income—
United States—Planning.   I. Dearborn•R&R Newkirk.
HQ1063.2.U6P75   1993
332.024′01—dc20
                                                    92-41257
                                                      CIP

■■■■■ Table of Contents

▪▪▪▪▪ Acknowledgments

T he publisher wishes to acknowledge and thank Carla Gordon, CFP, CEBS, of Constructive Financial Planning and Training, as the principal author of this text. Ms. Gordon currently designs training materials and presents training in various areas of financial planning for financial services professionals.

We also wish to thank the following individuals for their perceptive reviews, comments and recommendations, which were invaluable in the development of this text:

Eugene K. Ingalls, CLU, ChFC
Errold F. Moody Jr., BSCE, LLB, MBA, MSFP, PhD
Richard J. Moore, LUTCF
Ann Myers, CLU

····· Introduction

Retirement planning consists primarily of estimating one's future income and other needs and then determining how to meet those needs when one is no longer working. Although many people will rely on Social Security and employer-sponsored retirement plans for retirement income, they also realize that supplemental sources probably are necessary to maintain a suitable lifestyle in retirement. With the realization that they will spend 20 years or more in retirement, many people are looking for professional advice about ways to fund a comfortable retirement.

As a life agent, you can be an important source of retirement planning information for your clients. Our objective in writing *Principles of Retirement Planning* is to familiarize you with the retirement planning process; to impart a good understanding of that process; and to give you a comfort and security level that will motivate you to interest your clients in retirement planning. The text provides you with methods to assess your clients' postretirement needs and income and suggests ways to plug any gaps you may find.

An understanding of the retirement planning process offers you an opportunity to not only be of service to your current clients, but also to earn additional income by selling more products to a wider range of clients. Although this *Principles of Retirement Planning* text will provide you with an introduction to the retirement planning process, this course alone cannot make you a seasoned retirement planner. But it will help you take a major step in that direction.

On a final note, we hope that the material in this text will give you a foundation on which to build a better understanding of your clients' retirement needs and, in the process, improve upon the important range of services you offer to your clients as a life insurance professional.

Diane M. Lamyotte, CPCU, AU
Editor

1 Introduction to Retirement Planning

R etirement planning today is quite different from that of yesterday. In fact, some could argue that in the past, there was not much "planning" to be done. At one time, retirees did not have high expectations—a company pension and Social Security were about all that were necessary for a comfortable retirement. A retiree's income was not subject to steady erosion by inflation. And, because a retiree could expect to live only about five years into retirement before dying, there was little need—and little opportunity—to actively plan his or her future financial affairs. Such is not the case today. Increasingly, Americans are becoming aware of certain retirement realities. Many are apprehensive about the financial problems they may face during their retirement years. This, in turn, offers tremendous opportunity for the retirement planner.

■ ■ ■ ■ ■

■ THE IMPORTANCE OF RETIREMENT PLANNING

This opening chapter focuses on the importance of retirement planning for every person, regardless of income or social status. You will see how agents working in the retirement planning market can assist clients in preparing a comprehensive and effective retirement plan. We will begin our discussion with the growing need for retirement planning services and the important role the life insurance agent can play in this arena. Those who want to become actively involved in this market must wear many hats in order to create a financial plan to help clients achieve their goals. In addition, we will introduce ways to help you master the art of retirement planning.

Why is retirement planning important? We will answer this question throughout the text, but to begin, consider the following: At one time, the 65-and-older age group were considered to be "old." For many people, old age and retirement meant a few years of declining activity, followed by chronic illness and finally death. But, thanks to medical technology and better health care, people are living much longer after retirement. In fact, by the middle of the 21st century, the 76 million "baby boomers" (those born between 1946 and 1964), will be retired and will constitute one-fourth of the population. Without cash inflows from savings and adequate retirement planning, these future retirees should be as concerned about living "too long" and outliving their financial resources as they are about dying too soon.

Some people begin to plan for their retirement as soon as they begin their first job, but most people wait until their 40s and 50s to begin their retirement planning. They may feel that saving for retirement will be easier after the children have left home and expenditures decrease. By waiting they may reach their peak earning power and be able to set more aside. Unfortunately, however, the money saved will have fewer years to earn interest or accumulate returns until it is needed for retirement.

Many people feel that retirement planning is only for the wealthy, but nothing could be further from the truth. Everyone can benefit from an effective retirement plan to help them maintain a comfortable standard of living after retirement. Retirement planning is important for several reasons:

- Even with an employer-sponsored retirement plan and Social Security benefits, an individual and his or her spouse may not have adequate funds to maintain a preretirement standard of living during the retirement years. Changes in tax rates, interest rates and inflation rates will affect spending power.

- Although statistics regarding medical care for older Americans may be improving, many individuals and couples over age 65 still have to deal with poor health during their retirement years. Poor health means increased medical bills for services, medicine and equipment. For example, an extended hospital stay or round-the-clock nursing care can quickly deplete a lifetime of savings.

- A person's cost of living does not automatically decline at retirement. In many cases, routine living expenses, such as rent, utilities and food, may consume all the available dollars. There is nothing left for "luxuries," such as travel and entertainment.

- Employer-sponsored retirement plans rarely provide 100 percent of the income needed for retirement. Even under the most generous employer-sponsored retirement plans, the employer typically replaces only a fraction of an employee's salary. Even retiring executives with special arrangements, such as deferred compensation plans, may face shortfalls.

- People who count heavily on Social Security benefits for retirement income and financial security are sure to face pitfalls. Social Security provides a minimum benefit, its intent being to replace only a portion of an individual's preretirement income. In fact, the higher an individual's pay, the less he or she will receive proportionately in Social Security retirement benefits. Furthermore, the future capacity of the Social Security system is in question. The system may be unable to support economic strains in the wake of the large "baby boomer" generation retiring as a group.

- Inflation is a very real problem. Although the general trend is upward, prices have risen faster in some years than in others. Rising prices mean that retired individuals on fixed incomes have to struggle to replace their decreased purchasing power.

■ THE ART OF RETIREMENT PLANNING

Today's retirement planner recognizes that successful retirement planning is a multi-faceted, complex undertaking. The effective professional must have a knowledge of financial planning and retirement-related topics as well as an understanding of how to apply this knowledge to each client's unique situation. He or she must be able to help prospects identify their goals and then develop strategies to meet those goals.

Counseling clients about achieving their financial and personal objectives requires a great deal of skill and sensitivity. The client must be comfortable enough with the planner to answer a series of personal questions. For example, in order to formulate a retirement plan, the retirement planner may begin by asking a prospect three basic questions:

1. What do you have now?

2. What do you want to have in the future?

3. How do you currently plan to get what you want?

The answers to these questions will help the planner determine an appropriate plan for that prospect.

Although many prospects have successful careers, they probably also have a mortgage, bills to pay, children to educate and concerns about their financial future. They may wonder about how they can achieve important financial objectives such as maintaining their preretirement standard of living, becoming economically self-sufficient or minimizing taxes on retirement distributions. Among their personal objectives, clients may be concerned about taking care of a dependent parent or the special health needs of a spouse or child during both the preretirement and postretirement years. Many will feel they lack the disposable income, discipline or commitment to save for retirement.

The retirement planner must be able to understand an individual's financial and personal objectives, attitudes and preferences. He or she must then use this information to help the person choose from among various planning alternatives. Because meeting an individual's needs and objectives requires a variety of skills, including understanding, careful analysis and compassion, retirement planning is often more an art than a science.

ILL. 1.1 ■ Sources of Retirement Income

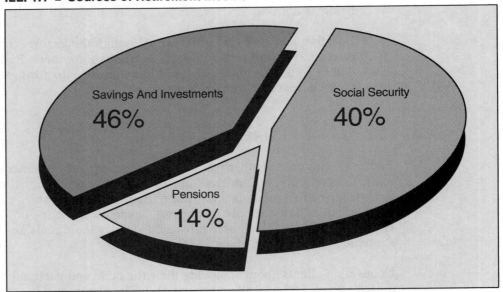

■ THE ROLE OF THE RETIREMENT PLANNER

The growing awareness of the need to plan for retirement has created a large market for today's life insurance agent along with unique opportunities for sales and service. A recent study by the Social Security Administration revealed that a retiree's income is provided as follows:

Social Security	40 percent
Pensions	14 percent
Savings and Investments	46 percent

Thus, as you can see, much of a retiree's income—46 percent—comes from *personal* investments and savings. A large part of that income is spent on long-term health care. The average annual cost of nursing home care is approximately $30,000. If inflation continues at current levels—approximately 4 percent—these annual costs are expected to reach more than $86,500 by the year 2020.

It is the role of the retirement planner to assist the client by developing a financial profile, determining retirement needs and developing strategies to meet those needs. Individuals who work in the retirement market know that finances, although vitally important, are only one of many issues the client must face. These professionals must take a broad view of retirement planning, and put financial matters into a proper context.

It is important to understand that financial matters cannot and should not be separated from personal and emotional issues. Although the focus of the retirement planner's recommendations may be financial, he or she may also be asked to act as an adviser about the nonfinancial aspects of retirement. For example, a client who has no hobbies or interests other than work may find himself or herself feeling "useless" after retirement. A financial planner who can suggest

ILL. 1.2 ■

Current Trends in Retirement Planning

Current trends and realities in retirement planning point to one conclusion: an individual's future financial security depends on what he or she does now. Those who understand the need to plan now and start saving now will be those who can look forward to a comfortable retirement.

What's Happening	What It Means
• *People are living longer.*	The average life expectancy for 65-year-olds is almost 20 years; future generations of retirees can expect to live this long and longer. This means retirees will have to provide for living expenses over a longer lifetime.
• *Inflation is a fact of life.*	Even at modest levels, inflation has a severe impact on fixed costs. If the cost of living rose at a steady 5 percent a year, the spending power of a $35,000 fixed income would be reduced by over 60 percent in 20 years.
• *Couples are postponing having children until they are well into their 30s.*	The major financial commitment of funding a child's education will come when the couple is in their 50s—traditionally the time devoted to saving heavily for retirement.
• *Social Security benefits may be scaled back.*	In the next two decades, the baby boom generation will move into retirement. It is estimated that this future swell of retirees will be supported by a greatly reduced workforce, requiring changes in the way Social Security benefits are funded. In anticipation of this, Congress has steadily increased the tax on earnings and has extended the age at which a worker can receive full benefits. Normal retirement age for individuals born after 1938 will rise gradually to 67 by the year 2026.
• *Employers are cutting back on health benefits for their retirees.*	Although many companies now pay part or all of a retiree's health insurance, this trend will probably not continue into the 21st century. Health costs typically increase about 20 percent per year—a cost that most companies will be unwilling to absorb. Retirees may soon have to pay a larger percentage (or perhaps all) of the cost of their group health insurance.
• *Fewer and fewer companies are offering defined benefit plans.*	The defined benefit pension plan, which promises a specific monthly benefit to retiring employees and places the burden for assuring the benefit on the employer, is being replaced by other types of plans, such as defined contribution plans. These plans do not guarantee any specific future benefits; in fact, many require that the employee assume much of the responsibility for his or her future payout, since the employee must contribute to the plan and/or direct how the funds are to be invested.

worthwhile activities, such as volunteering, to a client may provide the greatest single enhancement to that individual's retirement. The successful retirement planner will strive to meet the client's financial, personal and emotional needs to assure a happy, comfortable retirement.

When formulating a retirement plan the planner must address three key areas:

1. Determine how much income will be needed and how a client can accumulate that income;

2. Evaluate health care and health care insurance coverages; and

3. Formulate an estate plan for wealth distribution.

Each of these areas will be discussed in greater detail in later chapters; however, the retirement planner's function is briefly discussed in the next sections.

Develop a Financial Profile

Before the retirement planner can develop a retirement strategy, he or she must analyze a client's current financial situation and financial resources in relation to future retirement goals and objectives. The planner often begins by analyzing a client's financial statements and budget. An *income statement* shows where the client has been financially over a certain time period (usually one year); a *balance sheet* shows the current financial position; a *budget* expresses where the client would like to be in the future. These financial statements give the planner an indication of the client's available financial resources.

The financial planner will ask about the type of savings and investment program the client wishes to establish. Such a program should take into account the client's short-term and long-term objectives. It should also consider the client's feelings about the investment factors of risk, growth, liquidity and income. In addition the planner must ask about the client's future plans, aspirations and goals. Using all this information, the retirement planner will develop a financial profile, an overview of the client's current needs and future objectives.

Determine Retirement Needs

The retirement planner will also ask the client to list his or her retirement goals. Most people's goals will include both financial objectives, such as maximizing retirement income, and nonfinancial goals, such as learning to adjust to leisure time. Five of the most common retirement goals include:

1. *Maintaining a Comfortable Standard of Living.* For most clients, one of their primary goals after retirement is to maintain the same standard of living that they enjoy during their working years. In fact, many clients see retirement as an opportunity to enhance their lifestyle through travel and entertainment. You can help them to achieve their goals by developing saving and investment strategies in both the preretirement and postretirement years.

2. *Maintaining Economic Self-Sufficiency.* Many retirement planning clients will readily agree that the possibility of becoming financially dependent on others, particularly their children, is a real concern for them. Consequently, maintaining financial independence during retirement is a key goal in the retirement process. Most people regard the following as essential for economic self-sufficiency after their retirement:

- obtaining coverage for health care costs not covered by Medicare;

- investing money in such a way as to minimize potential losses;

- making sure that retirement income keeps pace with inflation's shrinkage of buying power; and

- keeping a family business under family control or effectively disposing of a closely-held business with maximum gain.

3. *Providing for Family Members.* After retirement, many clients will continue to have the financial responsibility of providing not only for themselves, but for a loved one, usually a spouse. The need to provide adequate income or care becomes more significant if the loved one requires expensive medical treatment or has other special needs.

4. *Transferring of Wealth.* Another common objective is to transfer as much of an individual's estate as possible to selected beneficiaries. A key factor in maximizing this goal is to reduce, or eliminate, federal income taxes, estate taxes and state death tax liabilities. Although every retirement planner is not a practicing tax professional, he or she should have a basic knowledge of how taxes will affect the distribution of a client's wealth during his or her lifetime and after death.

5. *Satisfying Nonfinancial Goals.* In addition to financial goals, most clients also have several nonfinancial or personal goals. These goals may include:

- selling the family home and relocating after retirement;

- maintaining health and fitness after retirement;

- learning to cope with leisure time and adapting to a nonworking lifestyle; and

- planning for future lifestyle changes.

It is the role of the financial planner to help formulate and implement a plan to achieve both these financial and nonfinancial goals and objectives.

Develop Strategies to Meet Retirement Needs

Because people are often dealing with an uncertain future, many of them will regard today's problems and responsibilities as far more important than the projected issues of 10, 20, 30 or even 40 years from now. It is the retirement planner's job to impress upon his or her clients that if they live to retirement they will probably live to be 85 or older. Consequently, if they expect to have a secure, comfortable retirement, they must begin to implement a savings and investment plan today.

Although most people understand that saving for retirement is important, they can usually find one or more reasons not to save. Some may say that their pension benefits will be enough or that they will save more when they get older.

The financial planner must overcome these obstacles to successful retirement planning. Some of the most common obstacles include:

- *Failure to Establish an Emergency Fund.* Every person should establish an emergency fund to pay for unexpected expenses such as home or auto repairs, medical bills or loss of employment. Most financial planners agree that the amount of the fund should be enough to cover a minimum of three (and preferably six) months of living expenses. Without an emergency fund, there may not be money to build a retirement fund or the retirement fund may be depleted to pay for emergencies.

- *Inadequate Insurance.* It has long been a fact of American life that most individuals are inadequately insured. This shortfall means that survivors are not protected if the insured's death is premature. There may be no insurance to provide cash values for emergencies and income for retirement.

- *Tendency to "Buy Now/Pay Later."* One of the most significant differences of today's generation is the overwhelming tendency of many to use all their current income, and even go into debt, to support a desired lifestyle. Not only is there no savings available for a secure future, but the desired lifestyle itself is in jeopardy because current debt will have to be paid out of future income.

- *Changes in Employment.* Americans have always been on the move from one job to another, often from one area of the country to another, in their quest for better opportunities. Recently, a new reason for mobility has been added: most Americans can no longer count on secure employment with a particular employer. Mergers, leveraged buy-outs, acquisitions and the "lean and mean" philosophy of senior corporate management have created situations in which individuals no longer stay with an employer long enough to become entitled to benefits from the company's retirement plan. Even if they do attain full vesting, employees who are laid off may have to spend their accumulated funds rather than investing them or rolling them over for retirement.

- *Divorce.* The divorce rate in the U.S. is rapidly approaching two out of every three marriages. One of the unfortunate results of a divorce is that one or both spouses could be left with little accumulation of personal assets—assets that could have been used as a source of retirement income. Also, alimony or extra child support payments may limit an individual's ability to save for his or her own retirement.

- *Retirement Myths.* Finally, there are many myths surrounding retirement which pose obstacles to adequate planning. For example, many people assume that their taxes will be lower once they retire. But, although a retiree's tax bracket may be lower, the effective tax rate he or she pays may not change at all. Over the years, the value of exemptions and deductions has declined, while state, local and property taxes have gone up and Social Security benefits are now subject to tax.

Another myth is that Medicare will cover all necessary health care

ILL. 1.3 ■ Future Income Needed to Maintain $30,000 Annual Income in Current Dollars (Based on 6 Percent Annual Inflation)

The need for retirement planning can be demonstrated by the erosion of buying power that results due to inflation. As illustrated below, a 65-year-old person who retires in 1993 and lives 15 years into retirement will need over $70,000 just to stay even with inflation. Retirement planning can guarantee that the needed income will be available for retirement.

Year	Retiree's Age	Future Annual Income Needed
1993	65	$30,000
1994	66	31,800
1995	67	33,708
1996	68	35,730
1997	69	37,874
1998	70	40,147
1999	71	42,556
2000	72	47,109
2001	73	47,815
2002	74	50,684
2003	75	53,725
2004	76	56,949
2005	77	60,366
2006	78	63,988
2007	79	67,827
2008	80	71,897

costs, including the costs of a nursing home. In fact, Medicare does not cover lengthy nursing home stays, and it does not cover custodial care at all. Finally, there is the persistent myth that Social Security benefits will replace a large portion of an individual's preretirement income. The fact is, the higher one's wages are, the less Social Security will provide proportionately. For example, when they retire individuals who have always earned the maximum taxable income can expect to receive only about 24 percent of that portion of their pay subject to Social Security taxes.

In order to achieve their retirement goals, clients will have to overcome these obstacles. They will also need adequate insurance and investment income to supplement their Social Security benefits and company pension plan. A retirement planner can help clients understand how insurance, investments, company benefits, Social Security benefits and estate planning can be used and integrated to assist them in meeting their retirement goals.

■ THE ROLE OF THE LIFE INSURANCE AGENT

As a life insurance agent, you are already aware of the vital role you play in your community. You know that life and health insurance provide a practical solution to the economic losses associated with sickness, accidents and death. But, did you know that as a life insurance agent, you are uniquely qualified to assist your clients with their retirement planning?

A life insurance agent is in a unique position to provide retirement planning for the consumer. First of all, an agent understands how to recognize and communicate about needs. This ability is vital for the retirement planning market. Secondly, the products and services the agent represents, from insurance to annuities, are ideal to meet retirement needs. Thirdly, agents understand how to create a comprehensive plan, put it into place, and then follow-up with periodic reviews and service. Finally, agents know how to disturb a complacent client—one who is not aware of the potential pitfalls he or she may be facing—and can propel that individual to take action.

Create a Plan for Today's Needs

Your primary role as a life insurance agent is to identify your clients' personal, financial and business needs and, whenever possible, to satisfy those needs with life and health insurance products. Most commonly, your clients will need funds to protect their families in the event of a premature death, a disability or for other financial contingencies. Your clients may also ask your assistance in choosing investments, protecting their business and funding their retirement.

As a life insurance agent, your goal will be to meet those needs by providing insurance products to:

- strengthen a client's financial worth;

- provide for final expenses and dependents' support;

- accumulate income for investment and retirement;

- protect business interests; and

- provide for an effective estate transfer.

Assist in Retirement Planning

From a retirement planning perspective, you are able to offer insurance products with certain unique characteristics. All life insurance policies provide payment at the insured's death, but many can also be used to provide retirement income. For example, funds that have accumulated in a cash value policy can be used to purchase a single-premium annuity that will guarantee a series of payments for a limited period of time or for life.

When you are assisting with estate planning, you may be able to minimize or eliminate such expenses as taxes that are associated with transferring assets at your client's death. By providing the cash needed to pay final expenses and other costs, life insurance can help transfer estate assets to your client's dependents, friends or organizations according to his or her wishes.

Retirement planning goes far beyond simply selling a product. It is a multidimensional approach to evaluating and achieving long-range goals and objectives. It involves prioritizing needs, coordinating assets and filling the financial gaps—tasks that the insurance agent has been trained for and is qualified to do.

■ **SUMMARY**

Retirement planning is the most important means of achieving the goals most people have for their future financial security. You can serve your clients by assisting them in identifying their goals and developing strategies to meet those goals.

Your clients may vary range in age from 25 to 65 and older, and their needs and objectives will be as different as their ages and lifestyles. As a result, your strategies and product recommendations must vary according to your clients' objectives. In Chapter 2, we will discuss how to identify your market, determine its needs and sell the appropriate product to meet those needs.

■ **CHAPTER 1 QUESTIONS FOR REVIEW**

1. What percentage of the population will be age 65 and older by the middle of the 21st century?

   a. 10 percent
   b. 25 percent
   c. 40 percent
   d. 50 percent

2. Which of the following statements regarding sources of retirement income is/are correct?

   I. Inflation only impacts individuals in the preretirement accumulation years.
   II. Employer-sponsored retirement plans are seldom structured to provide 100 percent replacement of preretirement income.
   III. The ability of Social Security to pay retirement benefits far into the future is sometimes questioned.

      a. I only
      b. I and II only
      c. II and III only
      d. All of the above

3. Which of the following is NOT part of the agent's role in helping a client formulate a retirement plan?

   a. Developing a financial profile
   b. Writing a will
   c. Determining ways to enhance wealth
   d. Discussing personal goals

4. Which of the statements below regarding obstacles to retirement planning is correct?

   a. Most financial planners agree that a household should maintain an emergency fund equal to 24 months of its typical expenditures.
   b. Financial expenditures resulting from inadequate insurance protection have little impact on the achievement of financial retirement goals.
   c. The tendency of Americans to spend up to, or even beyond, their current means is increasingly rare.
   d. The tendency for job changes means many workers leave an employer without becoming entitled to employer-sponsored retirement benefits.

5. Which of the statements below regarding the ability of the life insurance agent to provide retirement planning for clients is/are correct?

   I. Life insurance agents are generally familiar with identifying and assessing needs.
   II. Life insurance agents are generally comfortable with providing periodic reviews and adjustments that are often necessary with retirement plans over time.

   a. I only
   b. II only
   c. Both I and II
   d. Neither I nor II

2

Opportunities for Retirement Planning

T oday's aging population, coupled with a growing awareness of the need for retirement planning, creates opportunities for the life insurance agent who can map out an effective retirement strategy, based on a client's needs and objectives. As every good agent knows, each situation is different; what may be an effective approach for one client would not be appropriate for another. In this chapter, we will discuss various market segments for retirement planning products and services. We will examine the characteristics and profiles of these market segments and look at some of the unique issues associated with each one. We will also discuss some marketing and product strategies that have been implemented by many successful retirement planners.

■■■■■

■ TRADITIONAL INSURANCE CONSUMER VS. THE CONSUMER OF THE FUTURE

Until recently, most life insurance agents were trained to be just that—agents who provided protection for families against losses brought about by the untimely death or disability of the principal wage earner. The traditional life insurance "customer" has been a family, headed by a male in his 30s or early 40s, who provides most if not all of the family's income. The primary product solution has been permanent life insurance, often supplemented by term. Only secondarily have the accumulation aspects of permanent life insurance been touted or have the future living needs of the client been addressed. But times are changing and so are the demographics of the traditional insurance market.

In fact, there are fewer and fewer individuals in the traditional 30-year-old to early 40-year-old age group. There are more two-income families now than ever before; and there are many, many more single-person households. What used to be just a secondary market for the insurance industry—serving the needs of older people or the anticipated future living needs of middle-aged people

ILL. 2.1 ■

The Retirement Planner's Many Roles

A retirement planner will be called upon to play many roles:

1. *Teacher*—A good retirement planner educates prospects and clients about the real potential for a retirement income shortfall. He or she must be able to explain clearly and simply how this unpleasant shortfall can occur. More importantly, the retirement planner must be able to communicate the processes and discipline involved in successful retirement planning.

2. *Provider*—A good retirement planner provides the best in retirement planning products and services to clients. He or she provides reliable follow-up service and is able to adjust the existing retirement plan when a client's situation requires that it be changed.

3. *Team Captain*—A good retirement planner will coordinate with each member of the retirement planning team. In addition to the client or prospect, that team includes the client's accountant, attorney and more. The retirement planner refers clients to other financial professionals when it is appropriate.

4. *Counselor and Friend*—A good retirement planner is a good listener. He or she is aware that those awaiting retirement may have nagging concerns. These worries are usually about finances, but, occasionally, they are about nonfinancial

through the accumulation and income-producing aspects of life insurance products—may soon become just as dominant as the traditional primary market.

■ UNDERSTANDING THE OLDER PROSPECT

Financial professionals would do well to avoid assumptions about those older Americans whom they seek to serve. Although older people share some similar characteristics, gerontological research shows that people become more dissimilar as they age. For example, some will be healthy; some will face health problems. Some will retire while others will continue in the work force. They may be married, widowed, divorced or single. The financial profiles vary from the impoverished elderly subsisting on welfare to a large number of "semi-millionaires" between the ages of 50 and 70. Most older Americans fall somewhere between these two extremes. The challenge to financial services professionals is to provide products and services that will satisfy a large, diverse group of aging people. Each client and prospect has unique personal and financial needs and concerns to which his or her financial advisers must respond. Let's take a look at how the retirement market breaks down.

■ THE BABY BOOM GENERATION

Despite what one may think, the retirement market does not consist solely of individuals in their 50s or 60s. Like no other generation before them, baby

ILL. 2.2 ■ The Aging of America

During the next few decades, the United States will consist of a very large, older population. As the chart indicates, the total number of people between the ages of 50 and 75 will rise dramatically within the next several years. For example, people in the age 50 to 59 group will increase from approximately 64 million in 1990 to almost 85 million persons by 2005. This demographic change will present some unique opportunities for life insurance agents interested in retirement planning.

Age	1990	2005	Percent of Group Change
50-59	64.1*	84.5*	32.0
60-64	42.0	47.8	13.8
65-74	31.3	35.1	12.0
75 and older	13.1	17.1	30.7

*Figures in millions of persons.

boomers (those born between 1946 and 1964) have made significant impacts socially, culturally and economically. It is estimated that there are more than 82 million men and women who fit into this demographic category, and when these individuals begin to reach age 65, the United States will experience the largest retired population in its history. It makes sense that the agent who focuses on this group as they move from middle age to retirement has tremendous opportunities for successfully marketing his or her products and services.

Group Profile

The huge post-World War II generation—the baby boomers—usually begins to think seriously about retirement around age 45. Even with higher lifetime earnings than their parents, baby boomers may have difficulty saving for retirement. Financial resources are often allocated into shorter-term goals such as homeownership and funding education for their children or themselves. As a generation used to "playing now and paying later," baby boomers feel comfortable with the easy use of credit to purchase items now while deferring payments until tomorrow thereby reducing the amount of money available for retirement. Baby boomers are greatly concerned about the financial and personal impact of living into their 80s and even their 90s. They are also the first generation for whom divorce has become socially acceptable and for whom divorce settlements impact on their total available retirement income. In addition, baby boomers may already be supporting their own aged parents, facing a strain on their financial and personal wherewithal. Because the responsibility for caring for elderly parents usually falls on women, they often feel "sandwiched" between caring for their own children and elderly parents. In fact, women in the baby boomer generation are likely to spend more hours caring for their parents than for their own children.

If baby boomers implement a retirement plan by their early 40s, they have between 20 and 30 years before the funds will actually be needed. Though this may seem like a long time, they will still have to begin investing relatively large sums of money at regular intervals to have a significant nest egg for their retirement.

Needs and Objectives

Like most other groups, baby boomers' retirement needs include both financial and personal objectives. They want to maintain their current lifestyle at retirement and to provide for adequate health care, including long-term care, to protect themselves in the future. In general, baby boomers have little confidence that Social Security and Medicare will be substantial enough to support them when they retire. They recognize that they will have to rely primarily on company pensions and personal savings and investments for retirement.

Unfortunately, many baby boomers have failed to consider that their personal income during retirement will have to be quite substantial to offset their inability to save now for retirement. Moreover, they have several problems facing them—increased longevity, changes in Social Security benefits and company pensions and rising health care costs—that will increase the amount of personal income needed during retirement. As stated earlier, this group of retirees can expect to live into their 80s or 90s. What many have not considered is that this increased longevity cannot be fully funded by Social Security or their company pension.

By the 21st century, the Social Security full-benefit retirement age will be 67, not 65. In addition, many defined benefit programs will be discontinued as companies struggle to meet the heavy expenses of complying with the federal regulations and administrative costs of these programs. Companies that now pay all or some of their retirees' group health plan will probably decline to do so in the future. Retirees will have to pay for their own insurance and any additional medical costs not covered by insurance. Finally, those who wait until their late 30s or early 40s to have children will have less disposable income to save for retirement. Money previously earmarked for retirement will be spent on educating their children.

Product Recommendations

Those who have waited until their mid-40s to begin retirement planning usually have found it difficult to save for retirement on a regular basis. In most cases, however, conservative investments are useful for this group.

Any retirement plan for this age group should begin with traditional insurance products, such as whole life insurance. Life insurance offers a safe investment with a guaranteed return. If the client dies prematurely, life insurance will provide protection for financial obligations, such as a mortgage commitment and

**ILL. 2.3 ■ Percent of People in Each Age Group Seeking Personal
Retirement Planning Advice**

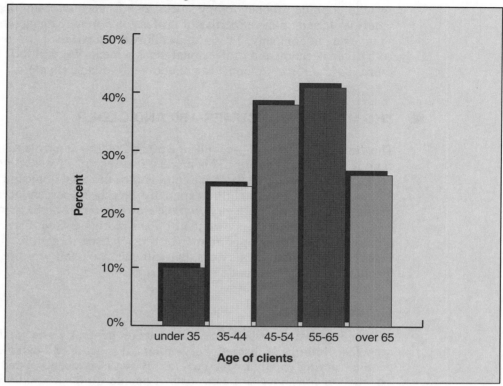

Source: American Society PULSE Survey, Fall 1991.

the childrens' education. Or, when the client reaches retirement, cash values can
provide additional retirement income. If the cash values are not depleted, a
death benefit will be available for survivor income or estate planning purposes.

Qualified plans (employer-sponsored plans, Individual Retirement Accounts,
Keoghs) remain an important source of retirement income. Employer-sponsored
plans, such as defined contribution plans and defined benefit plans, permit contributions to accumulate tax free until the employee actually receives them.
However, even a very generous employer-sponsored plan may be inadequate to
meet income needs. For those who are eligible, an IRA provides another way
for individuals to make tax-deductible contributions to a trust or custodial account for their retirement. Finally, self-employed individuals and their employees may contribute to a Keogh plan for their retirement.

Another financial product well-suited to the baby boomer's current and future financial needs is an annuity. The plan's somewhat compulsory savings features
and the lifetime guarantee of income are appealing to baby boomers. Although
it provides no life insurance protection, an annuity offers competitive rates, tax-
deferred growth and a regular, guaranteed lifetime income through distribution
of invested capital. Even modest savings, when compounded tax deferred over
20 or 30 years, can result in an impressive retirement nest egg.

Mutual funds can also be excellent vehicles for long-range retirement funding for this market. A *mutual fund* is an investment alternative available to individuals who pool their money to buy stocks, bonds, certificates of deposit and other securities based on the expertise of professional money managers who work for an investment company. These funds allow the small investor to benefit from both diversification and professional management. We will look at each of these sources of retirement income in greater detail in later chapters.

■ THE MATURE CONSUMER—50 AND OLDER

The "mature consumer"—people age 50 and older—controls more than 75 percent of the nation's wealth. This market also accounts for 42 percent of all after-tax income—which translates into one-half of the total domestic discretionary income—or around $160 billion annually. Nearly 75 percent of households falling into the "mature" category own their own homes—and a whooping 80 percent of these homeowners own their homes mortgage-free. Clearly, this market provides a remarkable opportunity for financial services professionals to provide those products and services that will enhance quality of life during these "mature" years and beyond.

Group Profile

Although we've described the mature market generally as a wealthy group that represents billions of discretionary dollars, it is actually a diverse group of people, varying widely by income, family status, occupation and social class. The mature consumer group consists of people from ages 50 to 60 who are: working, semi-retired and retired; healthy and frail; married and widowed; and sometimes beginning second careers and/or families. Obviously, the needs of a 50-year-old businessperson with no children at home will be quite different from a 50-year-old who has remarried and is beginning a second family.

Retirement planners and life insurance agents should recall that the 50 and older age group is healthier, more active and better educated than were their parents or grandparents. Studies have shown that mature buyers of goods and services are strongly influenced by quality and service—and not just price. Most consumers are interested in fully understanding a product and what a product will do for them.

Needs and Objectives

In the past, people who reached age 50 could look forward to a few more years of employment, a short retirement and a relatively early death. But as we've discussed, because of advances in health care and increased longevity, the needs of the mature market are clearly shifting from preparation for death and financial protection for their family to preparation for longer life and financial protection for their own personal needs. The key needs of this group are maintaining preretirement standards of living; providing for adequate current and long-term health care; and planning for the distribution of their wealth after death.

Product Recommendations

Most retirement planners will agree that long-term health care coverage is an important need for this group. The mature group will have seen at least one parent decline and die, perhaps without adequate medical insurance. They are concerned that their current insurance will not handle their medical needs in the future. Most life insurance agents will recommend disability income protection for present insurance needs and supplementary Medicare coverage to fill the gaps in Medicare benefits after retirement. If a plan is available in the prospect's state, an agent may also recommend a long-term care policy. These policies allow people to set aside a portion of today's income for the day when long-term health care may be needed. (You will learn more about these policies in Chapter 11.)

Although the mature consumer may have the means to purchase many products to supplement personal income, those close to retirement are often conservative and risk adverse. They generally seek investments that guarantee safety of principal and relatively certain returns. Life insurance remains important, although intergenerational wealth protection may become a higher priority, replacing dependent income needs as the number one reason for acquiring and maintaining life insurance. For example, the reasons for keeping the coverage may change from protecting a child's education fund to providing resources for an aging survivor spouse.

▪ THE SENIOR CONSUMER—65 AND OLDER

The senior consumer group consists of approximately 29 million people who are age 65 and older. In many cases, they will have enjoyed their peak financial years just prior to retirement. In the early phases of retirement, seniors will be active and probably spend much of their disposable income on travel, recreation and leisure activities. As they age, retirees often become less active and will begin to face the problems that come with increasing infirmity and illness.

Group Profile

In general, seniors have the highest net worth of any other age group. Approximately 90 percent of those with household incomes of more than $30,000 own their own homes. They have paid off their mortgages, have little or no installment debt and often have large sums of money to invest. Although they want to maximize the return on their money, they are also risk-adverse and prefer rather conservative investments. Their primary concern is safety. For example, most seniors maintain bank savings accounts or certificates of deposit rather than other investments for their retirement funds.

Needs and Objectives

Many retirees feel that they have earned a comfortable retirement after working all their lives. In fact, many expect that their standard of living will improve after they retire. In order to meet this expectation, retirees must find ways to invest their dollars wisely while protecting their capital. They often seek professional investment advice from their insurance or retirement planner.

Many seniors express concern about being able to maintain their current home. They may lack the funds, energy or desire to continue living in a large house once they have retired. Children have grown and left home, a spouse may have died or the neighborhood is no longer desirable. Relocation may therefore become an important issue during this period, along with the problems of leaving family, friends and favorite current activities for warmer or less expensive areas.

Probably the greatest need facing seniors is the lack of adequate health care insurance. Although many retirees have some coverage, the cost for long-term care services is projected to rise as the number of elderly increases. A larger share of the costs will be borne by the retiree who may or may not have adequate insurance coverage.

Finally, seniors are concerned about creating a definite plan for the disposition of their property while they are alive or after they have died. A life agent can provide a valuable service by helping a client develop an estate plan according to the client's objectives. However, the estate planning documents that support the plan—a living will, a will to transfer assets at death, a trust and so on—should be prepared by an attorney.

Product Recommendations

As a financial adviser, you might recommend that one of the best ways to preserve purchasing power and create value while minimizing the impact of risk is to balance risk and return. A person's investment portfolio might consist of high risk/high return investments such as commodities; average risk/average return investments such as stocks and bonds; and low risk/low return investments such as bank accounts. By diversifying their investments among investment categories, investors spread their risk and minimize their chance of loss. For example, assume that a person purchases mutual funds and corporate bonds. As inflation rises, the value of the mutual fund rises, but the value of the bond declines. The negative effect of rising inflation on the bond's value is offset by the positive effect on the mutual fund.

Life insurance—either traditional whole life or interest sensitive policies—often plays an important role in an individual's retirement program. Because of a remarkable Internal Revenue Code (I.R.C.) provision known as a *Section 1035 exchange,* certain kinds of policies can be exchanged with another plan without the gain being taxed. For example, a cash value life insurance policy (offering death protection) can be converted to another plan (such as an annuity, which offers retirement income) to coincide with the changing needs of an individual. Life insurance products like survivorship insurance, long-term care and living benefits riders in life insurance policies are also available options.

Both preretirees and retirees will be very concerned about health care benefits after retirement. Clients and their spouses about to turn age 65 will be eligible for government-subsidized medical expense insurance under *Medicare.* (Medicare coverage is explained in detail in Chapter 11.) However, as discussed for the baby boomer market, the retirement planner must make clients aware that Medicare, even with supplemental Part B coverage, does not fully address a retiree's exposure to all medical expenses. Additional insurance, such as Medicare supplement insurance (or medigap) insurance, may be used to fill these gaps in coverage. A few employers may provide this coverage to retirees, but in many cases, retirees will personally need to acquire such coverage to protect against deductibles, coinsurance and other expenses not covered by Medicare. In order to advise clients on the most appropriate coverages, a financial professional specializing in serving retirees should become familiar with the costs and features of the different medigap policies provided by insurers.

Those seniors who elect to sell their homes and move to smaller quarters or a warmer climate will have some financial concerns. The financial professional may be asked to comment about the pros and cons of electing the *Code Section 121 exclusion* on the gain on the sale of a primary residence. Under this exclusion, each taxpayer has a once-in-a-lifetime opportunity to exempt up to $125,000 in capital gains from the sale of his or her home. That is gain on the sale, not the price of the house. There are some requirements. The taxpayer or the taxpayer's spouse must be age 55 or older before the date of the sale, and the taxpayer claiming the exemption had to have lived in the residence for at least three of the five years immediately prior to the sale. Whether a Code Section 121 election makes sense for a particular client will depend on his or her relocation and estate plans. Each client's situation must be carefully analyzed.

Seniors also become increasingly concerned with estate planning issues. Estate plans and documents should be reviewed periodically, especially with the ever-changing tax laws. For example, estate plans made prior to September 13, 1981, may have to be reconstructed in order to take advantage of a number of newer, favorable estate tax laws. Both preretirees and retirees tend to be especially concerned with income for survivors. You will learn more about estate planning in Chapter 12.

■ BUSINESS OWNERS

When prospecting for retirement plan sales, small businesses should not to be ignored. Owners are often looking to begin retirement programs that provide security as well as tax breaks that positively impact their personal financial scenarios. The ages of the principals in a business and differences in ownership interests provide useful clues to a financial professional as to what type of retirement program to recommend.

Group Profile

Small businesses may be organized as sole proprietorships (a business owned by one person), partnerships (a business organization of two or more individuals) or corporations (an artificial legal entity). Sole proprietorships outnumber both corporations and partnerships by three to one. Many agents prefer to concentrate on the sole proprietorship market since corporate sales generally take longer to close and many layers of review may be required before actual decisions can be made.

Needs and Objectives

Some business owners seek retirement arrangements that benefit themselves alone. Others seek benefits for just a few select employees; still others will want to benefit all their employees. Some owners will simply want to sell their interest in a business at retirement. Other owners may be motivated to minimize estate taxes, to provide cash for estate settlement costs or to assure successor management for the business. Without adequate retirement planning, the business may be unable to continue or may be inadequately funded when the owner retires.

People may be uncomfortable admitting that their personal retirement concerns outrank their altruistic objectives, but clients have every right to allocate their retirement dollars in any legal manner they deem appropriate. The owner(s) should have clearly definable needs that an agent can address when making a product recommendation. To determine what these needs are, questions must be asked. For example, the agent might ask: "Is a plan currently in place? Do you want to cover everyone? Are you looking for a 'low-cost' plan?" Honest answers to these and other questions will become invaluable tools in the selection of the most appropriate retirement plan.

Product Recommendations

Business owners are often looking to begin retirement programs that provide both future security and current tax breaks. The purpose of a program may be to maintain a business as a going concern or to retain the values of the business for the benefit of an owner's estate following death or disability. In most cases, insurance can be used to protect the surviving members of a business where the loss of an owner or key employee could dissolve the business, adversely affect control of the business or decrease the value of the business. For example, sole proprietors, whose dependents rely on the business for their income, may be particularly eager to provide for their family's future. It is not surprising then that a business owner wants to spend more time discussing his or her personal financial planning needs than he or she does discussing financial issues that relate to employees.

If the purpose of the plan is to fund his or her own retirement, the owner may be able to use an executive bonus plan, a salary continuation plan or other nonqualified deferred compensation plan. But, if the purpose of the plan is to assure business continuity, the owner may select a buy-sell agreement so that the business is sold to the right people, at the right time and at the right price.

The purpose of the retirement plan may also be to ensure employee satisfaction. Businesses that require more than average expertise or technical ability are anxious to establish the kinds of employee benefit plans that historically attract quality employees and diminish employee turnover. Businesses with a relatively wide range of employee ages and salaries often select defined contribution approaches, such as profit-sharing and money purchase retirement plans.

When an older owner's number one priority is to maximize the amount of money that can be tax-favorably shifted into the future, the defined benefit approach is often the road to follow. Nevertheless, some plan sponsors will be so put off by the increasing complexity of government regulations associated with these plans that their priorities will change and defined contribution plans will have the greatest appeal.

Many business owners also offer 401(k) plans. Because of their salary-reduction feature, potential for employer-matching funds and the provision for employee loans, 401(k)s are now the most popular retirement plan.

Businesses with fewer than 25 employees may prefer the operational simplicity of a simplified employee pension (SEP) plan. These plans encourage small businesses to provide retirement benefits to employees. Basically, the employee sets up an IRA account to which the employer may contribute. These plans are discussed in more detail in Chapter 8.

■ STRATEGIES FOR THE RETIREMENT PLANNER

As a life insurance agent, you know that your job is to solve problems by meeting the financial needs of a variety of people. If you are new to the retirement planning area, you may be concerned about where to begin. You may be surprised to learn that you may already have the knowledge and skills needed to provide your prospects with insurance products that can help them enjoy a comfortable retirement.

Determine Financial Needs

As a life insurance agent, your first step will be to determine your prospects' retirement needs and to fill those needs successfully with your products and services. As we've seen, most people facing retirement will have several needs to which you can respond—health care, income needs, final expenses and estate planning. In many cases, the best solution to a need that exists because someone has lived, or because someone has died, is life insurance. In addition to providing protection against financial loss in the event of a policyowner's death, life insurance can serve as a means to accumulate assets for a variety of financial goals, such as building a retirement program.

Identify the Market

You probably have a good list of quality prospects among your current life insurance clients. You also may choose to prospect within a specific market segment comprised of prospects with similar needs and overall characteristics. To do so, select a geographic area where you would like to work, choose a specific group, learn their needs and determine which of your products and services fit its needs. For example, you may decide to concentrate on selling annuities to the senior market within a 25-mile radius of your office. Your goal will be to become *the* agent in that area. By focusing your efforts in one area, you will increase your effectiveness, productivity and earnings.

Sell the Product

There are many ways to successfully prospect, market and sell retirement products and services to both individuals and businesses. You may choose to use natural contacts, direct mail, telephone solicitations, referrals or a combination of methods. For example, *referrals* from satisfied clients and colleagues can, indeed, be a major source of business. But don't be surprised when an older party to whom you have been referred suggests that you contact their children. There may be more concern about retirement security among baby boomers than there is among 60-year-olds.

Retirement planning seminars presented to open enrollment or select employee groups as well as church or civic organizations can be an effective way to reach large groups of people. The best seminars emphasize information that is supported with data and examples to which the particular audience can relate. There should be no pressure about falling interest rates or "one time only" investment opportunities. Only use the "hard-sell" approach at a seminar if your objective is to turn people *off.*

Most employees are baffled by their employee benefit booklets and by "expert" explanations of their retirement plans and their options. If you can simplify complex concepts by breaking them into smaller steps and checking for client feedback and questions along the way, you can expect to be a sought-after employee retirement and benefit seminar presenter.

Your company may offer prepackaged retirement seminar presentation kits, complete with "scripts" and overhead transparencies or transparency masters. If you plan on presenting retirement planning seminars, such a kit will save you quite a bit of work. Have your business name and telephone number appear on all handout literature.

When you make your presentation, think of yourself as a "teacher" rather than a salesperson. Demonstrating the real possibility for a retirement income "gap" encourages your participants to listen to the rest of what you have to say. Clients become particularly interested when they can see that their pension, current savings and Social Security aren't going to give them sufficient income replacement. You may wish to design or purchase work sheets that help the attendees calculate for themselves how great a gap exists between what they have and what they need. You can then show your listeners that this gap can be addressed by:

- increasing savings;

- increasing investment returns; or

- lowering retirement lifestyle expectations.

Encourage your prospects to ask questions about anything they do not understand. Be prepared to answer a variety of questions about diverse topics from options for substantial lump-sum rollovers to maximizing pension benefits. Questions often act as a barometer to measure whether you are on the right track with the sales process. After handling any objections, motivate the prospects to solve their retirement problems by purchasing your products and close the sales by collecting premiums. Finally, ask for referrals for future sales calls.

Service and Follow-up

Your clients' retirement planning will not end with the delivery of a policy. After clients retire, their needs will change and you should be available to assist them. Arrange an annual review to assess your clients' current needs with their current coverage and make any necessary changes to accommodate new beneficiaries, revised settlement options or estate planning needs. As an insurance professional, your future depends on your client base. The interest you show in your clients will strengthen the relationship between your company, you and your policyowners.

■ SUMMARY

A successful, comfortable retirement doesn't just happen—it takes careful planning and continual adjustments. As a retirement planner, you can help your clients understand and become more comfortable with the retirement process and gain some control over their financial future. By identifying your market and its needs, you can map out an effective strategy for your clients whether they are part of the baby boom, mature or senior consumer group.

In Chapter 3, we discuss ways to determine how much income your clients will need to fund a comfortable retirement. We'll also review various sources of retirement income that may be available to your clients.

■ CHAPTER 2 QUESTIONS FOR REVIEW

1. Which of the following is/are common nonfinancial retirement objectives?

   I. Occupying increased leisure hours
   II. Staying healthy and fit
   III. Addressing the postretirement tendency for increased investment speculation
   IV. Deciding whether to move to a new community during the retirement years

   a. I only
   b. I and II only
   c. I and III only
   d. III and IV only

2. By the year 2000, the median age of the U.S. population is expected to

   a. decrease.
   b. increase.
   c. remain the same.
   d. neither increase nor decrease since median age cannot be forecasted.

3. All the following statements regarding age 50 and older, or mature consumer, are correct, EXCEPT:

    a. Mature buyers tend to pay attention to the quality of a product—not just its price.
    b. The population over age 50 holds almost half of America's corporate stock and two-thirds of all investment portfolios in excess of $25,000.
    c. Mature buyers are less concerned about long-term health care than any other group of consumers.
    d. Investors tend to be conservative and relatively risk averse

4. Which of the following is/are financial issues commonly affecting the baby boomer generation?

    I. A high frequency of divorce
    II. Conspicuous consumption of goods and services
    III. Support of aging parents and children
    IV. Concern about experiencing longevity that might cause them to outlive their income

        a. I only
        b. I and III only
        c. III and IV only
        d. All of the above

5. A planner at a retirement seminar should think of himself or herself primarily as a

    a. teacher.
    b. salesperson.
    c. tax expert.
    d. student.

...

3

Analyzing Retirement Income Needs

T he old saying, "People don't plan to fail; they fail to plan," certainly applies to retirement. Although people make plans which affect their education, careers, marriage and children, most of them fail to adequately plan for the day when they will no longer be working.

As a financial professional, you know it is never too early for your clients to begin planning for retirement. The longer they wait, the less control they will have over the shape of their lives during retirement. Your goal is to help your clients analyze their long-term retirement objectives and formulate plans to meet those objectives. In this chapter, we will discuss ways to determine how much income your clients will need for retirement. We will also review the three important sources of income that can be used to satisfactorily fund their retirement.

■ ■ ■ ■ ■

■ RETIREMENT CONSIDERATIONS

Before you can determine *how* your client should fund his or her retirement, you will need to know *how much* your client will need for retirement. The amount needed will vary based on your client's desired standard of living after retirement, projected retirement age and a variety of economic factors. In the following sections, we will discuss how three items—life expectancy, inflation and the time value of money—will affect your client's retirement planning.

Life Expectancy

In order to adequately fund a retirement plan, certain assumptions must be made that will affect the size of annual deposits that must be made now to savings accounts and other retirement plans. Obviously, the sooner your clients begin to save for retirement, the longer they have to invest and earn income. But how much they will actually need for retirement is also a function of how long they live.

You cannot be absolutely certain of a person's life span, but you can estimate how long the average retiree will live after retirement and the total income that will be needed to fund that retirement. For example, statistics show the current average life expectancy is about 75 years; however, actuaries know that many people live longer than the average life expectancy. Therefore, you must plan for the possibility that your client will live many years past the projected life expectancy when formulating retirement plans.

Inflation

It will come as no surprise to you that prices generally rise each year. *Inflation,* a general increase in prices, means that the buying power of a dollar decreases and buys less over time. Even a low rate of inflation can significantly affect the price of things. If prices rise only 5 percent in a year, items that cost $100 today will cost $105 a year from now. Over a ten-year period, those same items that cost $100 today will cost almost $163. Due to inflation, the cost of those goods will have risen almost 63 percent during that period.

The most commonly accepted measure of inflation is the *Consumer Price Index (CPI).* It is compiled by the Bureau of Labor Statistics and provides an accurate picture of changes in the prices of over 400 goods and services. According to the CPI, consumer prices have risen in all but one year since 1950. Retired persons on fixed incomes are especially affected by inflation because their financial resources are limited. Thus, each year a larger percentage of income is spent for necessities such as food, shelter and medical care as inflation rises. Although Social Security and many employer-sponsored retirement plans make periodic inflation adjustments to retirement and other benefits based on changes in the CPI, the increases may be inadequate to offset rising costs.

The Time Value of Money

As we illustrate later in this chapter, your clients will need to set aside a certain amount of money in retirement plans, savings accounts and other investments that will grow in value over the years to partially offset the effects of inflation. As you know, an amount of money invested today will increase as a result of earned interest. This concept, called the *time value of money,* is based on the fact that a dollar received today is worth more than a dollar received a year from now. The dollar received today can be invested immediately and when combined with the interest earned will, therefore, be worth more a year from now. Conversely, a dollar that will be received a year from now is worth less than a dollar received today.

Since you are already familiar with this concept because of your life insurance experience, you know that the time value of money consists of two aspects: present value and future value. The *present value* of a sum of money is simply the amount invested today. The *future value,* also referred to as "compounding," is the amount to which a current sum will increase based on a certain interest rate and period of time. In order to determine how much a client's money will grow if he or she invests it today and leaves it for a specified number of time periods, assuming it earns a specified rate of return each period, you need to find the future value (FV) of a sum of money. You may use the FV formula:

$$FV = PV \times (1 + i)^n$$

where FV = the future value,
PV = the present value (amount invested today),
i = the interest rate and
n = the number of periods the money is to be invested at the interest rate.

For example, $1,000 invested for three years and earning 10 percent per year grows to $1,331 ($1,000 × 1.331).

The other option for finding FV is to refer to a future value or compound interest table that shows the future value of $1 for various investment periods and rates.

Present value is the current value of a future sum based on a certain interest rate and period of time. To find the present value (PV) of a single payment, a formula reversing the process of finding the future value is used:

$$PV = \frac{1}{(1 + i)^n}$$

Again, tables can also be used to calculate the PV.

After you have reviewed your prospect's retirement objectives, you can use future value tables to illustrate how investments made today can grow over time to accomplish those objectives.

■ PROJECTING RETIREMENT INCOME NEEDS

An analysis of retirement income needs generally begins with a review of the prospect's existing income and expenses. The current budget is the springboard for creating a retirement budget since it will give you an indication of current spending and saving patterns. From this information, you can predict the amount and type of retirement expenses your prospect is likely to have and you can forecast the amount of income needed to meet those expenses.

When planning for retirement, a person may make the mistake of thinking that less income will be needed to maintain his or her current standard of living. Many people realize that expenses such as mortgage payments, transportation, dependent care and food and clothing costs for work will be eliminated. What they do *not* consider is that some expenses remain constant or may even increase after retirement. For example, property taxes, repair and maintenance expenses, recreation costs and medical costs will probably increase and take up a larger portion of a retiree's income. In most cases, overall expenses remain at about 70 to 80 percent of preretirement expense dollars.

Replacement Ratio

There is some disagreement among retirement planners about the amount of income needed during the retirement period. Many planners use a ratio of retirement income to preretirement income called a *replacement ratio* to estimate needed income. Some of these planners feel 60 to 75 percent of preretirement income is needed. According to these estimates, a person earning $50,000 annually with an estimated retirement income of $20,000 has a 40 percent replacement ratio ($20,000/$50,000). He or she would need an additional income of between $10,000 and $17,500 to be within an acceptable 60 to 75 percent range.

Maintaining the prospect's preretirement lifestyle is an important goal of retirement planning. Therefore, some planners feel that 100 percent of preretirement income is needed after retirement, since that is the amount the retiree currently needs to maintain his or her standard of living. It may, therefore, be more effective to base retirement funding on the prospect's current standard of living rather than a replacement ratio.

Expense Method

Because current expenses often determine retirement expenses, you might use the *expense method* to project a retiree's future expenses. This method considers current living expenses in relation to future expenses. For example, assume a prospect earns $35,000 and maintains a comfortable lifestyle. After retirement the client will continue to have expenses for housing, health care and utilities. If that retiree plans to have monthly expenses of $2,000 (or $24,000 annually) after retirement, then his or her retirement income must remain at $24,000 worth of purchasing power in today's dollars. Even if none of your prospect's expenses decrease after retirement, inflation, increased medical costs, increased recreation costs and unforeseen expenses may require between 70 and 90 percent of his or her final average salary in order to maintain the preretirement standard of living.

Protecting Needed Retirement Savings

Both the replacement ratio and the expense method are useful in determining a prospect's income needs at retirement. Unfortunately, they do not provide a means for determining the amount of savings your prospect will need to supplement any Social Security and pension benefits. In order to determine the amount of *needed retirement savings,* you must consider current savings, projected needs and projected inflation. In most cases, you'll use an average anticipated inflation rate to predict future investment outcomes.

For example, assume your client, Carrie Moore, will be 65 in three months and you have determined she needs $45,000 of retirement income annually to maintain her current standard of living. But consider how inflation might impact on your calculations. Rising inflation decreases purchasing power. If the inflation rate is only 4 percent annually over her retirement, Carrie's income will have to increase to $54,752 by age 70 and $81,041 by age 80 to maintain her lifestyle. Obviously, if inflation rises or interest rates fall, Carrie will need even more income in order to meet her future needs.

ILL. 3.1 ■ Current and Projected Annual Expenses

Current and Projected Annual Expenses
(Using "Today's Dollars")

Fixed Expenses	Current	Projected Retirement
Mortgage/Rent	$	$
Income Taxes		
Property Taxes		
Life Insurance		
Property Insurance		
Automobile Loan		
Variable Expenses		
Food		
Clothing		
Business Expenses		
Utilities		
Car Expenses (gas, etc.)		
Medical Expenses		
Entertainment		
Vacations		
IRA Contributions		
Savings		
Charitable Contributions		
Gifts		
Miscellaneous		
TOTAL	$	$

Notes: _____

_____

_____

ILL. 3.2 ■ Retirement Tables

TABLE I (Inflation)	
Years to Retirement	**Factor**
5	1.3
10	1.6
15	2.1
20	2.7
25	3.4
30	4.3
35	5.5
40	7.0

TABLE L (Lump-Sum Needed)		
Years Capital Must Last	**Income* Portfolio Factor**	**Growth* Portfolio Factor**
20	16.8	13.3
30	23.1	16.6
40	28.3	18.6

TABLE R (Retirement)		
Years to Retirement	**Income* Portfolio Factor**	**Growth* Portfolio Factor**
5	1.4	1.6
10	2.0	2.6
15	2.8	4.2
20	3.9	6.7
25	5.4	10.8
30	7.6	17.4
35	10.7	28.1
40	15.0	45.3

TABLE D (Divisor)		
Years to Retirement	**Income* Portfolio Factor**	**Growth* Portfolio Factor**
5	6.8	7.4
10	18.1	21.2
15	36.4	46.2
20	65.1	89.6
25	109.2	163.9
30	176.0	288.8
35	276.1	496.9
40	424.5	840.8

*The income portfolio factor assumes high-quality fixed income assets (bonds and other debt instruments) at an average growth of 7 percent annually; the growth portfolio assumes high-quality stocks with the potential to earn an average return of 10 percent annually. Both factors incorporate a 5 percent inflation assumption.

One of the retirement planner's goals is to provide protection against decreased purchasing power due to inflation. As a first step, the planner should itemize the client's retirement resources and determine which of these resources are affected by inflation. In most cases, pensions and any shortfalls between what the client has and what he or she needs at retirement will have to be protected from inflation. Other resources, such as Social Security and Medicare benefits, may be indexed to reflect inflation and the planner will not have to protect these resources.

Your prospect will probably need to supplement retirement income from Social Security and employer-sponsored pensions with additional savings. Determining how much an individual should save to support a comfortable retirement may be calculated in a variety of sophisticated ways. Computers and high-tech financial function calculators can be programmed to accurately determine the return on retirement savings (after taxes, if any) and the impact of an average assumed rate of inflation over what can be a longer retirement accumulation period.

For our purposes, however, a simplified version of a retirement savings calculation is presented. Using the work sheet (see Ill. 3.1) and retirement tables (see Ill. 3.2), you can quickly calculate a person's retirement savings needs. These tables provide estimates of needed income, assuming certain increases in inflation and investment growth over time.

To illustrate how the work sheet and tables can be used to calculate retirement and savings needs, we have developed a case study for two potential retirees, Stanley and Laura Rivers. Based on the information provided, we have determined and calculated their savings needs as shown in Ill. 3.3 and Ill. 3.4.

■ CASE STUDY: STANLEY AND LAURA RIVERS

Stanley and Laura Rivers, both age 45 this year, plan to retire in 20 years. Stanley is the director of marketing for a company that manufactures garden supplies. His employer sponsors a pension plan under which Stanley is covered. Laura, an author of children's books, pays Social Security taxes but is not covered by a formal retirement plan.

Their current combined income is $73,500. At retirement, their expected annual Social Security benefits will be $20,964. In addition, they will have $24,000 annually from Stanley's employer-sponsored retirement plan when they retire in 20 years. At some point, they decided to invest some money either in income stock (stock with a high dividend rate) or growth stock (shares of a company that is expected to achieve rapid growth). Although the growth stock carries above-average risks, the estimated annual return is 10 percent. They have invested $11,000 in a growth portfolio of high-quality stocks. They also want to begin a savings plan for their retirement which, according to statistics, should last about 20 years.

As you can see from Ill. 3.3, Stanley and Laura currently have annual expenses of $73,500. They are assuming that certain expenses—the mortgage, auto loan and business-related expenses—will be eliminated by the time they retire. Other

ILL. 3.3 ■ **Calculating Retirement Income Needs**

Stanley and Laura Rivers
Current and Projected Annual Expenses
(Using "Today's Dollars")

Fixed Expenses	Current	Projected Retirement	
Mortgage	$12,366	$ 0	(1)
Income Taxes	21,406	13,627	(2)
Property Taxes	2,000	2,300	
Life Insurance	978	1,714	(3)
Property Insurance	1,150	1,150	
Automobile Loan	3,600	0	(4)
Variable Expenses			
Food	$ 5,800	$ 5,800	
Clothing	4,800	3,000	(5)
Business Expenses	1,000	0	
Utilities	1,200	1,500	
Car Expenses (gas, etc.)	2,400	1,800	(6)
Medical Insurance Expenses	800	1,000	(7)
Entertainment	2,400	4,100	(8)
Vacations	3,000	7,100	(9)
IRA Contribution	0	0	(10)
Savings	3,000	2,400	(11)
Charitable Contributions	1,200	600	
Gifts	2,800	2,800	
Miscellaneous	3,600	2,000	
TOTAL	$73,500	$50,891	

Notes:

(1) Mortgage paid off
(2) Lower taxable income and special deductions
(3) Premiums will increase when employer-sponsored life insurance is converted
(4) Auto loan paid off
(5) No business clothing needed
(6) No commuting; cost of auto insurance also decreases
(7) Estimated increase of at least 25 percent in insurance and out-of-pocket expenses
(8) More leisure activities
(9) More time for extended travel
(10) Currently do not make nondeductible contribution and cannot after retirement
(11) Reduced income; will save less

ILL. 3.4 ■ Calculating Needed Annual Retirement Savings

Step 1.	Enter the amount of the annual projected retirement expenses.	$ 50,891
Step 2.	Multiply the amount entered in Step 1 by the factor shown in Table I for the number of years to retirement. (Assumes 5 percent inflation rate.)	× 2.7 $137,406
Step 3.	Enter the annual retirement benefit provided by all employer-sponsored retirement plans.	$ 24,000
Step 4.	Multiply the amount entered in Step 3 by the factor used in Step 2. (Assumes 5 percent inflation rate.)	× 2.7 $ 64,800
Step 5.	Enter the amount of any Social Security retirement benefits.	$ 20,964
Step 6.	Multiply the amount entered in Step 5 by the factor in Step 2. (Assumes 5 percent Social Security cost-of-living increase.)	× 2.7 $ 56,603
Step 7.	Subtract the amounts determined in Step 4 and Step 6 from the amount determined in Step 2. (Represents amount to be provided by personal savings.)	$137,406 − 64,800 − 56,603 $ 16,003
Step 8.	Multiply the amount calculated in Step 7 by the appropriate factor in Table L. (Assume a retirement period of 20 years and a growth portfolio.) (Represents lump-sum amount to provide an annual income for 20 years.)	× 13.3 $ 212,840
Step 9.	Enter the total value of all currently owned assets that may be allocated to retirement distribution. (Current growth portfolio.)	$ 11,000
Step 10.	Multiply the amount entered in Step 9 by the factor in Table R for growth portfolios over a 20-year period. (Represents the value of invested assets at retirement.)	× 6.7 $ 73,700
Step 11.	Subtract the amount entered in Step 10 from the amount entered in Step 8.	$212,840 − 73,700 $139,140
Step 12.	Divide the amount shown in Step 11 by the factor in Table D for growth portfolios over a 20-year period. (Represents the annual retirement savings need.)	÷ 89.6 $ 1,553

expenses—income taxes and miscellaneous items—will be substantially reduced. Conversely, leisure expenses—entertainment and travel—will increase since they will have more free time during retirement. Based on these anticipated changes, Stanley and Laura have projected their annual retirement expenses to be $50,891 in "today's dollars."

You will recall from the case study that the Rivers' current combined income is $73,500. After retirement, their income—consisting of Social Security benefits ($20,964) and Stanley's company retirement plan ($24,000)—will fall to $44,964. Based on their projected retirement expenses of $50,891, the Rivers will have a shortfall of $5,927 ($50,891 – $44,964 = $5,927). Of course, their $11,000 stock investment should grow and produce additional income to meet this shortfall, but additional savings will be needed to provide additional retirement income.

How much should the Rivers save each year to meet their retirement needs? As you can see in Ill. 3.4, by using the projected retirement expenses and income from the Case Study and the factors from the Retirement Tables in Ill. 3.2, the Rivers have calculated how much additional retirement income they will need.

Let's take a closer look at these calculations. First of all, according to the case study, the Rivers have decided to retire in twenty years when they are both age 65. Therefore, their projected retirement expenses (Step 1), employer-sponsored retirement benefits (Step 3) and the amount of their Social Security benefits (Step 5) in "today's dollars" are multiplied by 2.7, the factor for twenty years to retirement from Table I in Ill. 3.2. To illustrate, their projected annual retirement expenses over twenty years will be $137,406 ($50,891 × 2.7).

In Step 7, the Rivers have subtracted their projected Social Security benefits and their income from Stanley's retirement plan from their projected retirement expenses. The resulting number shown in "today's dollars" is then multiplied by 13.3, the factor for the twenty years that this capital must last from Table L. Based on the calculation in Step 8, the Rivers should save an additional lump-sum of $212,840.

Fortunately, the Rivers have already begun to plan for their retirement by purchasing stock. To determine the amount of potential income that will be generated by their stock portfolio, the Rivers multiplied their current investment of $11,000 by 6.7, the growth factor from Table R. Based on this calculation, their investment will grow to $73,700 over the next twenty years as shown in Step 10.

In Step 11, their $73,700 investment income is subtracted from the needed $212,840 savings leaving a net amount of $139,140. This amount is then divided by 89.6, the factor for growth portfolios over twenty years, to determine the annual retirement savings need. Based on these calculations, Stanley and Laura Rivers estimate that they must save an additional $1,553 annually to meet their projected retirement income needs.

The Rivers should remember, however, that the *exact* amount of money they will need during retirement is impossible to predict. They should review and revise their plans as needed to assure that they can meet their retirement goals.

ILL. 3.5 ■ Three-Legged Retirement Income Stool

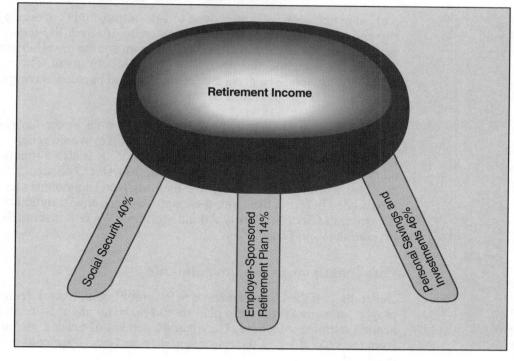

■ SOURCES OF RETIREMENT INCOME

Regardless of the amount of postretirement income needed, there are generally three sources to which individuals can look for retirement funds:

1. Social Security;

2. an employer-sponsored retirement plan; and

3. personal savings and investments.

Retirement planners compare these three sources of retirement income to a three-legged "stool" upon which your client can rest during retirement. Each of the three sources forms one "leg" of that stool, which, when combined at retirement, should provide the necessary benefits for a total amount of monthly or annual retirement income needed.

If one leg is weak or missing, the stool will collapse, leaving the client without adequate protection. The rest of this chapter is devoted to an overview of each aspect of this three-legged stool.

Then each of these sources of income will be discussed in greater detail in later chapters.

Let's begin our discussion with Social Security benefits, the first "leg" of the three-legged stool.

Social Security Benefits

Almost everyone who is employed or self-employed is covered by Social Security and will receive benefits when they retire, if eligibility requirements are met. Social Security benefits are an important source of retirement income, but they are not adequate to support a comfortable retirement. These benefits are intended to *supplement* a private pension plan and personal savings, the other two legs of the retirement income stool.

All monthly Social Security benefits are based on a worker's *Primary Insurance Amount (PIA)*. This is the amount the worker would receive if he or she retired at the normal retirement age, currently 65. It is also a function of the worker's *Average Indexed Monthly Earnings (AIME)* on which Social Security taxes have been paid. Although the monthly benefit amounts can be roughly approximated before retirement, the employee can request more accurate information from the Social Security Administration. (We will discuss Social Security in more detail in Chapter 4.)

Personal Savings and Investments

Depending on the client's income before retirement, Social Security and the employer-sponsored retirement plan should make up about 54 percent of the needed retirement income. The other 46 percent of needed income must come from the second leg of the retirement income stool—personal savings and investments.

Any savings or investment program should begin with the accumulation of an emergency fund that can be obtained quickly in case of immediate need. As we discussed in Chapter 1, the amount of money in this fund will vary, but most financial planners agree that it should be at least three months' salary (after taxes). In fact, many planners feel that six months' salary (after taxes) is a better safety cushion. The fund should be deposited in a savings account at the highest available interest rate.

After establishing an emergency fund, the client should begin to save additional money for investment purposes. One way to obtain these funds for investment is to pay bills first, set aside a specific amount for savings and then use the remainder for personal expenses. For those people who cannot save this way, some planners recommend that investors participate in an elective savings program through their employers. Many employees can have a specific amount of money withheld from their paychecks and deposited into savings accounts. In addition, any gifts, inheritances or federal income tax refunds can also be used to fund an investment program.

The Employer-Sponsored Retirement Plan

Another source of retirement income, the third leg of the retirement income stool, is the retirement plan offered by the client's employer. Many employers establish and maintain pension plans to provide financial benefits for their employees. Contributions to the plan are made by the employer (and often the employee) over a period of time. There are many types of plans that an employer can offer, and they can be as simple or as formal as the employer desires, depending on the employer's objectives.

In most cases, these plans are *qualified retirement plans* that meet government-mandated requirements. Taxed are deferred on employer contributions and the plan's interest earnings until the benefits of the retirement fund are received by the employee.

Qualified plans can be classed as defined benefit plans, defined contribution plans or a combination of the two. In essence, a *defined benefit plan* specifies the monthly benefit the employee will receive when he or she reaches retirement. The contribution is based on assumed investment returns and probabilities of the employee's survival.

Under a *defined contribution plan,* the employer establishes individual accounts for each employee into which the employer makes contributions. A specific benefit is not guaranteed and will depend on the investment performance of the retirement fund. When a plan participant retires or otherwise becomes eligible for benefits, his or her benefit is the total amount in the participant's account, including past investment earnings. Unfortunately, if investment results are poor, the employee may have inadequate retirement resources. We will discuss qualified plans in more detail in Chapter 7.

Unfortunately, only about 50 percent of currently employed people are covered by employer-sponsored plans. Those people who are not covered must find even more ways to supplement their Social Security benefits.

As you will learn in Chapter 5, successful investors begin by purchasing life insurance products to protect their dependents from the financial loss caused by their death and to create an immediate estate. After they have a solid insurance foundation that can also support retirement income objectives, investors can then decide whether to purchase stocks, bonds, mutual funds or other alternatives that make better use of their money than a passbook savings account. These investment options are discussed in more detail in Chapter 6.

■ SOLVING RETIREMENT INCOME SHORTFALLS

After you have determined your client's retirement income needs and calculated the various sources of income available, you will probably find that the client has some shortfalls. In order to close any income gaps at retirement, the client may choose any or all of the following options:

- save more money now;

- increase the rate of return on current savings or investments;

- delay retirement;

- work part-time during retirement;

- accept a lower standard of living; or

- consider a reverse annuity mortgage.

You can assist your client in choosing among these alternatives by explaining the advantages and disadvantages of each.

Save More Money Now

As mentioned earlier, many people use automatic payroll deduction or periodic payments to savings accounts to fund their retirement. You can illustrate the importance of regular savings by simply using the time value of money calculation. For example, the future value of $1,000 invested at 8 percent over ten years is $2,159; over 30 years, it grows to $10,062. Your demonstration should clearly show that saving more now will help to fund a comfortable retirement.

Increase the Rate of Return

Most investments involve *risk,* or the possibility of losing some or all of the original investment. As you recall from your economics or insurance classes, higher risk investments often promise higher potential return. In Chapter 6, we will discuss a variety of investments—from low-risk/low-return to high-risk/high-return—which you should understand.

Delay Retirement

According to the Social Security system, the normal retirement age (the age at which an individual is eligible to receive full benefits) is 65. By the year 2026, however, the normal retirement age will increase to 67. Those who delay their retirement past the normal retirement age receive a percentage increase in Social Security benefits (discussed in Chapter 4) and also have a longer time to save, invest and fund their retirement.

Work Part-Time During Retirement

Many people are choosing to work part-time for a variety of reasons after they retire. In addition to extra cash, part-time employment fulfills certain social and psychological needs. For people used to an active working life with long hours, retirement can be tedious. A part-time job helps to fill their days.

Unfortunately, additional income may reduce a person's Social Security benefits. In general, benefits are reduced if the earned income exceeds certain limits, as explained in Chapter 4.

Accept a Lower Standard of Living

If your client is concerned about maintaining a comfortable lifestyle after retirement, he or she may wish to curb spending and expensive lifestyle habits today. This may include selling the current family home and purchasing a smaller, less expensive house or trading down from a sports car to an economy car. In fact, there are tax advantages for the retiree who trades down—currently a one-time exclusion of up to $125,000 on the gain from a sale of a home for individuals age 55 or older.

For those who have already retired, a lower standard of living may be necessary to assure that they do not outlive their savings. This could mean less recreation, fewer vacations or a smaller retirement home than originally expected. It might also mean going without some of the luxuries they enjoyed during their working years.

Reverse Annuity Mortgage

Before making a decision to diminish a retiree's standard of living, the option of a reverse annuity mortgage should be explored. For most retirees, their home is the most valuable asset they possess and equity in that home can operate as a line of credit. A *reverse annuity mortgage* is an arrangement under which the equity in a home, owned mortgage-free, is liquidated in monthly installments over the retiree's statistically anticipated lifetime. Simply, the equity in the house is converted into periodic retirement income. Generally, reverse annuity mortgages are arranged with banks or other financial institutions that handle conventional home mortgage business. The gradual liquidation of the equity in a home can do much to provide a comfortable retirement for a retiree who has financial shortfalls in the postretirement years. However, such mortgages may not be available in all areas.

■ SUMMARY

Retirement, like all other phases of life, begins with realistic objectives and plans to achieve those objectives. As an insurance professional, you can assist your clients by helping them calculate their current and retirement income needs. You can project the amount of savings they will need to retire comfortably. Finally, you can suggest ways to fill any financial gaps left by Social Security, pensions and personal savings or investments.

Many people will expect Social Security to be the infrastructure that supports their retirement. Although it provides a base income for most retired persons, Social Security benefits were never intended to provide a decent retirement for anyone. In Chapter 4, we will discuss ways in which Social Security functions as the building block of retirement planning and how it can be used to fund *part* of your client's retirement.

■ CHAPTER 3 QUESTIONS FOR REVIEW

1. What is the most commonly accepted measure of inflation?

   a. Consumer Price Index (CPI)
   b. Producer Price Index (PPI)
   c. Gross National Product (GNP)
   d. Inflation Spiral Index (SPI)

2. Which of the following statements best reflects the time value of money theory?

   a. It is reasonable to expect prices to rise over time.
   b. A dollar received today is worth more than a dollar received tomorrow.
   c. The time value of money theory does not apply during periods of high inflation.
   d. Due to the effect of inflation, a dollar received today is worth less than a dollar received tomorrow.

3. Your client has just turned 21 years old. She wonders whether she should begin to make annual contributions to an Individual Retirement Account now or wait until she turns 40 to begin funding her retirement. If she begins contributions now, the difference in the amount she will have available at retirement will be

   a. inconsequential due to the time value of money.
   b. substantial due to the time value of money.
   c. impossible to determine because of the effects of inflation.
   d. dependent on the number of years she works.

4. An approach to providing extra retirement income by gradually liquidating a homeowner's equity in his or her residence is known as a

   a. tax-deferred annuity.
   b. shared appreciation mortgage.
   c. real estate liquidation trust.
   d. reverse annuity mortgage.

5. In order to fund a comfortable retirement, most people will need income from which three sources?

   a. Social Security benefits, life insurance and profit-sharing plans
   b. Personal savings and investments, an employer-sponsored retirement plan and part-time employment
   c. Social Security benefits, an employer-sponsored retirement plan and personal savings and investments
   d. Social Security benefits, part-time employment and personal savings and investments

4

Social Security

I t is important for a retirement planner to understand the role Social Security plays in an individual's retirement plans. As you learned in Chapter 3, Social Security benefits, as one leg of the retirement income stool, provide your client's base level of retirement income. These benefits must be supplemented by an employer-sponsored retirement program and/or personal savings if your client intends to maintain his or her current, or even an acceptable, standard of living.

Although Social Security provides benefits for retirement, disability and death, our focus will be primarily on its retirement benefits—those paid to workers and their dependents who meet retirement eligibility requirements. The chapter includes answers to commonly asked questions about Social Security, a brief explanation of how retirement benefits are calculated and taxed, and recommendations about integrating Social Security benefits into your client's retirement plans.

■ ■ ■ ■ ■

■ SOCIAL SECURITY: MYTHS AND FACTS

In 1935, Congress enacted a federal social insurance program called the Old Age, Survivors, Disability and Hospital Insurance Program (OASDHI). More commonly referred to as *Social Security,* this program is rarely understood by the people it serves. Social Security pays benefits in the form of monthly cash income when an individual retires, becomes disabled or dies. When an individual becomes entitled to benefits, other members of the family—including a spouse, children and other dependents—may also be eligible for benefits.

Some of the most common myths or misconceptions about the Social Security program include:

1. *Social Security benefits will cover all the income needs a person has at retirement.*

The Social Security system was *never* designed to meet all retirement needs. In fact, it was established to provide a minimal level of income for workers during their retirement years and to offer a small measure of defense against the financial burdens imposed by sickness, old age and death. Social Security is the basic foundation upon which other retirement plans such as employer-sponsored benefits and individual financial assets can be built. Unfortunately, for many people, Social Security comprises more than part of their retirement income; it is their only source of retirement income.

2. *The taxes an employee pays each year go into an investment fund where they accumulate for that employee's retirement years.*

Each worker does not directly fund his or her own retirement. The Social Security tax is simply a transfer of income from working Americans to those receiving Social Security benefits. The system is funded by means of a tax on wages, a tax enacted by the *Federal Insurance Contributions Act (FICA).* The actual amount of the Social Security tax rate and the wage limit to which it applies are frequently revised. Currently, this tax is a little over 71/2 percent on wages up to a certain amount. Both employee and employer are taxed this amount—but the employee gets all the benefits. Self-employed individuals must pay the entire tax themselves.

3. *Every retiree receives the same benefit amount.*

In fact, benefits decrease as a *percentage* of income as the level of preretirement income increases. Benefits are actuarially organized so that those in the higher income brackets receive a lesser return in benefits per dollar of Social Security tax paid. The actual retirement benefit amount is determined by quarters of coverage requirements and insured status, discussed later in this chapter.

4. *Retirement benefits begin automatically when a worker retires.*

Social Security will not begin benefits until an application is filed. The Social Security's national telephone number (800-772-1213) is the place to start. Applications will be sent to the potential retiree or may be taken over the telephone.

Even those people who understand the basics of the Social Security system will have questions about eligibility and the amounts and types of benefits available at retirement.

■ ANSWERING A CLIENT'S QUESTIONS

As a retirement planner, you must have a working knowledge of the Social Security system and the benefits it provides. These benefits supplement a retiree's income and, as such, impact on savings, pension and insurance plans. Because Social Security will not fill all a retiree's income needs, your client will need your assistance in formulating investment, insurance and possibly qualified pension plans to fill the gaps left by Social Security benefits.

For many reasons, the average American does not understand the Social Security system. Although there are many detailed books about the subject, few people take time to read and understand the material. Even the pamphlets provided by Social Security generally go unread because they seem dry or too complicated. Because most people feel that life insurance agents understand technical financial material, they may look to you to answer their questions about Social Security.

Some of the most frequently asked questions about retirement benefits are:

- Who is covered?

- How much will my benefits be?

- How do I get Social Security when I retire?

The questions are easy to ask but may be difficult to answer. In most cases, as you will see, the answer will depend on whether the individual meets certain eligibility requirements.

■ WHO IS COVERED BY SOCIAL SECURITY?

As previously stated, Social Security benefits are payable when a person retires, becomes disabled or dies. However, there is a difference between being covered by Social Security and being eligible for its benefits.

Persons Covered

Most employed or self-employed individuals contribute to, and are covered by, the Social Security system. There are a few exceptions:

- Most federal government employees hired before 1984 are excluded but are covered under the Civil Service Retirement Act. They do, however, have limited coverage under Medicare hospital insurance (discussed in Chapter 11).

- Some state and local government employees are covered by retirement plans offered by their state or local governments. Each government unit that has such a plan determines whether to join Social Security. All state and local government employees hired after March 1986 are covered by Medicare, even if not covered by Social Security.

- Railroad workers are covered by the Railroad Retirement system. However, some workers have coverage and coordinated benefits under both the Railroad Retirement and Social Security systems.

Persons Eligible

Although a person may be *covered* by Social Security, he or she may not be *eligible* for benefits. An individual's eligibility is determined by his or her "insured status": a worker must be either fully insured or currently insured. *Fully insured* is a status of complete eligibility that provides benefits for retirement, disability and death. A worker who is *currently insured* is not eligible for retirement benefits.

As you can see from these definitions, a worker's insured status determines the types of benefits that worker is entitled to receive. It depends on the number of a worker's quarters of coverage. A *quarter of coverage* is any three-month period commencing on the first day of January, April, June or October. Minimum quarter earnings are required and are based on national (adjusted) "average wages." The requirements vary depending on whether the worker needs to qualify for retirement, disability or survivors' benefits.

Eligibility for Retirement Benefits

A worker must be fully insured to qualify for retirement benefits. This means that the worker will need 40 quarters of coverage (the equivalent of ten years of covered earnings) to receive any retirement benefits. Quarters of coverage are credited on the basis of annual earnings. For example, in 1993, one quarter of coverage was credited for every $590 in earnings during the year, with four quarters of coverage for earnings of $2,360 or more annually. These amounts are subject to change every year. Workers born after 1928 will need 40 quarters of coverage to be fully insured. Those born prior to 1928 will need fewer quarters of coverage.

Eligibility for Disability Benefits

According to the Social Security definition, *disability* means that a person is so severely impaired, mentally or physically, that he or she cannot perform any substantial gainful work. The disability must be expected to last at least 12 months or to result in earlier death. This determination is based on medical evidence and is made by the government agency in the state where the disabled person applies for benefits.

To qualify for disability benefits, the worker must have earned a minimum number of quarters of coverage, some of which had to be in recent years. For example, individuals born after 1966 must have been covered by Social Security for at least 11 quarters after their 21st birthday. The requirement scales upward from there, depending on an earlier year of birth. For those born in 1957 to be eligible for disability benefits, for example, the requirement is 20 quarters of coverage out of the last ten years.

Eligibility for Survivors' Benefits

Survivor benefits under Social Security are payable monthly to the family or spouse upon the death of an eligible participant. In this case, eligibility is based either on the fully insured or currently insured status. The family of a *fully* insured participant is eligible for full survivor benefits; the family of a *currently* insured participant is eligible for some, but not all, survivor benefits.

A worker is fully insured depending on his or her date of birth and the quarters of coverage attained prior to death. In most cases, a worker needs 40 quarters or about ten years of work to be fully insured. Fewer quarters are needed by workers born before 1929. The longer the period between birth and death, the more quarters of coverage are needed for fully insured status. For example, if a worker was born in 1927, he or she needed 38 quarters of coverage to be fully insured in 1993. If a worker was born in 1960, he or she needed 10 quarters of coverage to be fully insured in 1993.

The monthly survivor benefits are based on the assumption that the participant worked steadily and received average pay raises throughout his or her working career. Like other Social Security benefits, survivor benefits are increased periodically to reflect changes in the cost of living.

In addition to monthly benefits, survivors receive a lump-sum death benefit of $255 when the participant dies. Unlike other Social Security benefits, this amount seldom changes. The lump sum is payable to:

- a spouse living with the participant at the time of his or her death or

- to a spouse or children who are eligible for monthly survivor benefits.

■ HOW MUCH WILL MY BENEFITS BE?

Again, this question is easy to ask but difficult to answer. Whether you are asked to calculate potential benefits for disability, retirement or survivors, the calculations are complicated. Benefit levels are based on the participant's earnings history and his or her insured status. In addition, benefits are tied to cost-of-living indexes and are subject to periodic revisions.

The amount of the benefit depends in part on the individual's retirement date. According to Social Security, *normal retirement* is currently age 65, and this is the earliest age at which full retirement benefits are paid. (Normal retirement age is 65 until the year 2003, then gradually increases to age 67 after 2026.) If a worker retires earlier (as early as age 62), he or she receives reduced benefits. If he or she works beyond the normal retirement age, benefits will increase slightly. The percent increase can be as much as 8 percent for workers reaching normal retirement age in 2008 and after.

The amount payable to a retiree, disabled person or a survivor also depends on the size of the worker's *Average Indexed Monthly Earnings (AIME),* which is based on a lifetime earnings history. (These earnings take into account the wages on which a worker has paid FICA taxes over the years and a weighting factor to account for inflation and cost-of-living increases over those years.) The AIME is then used to calculate the worker's *Primary Insurance Amount (PIA)* at the time of the claim.

The PIA can be defined as the monthly amount an individual would receive as a retirement benefit if he or she retired at age 65. The PIA is determined by formulas set out in Social Security law and applied to the participant's credited earnings during prescribed earnings periods. Basically, the PIA is based on a worker's covered earnings, an indexing procedure to allow for price changes over that career and the year the worker reaches age 65. In general, the higher the credited earnings, the greater the PIA and the larger the benefits (up to stated maximums).

Obviously, if a worker decides to retire early, say age 62, and collect retirement benefits, the benefit amount would be reduced to 80 percent of his or her PIA. Conversely, for those who choose to work beyond normal retirement age the benefit amount will increase slightly. (Currently, the benefit amount is increased by about 3 percent for each year the worker delays his or her benefits.)

Social Security retirement benefits are also payable to members of a worker's family. The spouse and dependent children receive monthly benefits based on a percentage of the worker's PIA.

Approximate Retirement Benefits

As we've stated, Social Security benefits are indexed for inflation and, therefore, increase periodically. In December of each year, any changes in the cost of living that could affect Social Security benefits are calculated. An increase in benefits, called a *cost-of-living adjustment (COLA)*, is payable beginning every January.

ILL. 4.1 ■ Sample Social Security Retirement Benefits

		\$1,000	\$1,600	\$2,500	\$3,300
Monthly Retirement Benefit					
Individual's Age in 1993		**Current Monthly Earnings**			
35	Individual	\$488*	\$675*	\$902	\$1,034*
	Spouse	236	327	437	500
45	Individual	\$505*	\$698*	\$939*	\$1,074*
	Spouse	248	343	461	527
55	Individual	\$528*	\$728*	\$977*	\$1,102*
	Spouse	263	362	487	549
65	Individual	\$529	\$728	\$970	\$1,066
	Spouse	264	364	485	533

An individual who was 55 in 1993 and earned \$2,500 a month could expect to receive Social Security retirement benefits of about \$977 at age 65. His or her spouse would receive about \$487 when the spouse reaches age 65.

*Because the Normal Retirement Age is higher for these persons, these amounts are reduced for retirement at age 65.

A sample of estimated benefits is contained in Ill. 4.1 to show how retirement benefits relate to current earnings. These figures are used for illustration purpose only. They assume that the participant worked steadily and received pay raises at a rate equal to the U.S. average throughout his or her working career. In addition, those earnings, and the general level of wages and salaries in the country, are assumed to stay the same as at present until the worker retires. The table, therefore, shows the value of those benefits in today's dollars.

As mentioned earlier, the exact retirement benefit is based on the participant's AIME, a figure that is then used to determine the PIA. The higher the earnings, the higher the PIA and the larger the monthly retirement benefit. However, although those with higher AIMEs will receive larger monthly benefits, these benefits will be proportionately less than benefits paid to workers who earned less. For example, an individual whose AIME is $1,000 will receive a monthly retirement benefit under Social Security equal to 53 percent of those earnings. An individual whose AIME is $4,100 will receive a monthly benefit equal to 29 percent of earnings. The fact Social Security provides proportionately smaller benefits for higher wages is an important concept that an agent may have to explain to his or her prospects.

Early Retirement

Although the normal retirement age is currently 65, Social Security will provide "early retirement" benefits, beginning at age 62 for those who are fully insured. Once they elect early retirement, these people will receive a smaller benefit for the rest of their lives. The reduction in benefits is based on two facts. First, the worker's average earnings are probably lower since he or she will have worked fewer years than the normal retiree. Second, assuming the worker will live an average of 20 years into retirement, he or she will, in theory, receive more monthly benefit checks since they will begin before age 65.

The amount of reduction in benefits will depend on the worker's age when the benefits begin. The reduction is expressed as a percentage reduction of the PIA and equals five-ninths of 1 percent for each of the first 36 months of retirement prior to Normal Retirement Age, plus five-ninths of 1 percent for each month in excess of 36. For example, retirement at age 62 represents a 20 percent reduction in the monthly benefit (3 years × 12 months × .0056). If a worker chooses to retire early, this benefit reduction is permanent.

Delayed Retirement

Mandatory retirement at any age is discriminatory and illegal. Because people are living longer, healthier lives, delayed retirement may become a trend in the future. If a worker delays retirement beyond the normal retirement age, the PIA is increased by one-fourth of 1 percent for each month (3 percent per year) of delay. (As of 2008, workers reaching age 66 will receive a credit of 8 percent.)

Earnings after the normal retirement age may increase the worker's AIME and, therefore, the PIA. (Average monthly earnings take into account the wages on which a participant has paid Social Security taxes over the years and a weighting factor to create an equivalent standard for these wages and account for inflation and cost-of-living increases over these years.) Any increase in the PIA will increase the retiree's and dependents' benefits based on those earnings. The percentage increase for delayed retirement affects only the benefits of the retired worker and the surviving spouse.

Family Benefits

As stated earlier, when a worker retires his or her family members may also become eligible for Social Security benefits. Their benefits will be based on the worker's earnings records and will be figured as a percentage of that worker's PIA, subject to the Maximum Family Benefit. (This benefit limitation is discussed in the next section.)

The participant must apply for his or her benefit before family members can become entitled to benefits (except in the case of some divorced spouses). The benefits paid to family members are in addition to the participant's benefits. In order to receive benefits, family members must meet several qualifications.

Spouse

If the worker retires at age 65, is fully insured and married, the spouse, age 65 or older, may receive a benefit equal to 50 percent of the worker's PIA. If the spouse is at least 62, he or she may receive permanently reduced benefits of 37.5 percent of the worker's PIA. The worker must begin his or her benefit before the spouse can collect a benefit on the worker's work record.

If the spouse of the worker is caring for a child under age 16 or a child disabled before age 22, the spouse (regardless of age) may receive a retirement benefit of 50 percent of the worker's PIA.

Divorced spouses may receive benefits as early as age 62 if married for at least ten years to the retired worker. However, this benefit terminates if the spouse re-marries. If the re-marriage is to a person receiving Social Security benefits, the same restrictions apply as spouse's benefits if benefits begin before the normal retirement age.

Children

Children of a retired worker may also be eligible for benefits. These children may be legitimate or illegitimate natural children, adopted children, stepchildren and dependent grandchildren (if their parents are deceased or disabled). An *eligible* child must be unmarried and under age 18 (or 19, if still in high school) or any age, if disabled before age 22. Each child's benefit is based on 50 percent of the greater PIA of either working parent, but not on the total of both.

Limitations on Benefits

Social Security survivor, dependent and retirement benefits may be reduced by several limitations. One such limitation is the *Maximum Family Benefit (MFB)*. The total benefit that all members of one family may receive is based on the earnings records of one worker and is limited to an amount that varies with the

PIA. For example, for persons reaching age 62 in 1993, the MFB was 150 percent of the first $513 of PIA, plus 272 percent of the next $227, plus 134 percent of the next $226, plus 175 percent of the PIA in excess of $966. The MFB is increased annually to reflect changes in the cost of living. Social Security literature should be reviewed annually to determine the actual MFB for each individual and family.

A second important limitation on benefits is the *earnings limitation* or the *retirement test.* Basically, if a retired worker receiving Social Security benefits also earns income from employment beyond a specified limit in a particular year, Social Security benefits may be reduced. These earnings limits change annually. The worker can earn up to a certain amount each year without affecting his or her benefits. But once that limit is reached, Social Security will reduce the worker's and dependents' benefits. For example:

1. From ages 62 to 64, benefits are reduced by $1 for every $2 over the earnings limitation during the year ($7,680 in 1993).

2. From ages 65 to 69, the reduction is $1 for every $3 earned over the limit ($10,560 in 1993).

3. Beyond age 70, there is no reduction in benefits regardless of an individual's earnings.

4. If employed by a federal, state or local government and not covered by Social Security when employment ended, a worker will receive only the amount of Social Security benefit that exceeds two-thirds of the applicable government pension. In most cases, Social Security benefits are entirely eliminated.

In theory, the purpose of these limitations is to restrict Social Security benefits to people who are actually retired or, in the case of dependents, to those who were truly reliant on the worker. Those who are self-supporting or who can continue to earn income should receive reduced benefits because they have additional sources of income. In practice, however, these limitations have been criticized as penalizing those who worked for many years at low earnings and who must continue to work after retirement to meet their monthly expenses. In contrast, workers who receive large monthly pensions will probably receive a full Social Security benefit, since nonwage income does not reduce benefits.

After the worker retires, benefits received from Social Security are usually tax free. However, in 1983, some legislation was introduced to add financial strength to the Social Security system by increasing revenue. It was determined that those in upper income levels received disproportionately higher benefits which should be taxed in a similar manner as private pensions. Consequently, those with threshold income levels of $25,000 for a single individual or $32,000 for married couples filing joint returns must pay federal income tax on up to half of their Social Security benefits.

In addition, a worker who is retired and receiving Social Security benefits must pay FICA taxes on income from any work as an employee or self-employed individual. This tax is in addition to the reduction in benefits if earned income

ILL. 4.2 ■ Request for Earnings and Benefit Estimate Statement

Form Approved
OMB No. 0960-0466

SP

SOCIAL SECURITY ADMINISTRATION

Request for Earnings and Benefit Estimate Statement

To receive a free statement of your earnings covered by Social Security and your estimated future benefits, all you need to do is fill out this form. Please print or type your answers. When you have completed the form, fold it and mail it to us.

1. Name shown on your Social Security card:

First   Middle Initial   Last

2. Your Social Security number as shown on your card:

3. Your date of birth:

Month   Day   Year

4. Other Social Security numbers you have used:

5. Your Sex: ☐ Male   ☐ Female

6. Other names you have used (including a maiden name):

7. Show your actual earnings for last year and your estimated earnings for this year. Include only wages and/or net self-employment income covered by Social Security.

A. Last year's actual earnings:

$ ☐☐☐,☐☐☐.0 0
Dollars only

B. This year's estimated earnings:

$ ☐☐☐,☐☐☐.0 0
Dollars only

8. Show the age at which you plan to retire:

☐☐ (Show only one age)

9. Below, show the average yearly amount that you think you will earn between now and when you plan to retire. Your estimate of future earnings will be added to those earnings already on our records to give you the best possible estimate.

Enter a yearly average, not your total future lifetime earnings. Only show earnings covered by Social Security. Do not add cost-of-living, performance or scheduled pay increases or bonuses. The reason for this is that we estimate retirement benefits in today's dollars, but adjust them to account for average wage growth in the national economy.

However, if you expect to earn significantly more or less in the future due to promotions, job changes, part-time work, or an absence from the work force, enter the amount in today's dollars that most closely reflects your future average yearly earnings.

Most people should enter the same amount that they are earning now (the amount shown in 7B).

Your future average yearly earnings:

$ ☐☐☐,☐☐☐.0 0
Dollars only

10. Address where you want us to send the statement:

Name

Street Address (Include Apt. No., P.O. Box, or Rural Route)

City   State   Zip Code

I am asking for information about my own Social Security record or the record of a person I am authorized to represent. I understand that if I deliberately request information under false pretenses I may be guilty of a federal crime and could be fined and/or imprisoned. I authorize you to send the statement of earnings and benefit estimates to the person named in item 10 through a contractor.

Please sign your name (Do not print)

▲

Date   (Area Code)   Daytime Telephone No.

ABOUT THE PRIVACY ACT
Social Security is allowed to collect the facts on this form under Section 205 of the Social Security Act. We need them to quickly identify your record and prepare the earnings statement you asked us for. Giving us these facts is voluntary. However, without them we may not be able to give you an earnings and benefit estimate statement. Neither the Social Security Administration nor its contractor will use the information for any other purpose.

Form SSA-7004-SM-OP1 (9-91) Destroy prior editions

SAMPLE

Source: Reprinted with permission from the Social Security Administration, 1993.

exceeds the earnings limitation. Many states do not tax Social Security benefits, but retirees may want to consult a tax advisor to be certain.

■ HOW DO I GET SOCIAL SECURITY BENEFITS WHEN I RETIRE?

Your clients will want to get all the benefits to which they are entitled. You should remind them that Social Security benefits will not begin automatically; they must apply for benefits.

Those further from retirement should complete a "Request for Social Security Earnings and Benefit Estimate Statement." This form, called Form SSA-7004, is available from the Social Security Administration and documents a worker's earnings throughout his or her career. When the statement is received, any errors should be noted and reported to Social Security. Errors identified early may be relatively easy to correct. As stated earlier, information about Social Security can be obtained by calling a national telephone number: 800-772-1213. There is no charge for these calls.

■ FUNDING A COMFORTABLE RETIREMENT

As you have seen, monthly Social Security benefits will seldom be sufficient to support a comfortable retirement. Even with annual cost-of-living increases, these benefits are usually subsistence level. Additional retirement plans should be formulated to supplement Social Security benefits.

To illustrate this point, assume that your clients, Mary and Todd, are both age 55. Todd is the sole wage earner in the family. If Todd retires at age 65 with an annual income of $42,000, his monthly retirement benefit (based on Ill. 3.1) would be $1,066 and Mary's would be $533. Their total monthly benefit of $1,599 is about 46 percent of their preretirement monthly income of $3,500. Even if their expenses are reduced after Todd's retirement, this couple will need additional income to maintain their current lifestyle.

As a life insurance professional you must understand the limitations of Social Security, emphasizing the needs that these benefits do not address. Your responsibility is to help your clients fill these gaps through other sources: life insurance, annuities, pension plans and personal savings and investments. We will cover each of these subjects in later chapters.

ILL. 4.3 ■

The Limits of Social Security

Social Security does not fill these needs:

- Cash needs at death

- Total income needs for survivors

- Adequate retirement income for surviving spouse

■ SUMMARY

As a retirement planner, you are in a unique position to help your clients understand the Social Security program and the benefits they may receive. You are an important source of information and can use this information to help clients' begin to effectively plan for their retirement.

When estimating retirement income for your clients, you must consider the benefit amount that will be payable from Social Security. This amount will depend on a number of things, including the age at which your client plans to retire. Early retirement at age 62 can reduce Social Security benefits by 20 percent and that reduction is irreversible. This reduction must be offset by increased savings or investments.

Conversely, delayed retirement can increase Social Security benefits by between 3 and 8 percent for each year of delay after the normal retirement age. The increase is also permanent and impacts on the retiree's total retirement income. You should review current Social Security information annually to determine any changes or limitations in benefits.

In the next chapter, we will address how you can use life insurance to meet retirement needs. In addition to the living benefits provisions of permanent life insurance products, we will also look at ways annuities can be used to fund your client's retirement.

■ CHAPTER 4 QUESTIONS FOR REVIEW

1. Whether a person is fully or currently insured under the Social Security program depends upon his or her

   a. Average Indexed Monthly Earnings.
   b. quarters of coverage under the system.
   c. number of dependents.
   d. annual salary.

2. Which of the following is NOT a true statement regarding the Social Security program in the U.S.?

   a. It was established in 1935.
   b. It is widely understood by the American public.
   c. Practically everyone who is employed or self-employed is covered by the program.
   d. It is a nationwide group insurance plan providing retirement, disability and survivor benefits.

3. Ron is eligible for full death, retirement and disability benefits under Social Security. His worker status is

   a. completely insured.
   b. currently insured.
   c. fully insured.
   d. partially insured.

4. If a retired worker receiving Social Security retirement benefits earns income from employment, that income may be reduced based on the

   a. relationship between monthly benefits and retirement age.
   b. age at which the individual retired.
   c. Primary Insurance Amount.
   d. earnings limitation.

5. When a person retires, Social Security benefits will begin

   a. automatically.
   b. 90 days after retirement.
   c. after a retiree applies for benefits.
   d. after an employer files for benefits on behalf of the employee.

5

Life Insurance and Annuities

As any life insurance agent knows, one of the unique features of permanent life insurance, a characteristic that sets it apart from all other financial products, is its provision for living benefits as well as death protection. These living benefits, combined with the protection element, make life insurance ideal for retirement planning and meeting retirement needs. Annuities, because they accumulate funds on a tax-deferred basis and guarantee an income flow for life, are also excellent retirement planning tools. These two products, life insurance and annuities, serve as the cornerstone of many financial plans. The agent who understands and can apply the features and benefits of these tools to retirement planning will be able to serve his or her existing clients and approach new prospects with confidence.

■ ■ ■ ■ ■

■ THE ROLE OF LIFE INSURANCE IN RETIREMENT PLANNING

For most people, life insurance is an important component of a comprehensive financial plan. It provides needed financial protection during child-rearing years and when financial obligations loom large. When coverage is purchased at an early age, the rates are very affordable. Yet even though life insurance may have been purchased to provide protection in the event of death, policyowners who are now facing retirement will find that their coverage can be redirected to meet new and different needs. Retirement does not lessen the need for life insurance; rather, it represents another dimension that this product can aptly serve.

New Needs, Different Objectives

As individuals near retirement, many will find some of their original needs for life insurance such as paying off a mortgage or assuring a child's education are diminishing. They may find that estate liquidity instead has become an important concern. Others may require the same level of death protection, yet do not want to divert retirement dollars to premium payments. Business owners, whose primary focus has been on the day-to-day operation of a business, may find themselves confronted with the issue of what to do with their business upon retirement. Different objectives, brought on by changing circumstances, present an opportunity for life agents to serve their clients effectively by updating or expanding the life insurance plan currently in place or by evaluating the need for a new plan.

A Retirement Product from the Beginning

Most people will agree they have a difficult time consistently setting aside money over a long period of time. Yet they recognize that a nest egg is important if they want to get ahead financially and retire comfortably. In this case, their general problem is finding a cash accumulation plan that works. The solution to that problem may be life insurance.

The application of permanent life insurance for retirement planning begins long before the policyowner retires. It begins, in fact, when the policy is purchased. Again, even though a policy may be bought primarily for its death protection benefits, its accumulation or investment features also allow it to operate as a retirement vehicle in the following ways:

- *It builds cash value.* Depending on the type of policy, the cash value growth is guaranteed (traditional whole life) or will vary, depending on the underlying investment fund (variable life or variable universal life). These values belong to the policyowners and are available to help support their financial objectives.

- *The cash value growth is not taxed while it accumulates in the policy.* The cash value's compounded interest earnings combined with the tax deferral on these earnings can create a sizable sum over time.

- *Life insurance requires periodic contributions.* Many individuals do not have the discipline to invest or save on a regular basis. Moreover, some investments, such as savings accounts, are too readily accessible to properly serve as long-term retirement plans. The fact that life insurance requires periodic premium payments and its values are somewhat illiquid make it a good accumulation vehicle for retirement purposes. Because premiums are not considered spendable dollars, they are much more likely to be paid as they should be and can be used to generate a cash value fund for the future.

- *Life insurance is a safe investment.* Behind every life insurance policy stand reserving and nonforfeiture laws, state guaranty associations, rating organizations and the strength of the insurance industry itself. Because of these factors, life insurance is one of the safest, most secure investments.

Because life insurance can serve the dual role of providing protection and accumulating funds, it is a valuable retirement tool. Let's examine some of the ways in which different life insurance plans can be used to meet retirement needs. Though term insurance can play a role in this arena, our focus will be on permanent plans.

Traditional Whole Life

There is nothing new about the role of traditional whole life insurance in retirement planning. The premiums, paid over the life of the insured, remain level over the life of the policy. Whole life policies build cash values which, when they are not needed to support death benefits, can be used in a variety of ways for retirement. Cash values can be withdrawn, through a policy loan or policy surrender to provide income. They also can be used to purchase paid-up insurance or extended term insurance, relieving the insured of premium payments but allowing him or her to maintain insurance coverage. They can be left intact in the policy, the proceeds of which may be needed for estate liquidity. The policies can satisfy the continuing need for survivor benefits after retirement. And, finally, they can be used to purchase an annuity through a tax-free transaction known as a *1035 exchange* (explained later in this chapter).

If an insured purchases a participating life insurance policy, he or she will be entitled to receive policy dividends. These *dividends* represent the difference between the premiums charged and the actual costs incurred during the period for which the premiums were charged. Owners of participating policies who have been receiving dividends over the years may want to reconsider how they can or should be using these dividends. For example, should dividends that have been used to purchase paid-up additions through the years leading to retirement now be applied to reduce premium payments, if the existing level of coverage is

ILL. 5.1 ■

Retirement Planning—A Reason to Call

Middle age is often the period when people begin to seriously consider retirement planning and have the financial resources to start putting their plans into action. A review of your policyowner files will identify clients who could benefit from your advice and ideas.

As a starting point with these clients, you should review their current life insurance plan with questions like these in mind:

- "Are existing coverages adequate?"

- "Should current policies be consolidated?"

- "Are any new policies—with different features or different benefits—warranted?"

- "Does this current plan reflect the needs of this individual today? Are the types and amounts of insurance coverage in line with his/her current objectives?"

- "Are the beneficiary designations and policy ownership structure up to date?"

- "Has the need for life insurance been replaced by the need for health insurance or long-term care insurance? Is the client's health insurable?"

- "Does this current insurance plan support or counter the person's financial and retirement goals?"

adequate? Conversely, if current levels of life insurance are not enough to meet a survivor's needs or cover estate liquidity, dividends could be used to purchase more coverage, without increasing the insured's out-of-pocket expenditures.

Limited Pay Whole Life

For a number of people, the 15- to 20-year period preceding retirement may be a time when their financial obligations are great—children are in college, mortgages have not yet been paid off, a business may require additional investment—and their incomes may be relatively high. Although these people need permanent, whole life protection, they are also concerned about maintaining their lifestyle after they retire when their incomes may be drastically reduced. These prospects are candidates for *limited pay whole life policies.*

These excellent retirement planning tools provide faster-growing cash values than straight whole life policies offer. The premiums are adjusted to fit a specified period, such as the insured's anticipated retirement date. Premiums are paid during the insured's most financially productive years, with no premiums due after a specified period. At that time, the insured will have a fully-paid up policy—its values and benefits intact and available—and the premium dollars will be freed up to use for other needs.

Universal Life

A *universal life* policy can be an attractive alternative to a traditional whole life plan. It too is permanent insurance, but it differs from whole life by permitting flexible premium payments and adjustable death benefits. These features give the policyowner greater control over his or her plan.

Universal life policies allow the policyowner to select one of two death benefit options:

1. an increasing death benefit (the sum of a level term insurance amount plus the increasing cash values) or

2. a level death benefit (the sum of a decreasing term insurance amount plus the increasing cash value).

Based, in part, on the amount of insurance (the "amount at risk"), a premium rate is established. From the premium, a predetermined monthly expense charge is subtracted and the balance is directed into the policy's cash value. Each month, the cash value account is credited with a guaranteed interest rate as specified in the policy *plus* any excess interest earned by the insurer. The cost of the insurance is subtracted each month from the cash value account.

From the policyowner's perspective, the flexibility of universal life centers around the amount and timing of premium payments and the amount of insurance. Because the cost of the insurance is taken from the policy's cash value, premium payments can be increased or decreased or skipped altogether. As long as the cash values are sufficient to support the cost of insurance protection, the policy remains in force. The amount of the insurance and the death benefit can be increased (as long as the insured is healthy) or decreased to adapt to a policyowner's need. Finally, universal life policies typically allow for partial withdrawals of the cash value (though surrender charges could be applied).

Because of this flexibility, universal life has been described as a "cradle to grave" plan. For example, during the years when death protection is most needed, the amount of insurance can be adjusted upward to cover those needs. As the individual nears retirement and perhaps has a greater need for savings and accumulation, the face amount can be decreased. By decreasing premiums, the policyowner can divert the savings to another investment; by increasing the premiums, the insured will enhance his or her cash value growth. The fact that this growth is tax deferred is another benefit.

Variable Life

Variable life insurance is a good example of how a life insurance product combines a protection element with an investment element. And, for some people, variable life insurance could be an ideal retirement planning tool.

Like whole life, variable life has fixed, permanent premiums and a minimum guaranteed death benefit. Unlike whole life, which guarantees a certain rate of return on its cash values, variable life allows the policyowner to choose how the cash value will be invested from a selected portfolio of stocks, bonds or money market funds. To this extent, the policyowner assumes the risk of directing the investments. Cash values are not guaranteed with variable life; they will perform in relation to the underlying investment portfolio. If the portfolio does well, the return will be higher than what the policyowner otherwise would have received with a traditional policy. However, if the portfolio performs poorly, the policyowner could lose a portion of his or her investment funds.

The death benefit payable from a variable policy is also a function of how well the cash values perform. As noted, a minimum benefit is guaranteed; it is the initial face amount of the policy. The actual amount of the death benefit, however, is equal to the minimum death benefit plus the cash value. Thus, if at the insured's death the policy's cash value were $0, only the minimum death benefit would be paid. If the policy's cash value were greater than $0, the death benefit would be that value plus the minimum benefit.

Whether variable life is suitable for any given individual will depend on his or her risk tolerance. Variable life can be an excellent way to accumulate retirement savings while maintaining needed insurance coverage, as long as the individual can accept the risk. Because of the investment risk of these policies, they are considered "securities" and are regulated by state insurance law and the Securities and Exchange Commission (SEC).

Variable Universal Life

One of the most versatile products offered by insurers today, *variable universal life*, combines features of universal life and variable life into one policy. Specifically, variable universal life policies provide permanent, cash value insurance with flexible premiums, separate cash value investment accounts, no cash value guarantees and death benefit options. Cash values can be moved among the underlying accounts; within limits, death benefits can be increased or decreased to meet policyowner needs; and premiums can be increased, decreased or even skipped, as long as the cash value is enough to support the insurance amount. As in the case of variable life, the policyowner—not the insurer—assumes the investment risk for his or her cash values.

■ MEETING RETIREMENT NEEDS WITH LIFE INSURANCE

As the discussion above indicates, life insurance products are ideally suited for retirement planning. However, as agents active in this market know, the focus of retirement planning is not product-driven, but needs-driven. Before an agent can recommend a specific plan or policy, he or she has to understand the prospect's or client's goals and determine what is needed. The selection of the "best" policy or an appropriate change to an existing plan will depend on the individual's objectives and where he or she stands financially today. It requires that an agent ask, "At this point in his or her life, what does this client want and need and how can my products and services help?"

To answer these questions, an agent must analyze an individual's financial situation and weigh it against the client's goals and objectives. While every situation will be different, the following are typical retirement needs that can be met with life insurance:

- wealth accumulation;

- retirement income;

- business planning;

- pension maximization;

- additional insurance; and

- estate liquidity.

Let's examine each of these retirement needs and see how life insurance can be used to meet them.

Wealth Accumulation

A likely retirement priority for most people is to acquire or have access to enough wealth so that they can comfortably and confidently forego the salary or wage they had been earning prior to retirement. As we have learned, funds for retirement are accumulated through personal savings and investments, pension plans and Social Security. And as we have also learned, through its cash values, permanent life insurance provides an orderly and effective means to accumulate funds and contribute to the savings and investment aspect of the three-legged stool.

Some might argue that the rate of return on life insurance makes it unsuitable as an accumulation vehicle when compared to other investments that offer potentially higher returns. There are a number of ways to counter this argument. First of all, most experts agree that in the pursuit of retirement funds, individuals should diversify or balance their savings and investment mix. Life insurance provides a balance and minimizes loss because it offers safety of principal, liquidity and, with traditional policies, a guaranteed rate of return. Although many investments can offer a higher rate of return than life insurance, few investments are safer.

Second, life insurance accumulates values on a tax-deferred basis, which enhances its growth. Other investments, unless they too are tax deferred, will provide a return that is reduced by an amount equal to the individual investor's tax burden. Through tax-deferred earnings that are compounded year after year, a life insurance policy can generate sizable cash values for retirement purposes.

Third, certain types of life insurance policies, such as variable life and variable universal life, *do* offer the potential for higher returns. Through these plans, the life insurance industry has kept its products in pace with the changing needs and expectations of an increasingly sophisticated consumer base that wants long-term investments with appreciation potential.

Retirement Income

Being able to count on a certain income flow will be another retirement objective for many people. Social Security benefits will not provide the level of income needed to maintain a comfortable standard of living nor will most pension plans (if, indeed, the individual is entitled to a pension). Insurance can help provide additional income. For example, a policy's cash value can be used to purchase a single premium annuity, which will create a guaranteed income stream. Or, depending on the type of policy, these values can be withdrawn, surrendered or borrowed and used to pay off a large debt, such as a mortgage.

Business Planning

Life insurance plays a vital role in the retirement plans of business owners. For most business owners, whether they are sole proprietors, partners or close corporation stockholders, their businesses represent the largest source of their income and the most significant portion of their wealth. Planning for the orderly transition from or succession of their business is a major issue business owners must address.

A business owner can choose when to terminate his or her active involvement in a firm. Many plan to remain active until death. Others may choose to withdraw sooner, to make way for a younger family member or to enjoy the leisure of retirement. Regardless of when an owner withdraws, plans must be made so that the owner's departure does not reduce the value of the business or prevent the family from receiving its full interest at the owner's death. Consequently, retirement planning for a business owner should take into account that his or her involvement with the business will eventually cease and his or her ownership

ILL. 5.2 ■ How Life Insurance Meets Business Needs

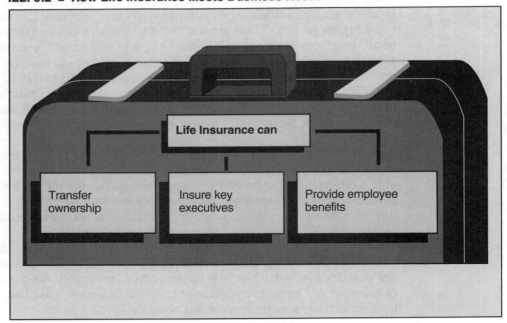

Life Insurance can

Transfer ownership

Insure key executives

Provide employee benefits

interest will have to be sold or transferred. These two certainties may or may not occur at the same time.

Life insurance is an effective planning tool that can address both eventualities. Though discussed thoroughly in Chapters 7, 8 and 12, we will briefly review its applications here:

- Life insurance can be used to fund plans that provide incentives to a key employee who the business owner views as a successor to the owner. These plans include deferred compensation, profit-sharing plans or split-dollar life insurance, for example.

- Life insurance can be used to fund retirement plans for the business owner, such as SEPs or Keoghs.

- Life insurance can be used to fund business buy-out agreements, guaranteeing the orderly sale and transfer of the business at the owner's death and providing his or her family with the assurance that they will receive a full and fair price for the business.

- Life insurance can be used to provide estate liquidity, an important consideration for business owners whose assets are tied up in their business.

Pension Maximization

Although employer pension plans can support some of the costs of retirement, they usually are not adequate to meet all of the retired worker's income needs. Another application of life insurance is to maximize a retiree's pension benefits.

ILL. 5.3 ■

> ### Meeting the Needs of the Elderly—Accelerated Death Benefits
>
> Until quite recently, traditional whole life insurance policies provided cash benefit payments only in the event of the insured's death. The only way the insured could access the policy's cash value while he or she was living was through a policy loan or policy surrender. In the event the insured was faced with a life-threatening medical condition, the life insurance policy, by design, could provide no immediate financial relief.
>
> Today, many insurers offer an *accelerated benefits rider* for their life insurance policies. This rider allows the early payment of some portion of the policy's face amount if the insured suffers from a terminal illness or injury. The death benefit, less the accelerated payment, is still payable. For example, a $250,000 policy that provides for a 75 percent accelerated benefit would pay up to $187,500 to the terminally ill insured, with the remaining $62,500 payable as a death benefit to the beneficiary when the insured dies.
>
> Recognizing the needs of the elderly, more and more insurers are beginning to offer accelerated benefits, either as policy riders or as provisions in the life insurance policies themselves. Accelerated payments can be made in a lump sum or in monthly installments over a specified period, such as one year. Innovative approaches such as accelerated benefits show how the insurance industry continually strives to address the problems and challenges facing our older population.

Upon retirement, a married worker who participated in a pension plan has two alternatives for the distribution of his or her pension benefits. He or she may either:

1. take the full pension benefit, which will be paid as long as the worker lives and will cease upon his or her death or

2. take a reduced pension benefit, which will be paid as long as either the worker or his or her spouse live.

The second alternative, known as the *spousal option,* obviously has an appeal because it covers two lives rather than one. It can be arranged in a number of ways. For example, the same benefit could be paid as long as either spouse is living or, upon the death of the worker, the spousal benefit can be reduced to half or two-thirds of that which was paid to both. In any event, the spousal option, because it covers two lives, will always produce a benefit less than the full pension benefit.

The reduced benefit may not generate enough retirement income for both worker and spouse and its potential benefit is effected only if the worker predeceases the spouse. An alternative may be life insurance and a technique called *pension maximization* or *pension enhancement.*

With pension maximization, the worker elects his or her full pension benefits. Then, using that larger benefit, life insurance is purchased in an amount that would provide the spouse with the desired amount of income at the worker's death. When the worker dies, the pension benefit ceases, but the life insurance proceeds take over and the spouse continues to receive an income. This approach has a number of advantages: both worker and spouse benefit from the higher pension benefits, the spouse is protected in the event the worker dies first and, if the spouse dies first, the worker still has an active insurance policy that can be used to supplement retirement income, provide benefits to heirs or provide estate liquidity.

Additional Insurance

For some individuals, an analysis of retirement needs may call for additional insurance. For example, an older person may be concerned about leaving his or her spouse with a small mortgage or final hospital or medical expenses. Although these commitments may not be substantial, the spouse nevertheless may lack the investment or retirement savings to meet these expenses. In the past, because of age, illness or the small amount of coverage needed, the 50-year-old and older market may have been unable to obtain life insurance to fund these small expenditures. However, many companies are now offering a "simplified issue" nonparticipating whole life insurance product created specifically for this market.

The product is designed for healthy prospects who can prequalify by answering "no" to a few broad medical questions about their health during the past three to five years. Usually, no medical exam is required, but the issuing company will likely conduct a Medical Insurance Bureau check and a telephone interview at a later date. Many of the policies contain an advance settlement option that allows the policyowner to receive a certain percent of the face amount upon a physician's confirmation that the insured has six months or less to live.

In some cases, a "second-to-die" policy may be in order. These policies are designed to cover two lives and pay a benefit at the death of the second individual. Such policies are especially useful for married couples who have accumulated substantial estates and who plan to take advantage of the unlimited marital deduction to pass the estate, untaxed, to the surviving spouse at the first spouse's death. It is at the second spouse's death that a large amount of insurance will be needed to provide estate liquidity to pay final expenses and taxes so that property and assets can be passed on intact to heirs.

Estate Liquidity

Finally, life insurance can be used to provide estate liquidity. Everyone has a need for estate liquidity and a plan to meet that need should be an integral part of any retirement program.

Death brings about certain financial obligations that must be met immediately with cash. Final expenses, hospital and medical costs, funeral and burial costs, unpaid debts, bills, taxes, probate costs, attorney fees—all of these obligations must be paid before an estate can be settled and before property and assets can be transferred to the decedent's heirs. Even the most modest estate will likely be faced with thousands of dollars in final expenses. If there is not enough cash in the estate to cover these costs, then assets may have to be sold or liquidated, often at less than market value. Life insurance, however, can provide that needed cash—and it is available at precisely the time it will be most needed. In planning to meet the liquidity need, no other vehicle is better than life insurance.

From this discussion, it is apparent that life insurance plays an important role in retirement planning. It can be used as an accumulation vehicle, as a way to distribute retirement income, as a means to assist in the orderly transition of a business interest, as a way to maximize pension benefits and as a way to provide an estate with needed liquidity at an owner's death. But life insurance agents also have another tool that can play a significant part in helping individuals meet their retirement needs and objectives. That tool is the annuity.

■ THE ROLE OF THE ANNUITY IN RETIREMENT PLANNING

An *annuity* is a regular, periodic payment for life or another defined period. It is a mathematical concept that begins with a lump sum of money that is deposited, earns interest over time and is paid out over time. Although annuities are issued by life insurance companies, they are not considered life insurance because they offer no insurance protection. While the principal function of life insurance is to *create* an estate (an "estate" being a sum of money) by the periodic payment of money into a contract, an annuity's principal function is to *liquidate* an estate by the periodic payment of money out of a contract.

Though annuities can be structured to provide benefit payments over any length of time, most are arranged to generate payments over a lifetime. For retirement planning purposes, the advantage of a structured, guaranteed life income is obvious and is one of the primary reasons the annuity is so popular. Many individuals, especially those in retirement, may be reluctant to use the principal of their savings, fearing it may become depleted. However, if they choose to conserve the principal, they run the risk of never deriving any benefit from it at all—and ultimately are obliged to pass it on to others at their deaths. An annuity is designed to liquidate principal—but in a structured, systematic way that guarantees it will last a lifetime.

Besides being able to guarantee a lifetime income, annuities make excellent retirement planning products for many other reasons. As accumulation vehicles, they offer safety of principal, tax deferral, competitive yields (enhanced by tax deferral) and liquidity. As distribution vehicles, they offer a variety of payout options, which can be structured to conform to certain payment amounts or certain payment periods. They can cover one life or two. They can be arranged so that a beneficiary will receive a benefit if the annuitant dies before receiving the full annuity principal. Like life insurance, annuities offer the advantage of flexibility, which is important to retirement planning.

Product Variations

Annuities exist to match virtually any need and objective. *Immediate annuities* are funded with a single, lump-sum premium and begin to generate periodic benefit payments within a short time after purchase. *Deferred annuities* are characterized by an accumulation period, during which time the annuity fund grows, tax deferred, for a payout at a future date. Deferred annuities can be funded with a single premium or with a series of periodic premiums over time. If the annuity is *fixed,* the insurer guarantees that a specific rate of return will be credited to the annuity funds. If it is a *variable annuity,* the premiums are invested in mutual funds and the annuity fund performs in relation to the underlying investments. With fixed annuities, the insurer assumes the investment risk; with variable annuities, the annuity owner assumes the investment risk.

Inevitably, an annuity combines two or more of the above features in its design. For example, an individual could purchase a single-premium fixed immediate annuity or a periodic premium variable deferred annuity. Basically, the variables are:

- when annuity payments are scheduled to begin—immediate or deferred;

- the method of funding the annuity—single premium or periodic premium; and

- the underlying investment account that supports the annuity—fixed or variable.

By matching these variables to specific needs, the agent can "create" a product that exactly meets an individual's retirement planning objectives. Let's see how.

The Need for Accumulation

When the need is to accumulate retirement funds, the *deferred annuity* offers a number of advantages. These include funding flexibility, tax deferral, investment options and liquidity.

Funding Flexibility

The deferred annuity can be funded with a single-premium payment or periodically over time, with a series of premium payments. For single-premium payments, most insurers require a minimum deposit of $5,000 or more; for periodic premium payments, an initial deposit of $500 or $1,000 may be required, but the annuity owner can then make future payments of as little as $25 or $50, as often as he or she wants.

Tax Deferral

Another advantage of a deferred annuity, one that is very important in retirement planning, is that the accumulating funds grow within the annuity on a tax-deferred basis. Tax deferral gives the annuity an edge over other products such as CDs or taxable bonds. For example, a CD that earns 6.5 percent will actually yield 4.68 percent to an individual in the 28 percent tax bracket. If that same individual purchases an annuity crediting 6.5 percent, he or she would actually realize a 6.5 percent return because of tax deferral. The combination of tax-deferred growth and interest earnings on the fund compounded over the deferral or accumulation period can generate significant retirement funds. Let's look at an example.

Assume John, age 50, deposits $50,000 in a certificate of deposit with his local savings and loan. Jane, also age 50, purchases a $50,000 single-premium deferred annuity from ABC Life. Both earn a 6.5 percent rate of return; however, because the earnings on the CD are taxed every year, John has fewer funds available for continued growth and compounding than does Jane with her annuity. For the sake of simplicity, let's say that both the CD and the annuity earn a constant 6.5 percent compounded annually over a 15-year period. The result, when John and Jane are ready to retire at age 65, is a fund of $99,295 in the CD and $128,592 in the annuity. The difference is attributed to tax deferral.

Investment Options

Third, the annuity as an accumulation vehicle offers the choice between a guaranteed rate of return (a fixed deferred annuity) or a variable rate of return (a variable deferred annuity). The decision should be based on an individual's objectives and his or her risk tolerance.

With a traditional fixed deferred annuity, the insurer guarantees a certain initial interest rate will be credited to the annuity for a specified period of time, such as one, two or three years. After that initial period, the annuity is "renewed" and a new interest rate is credited. It may be higher or lower than the initial rate, but it too is guaranteed for a specific period of time. By guaranteeing the interest rate, the insurer absorbs the investment risk with a fixed annuity.

In contrast, the variable annuity shifts the investment risk from the insurer to the annuity owner. Variable annuity premium payments are directed into non-guaranteed investments, such as stock, bond or money market funds and the value of the annuity fluctuates in response to how well or how poorly its underlying investments perform. If these investments do well, the annuity owner will likely realize growth that exceeds what a fixed annuity would offer. On the other hand, the lack of guarantees leaves the owner open to the ups and downs of the market inherent in investment risk. The theory behind variable annuities, which has generally held true over the years, is that by tying their return to the market they are able to outdistance or at least keep pace with inflation. Like variable life and variable universal life, variable annuities are considered "securities" because of the investment risk they hold for the consumer.

Liquidity

Finally, despite what many people think, the deferred annuity offers a number of liquidity options for those who need access to their funds prior to retirement. Because most annuities carry some kind of *surrender charge* (a charge assessed by the insurer for early fund withdrawals or contract surrenders), many people believe that once they purchase an annuity, their funds are out of reach until they retire or the product is annuitized. In fact, surrender charges for most annuities are of limited duration, applying only during the first five to eight years of the contract. Secondly, for those years in which surrender charges are applicable, most annuities provide for an annual "free withdrawal," which allows the annuity owner to withdraw up to a certain percentage of his or her annuity account with no surrender charge applied.

Deferred annuity owners can also take out loans from their contracts. Typically an annuity loan provision allows the owner to borrow up to a specified percentage of the annuity's fund value at comparatively low rates. Contract owners who consider this option should know that annuity loans are taxable and, if taken prior to age 591/2, they would be subject to a 10 percent penalty. This is explained later in the chapter.

As our discussion shows, annuities are ideal for accumulating retirement funds, offering many advantages not available with other investments. But they can also serve to create an income flow during retirement, through any number of payment or distribution options. In this way, they can address this other important retirement need.

The Need for Income

Annuities can be used to generate and maintain an income stream during retirement, for as long as the annuity owner desires. For this need, there are two options: purchasing an immediate annuity or annuitizing a deferred annuity.

An immediate annuity provides a way to convert an existing sum of money into an income stream very shortly after it is purchased. Most immediate annuities begin generating income payments within a few months; as such, they should be viewed solely as distribution products, not accumulation products. The *distribution period* is the time during which benefits are drawn from the annuity fund and paid to the annuitant. Deferred annuities can be annuitized and converted from an accumulation mode to a distribution mode.

The payout options are the same for both immediate and deferred annuities. The choice of option will affect the size and amount of the individual benefit payments. These options include:

- Straight life;

- Life with refund;

- Life with term (or period) certain;

- Joint life; and

- Term (or period) certain.

Straight Life Annuity

A *straight life annuity* pays the annuitant a guaranteed amount of income for life. When an annuitant dies, no further payments are made to anyone. If death occurs before the annuitant receives the return of his or her full principal, it is forfeited. On the other hand, if the annuitant lives beyond the point at which the principal has been paid out, payments still will continue as long as he or she lives.

Life with Refund Annuity

For those who do not want to risk the loss of principal in the event of the annuitant's early death, a *life with refund option* may be more attractive. This option offers two guarantees: the annuitant will receive benefit payments as long as he or she lives and, in the event the annuitant dies prior to receiving all of the annuity's principal, payment of the balance will be made to a beneficiary. This "refund" of principal can be in the form of a lump-sum cash payment or as continued annuity installment payments, until the principal is repaid. In either event, the beneficiary receives an amount equal to the original annuity sum less the amount already paid to the annuitant.

Life with Term Certain Annuity

A *life with term certain annuity* option provides income payments to the annuitant for life, but guarantees the payments for a specific number of years if the annuitant dies earlier. For example, a life with 15-year certain option would make payments to the annuitant for life and guaranteed payments for 15 years. If the annuitant dies prior to 15 years, payments continue to a beneficiary for the remainder of the 15 years. If the annuitant dies after the 15-year period, no more payments are made.

Joint Life Annuity

Joint life annuities are popular because they cover two lives and there are many variations. A *pure joint life annuity* pays benefits to two people, based on their joint life expectancy, and ceases payments at the death of the first to die. A *joint and full survivor annuity* makes benefit payments to two people and, at the death of the first, continues the same payments to the survivor until his or her death. A *joint and one-half survivor annuity* would pay a joint income to two annuitants and, when the first dies, would pay an income equal to one-half the original income payment to the survivor.

Term (or Period) Certain

Finally, there is the *term certain* or *period certain option*. This option is not based on life contingency; instead, it guarantees benefit payments for a certain period of time, such as 10, 15 or 20 years, whether or not the annuitant is living. At the end of the specified term, payments cease.

Which Option to Choose?

The choice of the best payout option depends, of course, on the annuity owner's needs and objectives. For any given annuity fund, the more guarantees the option offers, the less each benefit payment will be. For example, if Carl, age 60, purchased a $100,000 immediate fixed annuity and chose a straight life payout option, his monthly payments would be about $800. If he chose a life only with a ten-year certain option, the payouts would be approximately $730. A joint and full survivor option, covering his wife, also age 60, would generate about $600 a month.

A structured, fixed payout that guarantees a steady income stream for as long as the annuity owner desires can undoubtedly bring peace of mind to many retirees. However, a fixed income is subject to erosion due to inflation. As we have seen, even low inflation levels will significantly reduce the purchasing power of a fixed income stream over a number of years. For this reason, the variable annuity and its potential for higher annuity payouts may be appealing to some people. Let's take a few moments to consider how the structure of a variable annuity payout differs from that of a fixed annuity and also explore its advantages.

Variable Annuity Benefits

As explained earlier, the value of a variable annuity fluctuates in response to its underlying investments. This is also true after the contract has annuitized and benefits are paid to the annuitant. The amount of each benefit payment will vary, depending on how the contract's investments perform. Because of this, a different method to account for variable annuity premiums and variable annuity benefit payments involving *accumulation units* and *annuity units* is necessary.

During a variable annuity's accumulation or deferral period, premiums made by the annuitant are converted to *accumulation units* and are credited to his or her account. The value of each unit varies, depending on the value of the underlying investment. For example, if an accumulation unit is initially valued at $15 and the annuity owner makes a $150 premium contribution, he or she has purchased ten accumulation units. Six months later, the annuity owner makes another $150 premium payment, but during that time the underlying investments have declined and the value of the accumulation unit is $10. This means the $150 payment will now purchase 15 accumulation units.

At the point when the variable annuity benefits are to be paid to the annuitant, the accumulation units in the owner's account are converted into *annuity units*. This annuity unit calculation is made at the time of annuitization and, from then on, the number of annuity units remains the same for that annuitant. The value of a unit, however, can and does vary from month to month, depending on investment results.

For example, let's say our annuitant has 1,000 accumulation units in her account when she retires and these accumulation units have been converted into ten annuity units per payment. She will always be credited with ten annuity units—that number does not change. What does change is the *value* of the annuity units, in response to the underlying funds. Assume when she retired, each annuity unit was valued at $45. That means her initial benefit payment was $450 (10 × $45). Now assume that for each of the next three months, the value of an annuity unit was $47.50, $48 and $43.25. The annuitant would receive monthly payments of $475, $480 and $432.50, respectively.

Again, the principle behind the variable annuity and its benefit payment structure is that over a period of years, the benefits will keep pace with the cost of living and thus maintain their purchasing power at or above a constant level. Like the fixed annuity, a variable annuity offers a variety of payout options, including a life annuity, a life annuity with term certain, a unit refund annuity (similar to a cash refund annuity) and a joint and survivor annuity.

■ INCOME TAXATION OF ANNUITY BENEFITS

Annuity benefit payments are a combination of principal and interest. Accordingly, they are taxed in a manner consistent with other types of income: the portion of the benefit payments that represent a return of principal (i.e., premium contributions made by the annuity owner) are not taxed; the portion that represents interest earnings is taxed. The result over the benefit payment period is a tax-free return of the annuitant's investment and the taxing of the interest earnings on that investment.

The method used to determine the taxable and nontaxable portion of annuity benefits is known as the *exclusion ratio*. The formula is:

$$\frac{\text{Investment in the contract}}{\text{Expected return}}$$

The "investment in the contract" is the amount of premium contributed by the annuitant; the "expected return" is the total benefit amount the annuitant will receive. The resulting ratio is applied to the benefit payments to determine the amount of payment subject to tax. Let's say that Andy, age 60, invested $50,000 in an immediate fixed annuity and selects a ten-year certain payout, which will provide him with $525 a month for ten years. To determine the taxable and nontaxable amounts of his benefits, we would divide Andy's investment in the contract ($50,000) by the expected return ($525 a month × 10 years = $63,000). The result is 79 percent, which means that 79 percent of each $525 payment, or $415, would be considered a nontaxable return of principal and $110 would be taxable as interest earnings.

Taxation of Annuity Withdrawals and Surrenders

In order to encourage the use of annuities as long-term retirement products and discourage their use as short-term tax-deferred investments, the government has imposed a number of restrictions on the withdrawal, surrender or loan of funds prior to annuitization. When any of these options is taken, the money withdrawn is considered a distribution of interest and will be fully taxed. Only after all credited interest earnings have been paid out will principal be considered to be returned. A return of principal is not taxed. In addition, if a withdrawal, surrender or loan takes place prior to the annuitant's age 591/2, a 10 percent penalty is assessed on the amount taken. This penalty is waived if the distribution is taken due to death or disability or if the contract is annuitized over life.

■ 1035 EXCHANGES

As this chapter has shown, through life insurance and annuities, an agent is able to offer some very important retirement planning products and strategies to his or her prospects and clients. However, no discussion of life insurance, annuities or retirement planning would be complete without mentioning a method by which an insurance plan or an annuity can be exchanged for another annuity plan on a tax-favored basis. This is a *1035 exchange*.

Generally speaking, when an individual realizes a gain on an investment, that gain is taxed. For example, an individual who surrenders a life insurance policy after a number of years for its cash value will realize a gain to the extent that the cash value exceeds the premiums he or she paid. That gain is considered ordinary income and will be fully taxed. However, through Code Section 1035 of the I.R.C., certain kinds of policies and annuity contracts can be exchanged without the gain being taxable. Specifically, Code Section 1035 provides that no gain (or loss) will be recognized when:

- A life insurance policy is exchanged for another life insurance policy, an endowment policy or an annuity contract.

- An endowment policy is exchanged for an annuity contract.

- An annuity contract is exchanged for another annuity contract.

Consequently, when an analysis of retirement needs points to the exchange of a life insurance policy for an annuity, this can be accomplished without incurring taxes. However, as is the case when replacing any kind of permanent insurance or annuity plan, the agent has the responsibility to initiate such a transaction only when it is in the best interest of the policyowner or annuitant.

■ SUMMARY

Life insurance is a key element in any well-formulated retirement plan. Although its primary purpose may be to provide a financial safety net for dependent family members at the premature death of the insured, it can also be used to fund retirement. A variety of policies are available—each with its own premium payment, death protection and/or cash build-up structure. In addition, annuities can be used to protect against the possibility that the retiree will outlive his or her income.

In Chapter 6, you will be introduced to the "investment pyramid," a visual representative of an investment's risk and return, that many investors use when they are diversifying their investments. Investments at the base of the pyramid (such as life insurance and annuities) entail the least amount of risk to the investor's principal. We'll look at ways your clients can use additional types of investments to build on their solid investment base of life insurance and annuities.

■ CHAPTER 5 QUESTIONS FOR REVIEW

1. When a cash value life insurance policy is converted into an annuity in a nontaxable transaction, that event is generally known as a

   a. rollover.
   b. 1035 exchange.
   c. modified endowment.
   d. pension enhancement.

2. Which of the following is NOT a guarantee provided by a life insurance policy?

   a. An instant estate
   b. Cash to named beneficiaries
   c. Tax-deferred earnings
   d. A trust agreement for income settlements

3. Which of the following statements regarding annuities is correct?

   a. Interest earned by annuities is generally taxable in the year in which it is earned.
   b. Most annuity contracts are marketed by mutual fund sponsors.
   c. Each annuity payment represents only interest.
   d. Most annuities are designed so that the annuitant cannot outlive the income.

4. A technique under which a retiree and spouse reject joint and survivor distributions from a retirement plan in favor of a single life distribution payment while protecting the survivor spouse's income by acquiring life insurance is generally known as

   a. an election against the benefit.
   b. alternative distribution.
   c. pension maximization.
   d. rejection annuitization.

5. A type of annuity designed so that a second payee receives the balance of the policy proceeds should the primary annuitant die is generally known as a/an

   a. immediate annuity.
   b. life annuity with period certain.
   c. refund annuity.
   d. pure annuity.

6

Investing for the Future

A s you learned in Chapter 5, life insurance products can do more than provide death protection. Along with annuities, they are important investments that can provide additional income during an individual's retirement years.

In this chapter, we will move our discussion to the second "leg" of the retirement income stool—personal savings and investments. We will describe investment options and explain how several factors affect investment alternatives. By placing money into investments with the potential to grow and produce income, people are better able to accumulate the large sums of money that may be needed for a comfortable retirement.

■ ■ ■ ■ ■

■ INVESTMENT BASICS

As you learned in Chapter 5, life insurance needs must be met before beginning any investment program. Life insurance forms the foundation of a sound financial plan and, if not utilized or needed for death benefit protection, can be redirected to establish the basis for retirement plans and objectives. After your clients have purchased life insurance, they should establish an *emergency fund* for money that can be obtained quickly in case of immediate need. Only after this fund is established should your clients look at additional investments that offer higher potential returns.

An *investment* is any vehicle into which funds can be placed with the expectation that they will be preserved or increase in value and/or generate some returns. Cash stored in a mattress is not an investment, since its fails to earn any interest and its value will be eroded by inflation. The same cash placed in a savings account becomes an investment since it is earning interest over time.

The investor's goals, available funds and risk tolerance should determine which investments are selected. Young investors will be concerned with saving for a house, providing a college fund for their children and building an estate. They may be willing to take some investment risk to generate larger returns to fund these long-term goals.

As your clients approach retirement, however, it's likely that their goal will be to *preserve* the money they have and to make it grow and last throughout their retirement years by investing. Safety of their principal will probably be very important to them. They may choose from a variety of low-risk investments—CDs, life insurance, savings accounts—and moderate-risk investments—stock, bonds and mutual funds. Speculative investments—commodities, precious metals, and collectibles—are usually not recommended for their retirement planning. (We'll look at the advantages and disadvantages of various investments later in this chapter.)

Most investments yield some sort of cash flow or return on investment. The *return on investment* is defined as the pretax profit on an investment, expressed as an annual percentage of the investor's original capital. There is a trade-off between the return an investor can expect on an investment and the amount of risk he or she must take to earn that return. In general, investors seeking high returns must be prepared to assume high risks. Failure to understand investment *risk and return* is the primary reason many investors choose the wrong investments and face catastrophic results.

■ UNDERSTANDING RISK

Risk is the potential that actual returns will differ from those expected. In general, the greater the variation in potential gains or losses, the greater the investment's risk. The smaller the range, the smaller the risk. Therefore, low-risk investments usually mean lower expected returns.

An investment's returns are affected by a variety of changing economic and business conditions. The most important factors that widen an investment's range of possible return are:

- inflation risk;

- interest rate risk;

- market risk; and

- business risk.

Inflation Risk

Inflation—the general rise in prices over a period of time—tends to reduce purchasing power. As prices increase, the purchasing power of a fixed amount of principal declines. Therefore, investors must seek investments that produce a rate of return that compensates for lost purchasing power. Although there are no guarantees, in times of low or moderate inflation, a portfolio of equity investments can provide some hedge against inflation. However, the value of stocks tends to fall in times of rapid inflation if the government uses monetary policy to fight inflation.

Interest Rate Risk

The interest rate risk associated with investments in stocks and bonds is a result of changes in the overall interest rates in the economy. Increases or decreases in interest rates result from a fluctuation in the supply of or demand for money. This demand inversely affects fixed return investment values. As interest rates decline, investment values tend to increase; when interest rates increase, investment values decline.

For example, assume that a $1,000 corporate bond matures in 20 years and pays 9 percent interest ($90) each year. If bond interest rates increase to 12 percent on comparable bonds, the value of the 9 percent bond falls because people can purchase bonds paying a higher return. As a result, the original bond must be sold for less than $1,000 or held until maturity.

Market Risk

The price of stocks, bonds and other investments may fluctuate because of economic, social or political conditions. These changes in market conditions affect the value of the securities market. For example, real estate investments may be difficult to sell during a recession. As a result of market risk, market growth is not as predictable and systematic as most investors would like to believe.

Trends in the market are summarized as either *bull* (rising) or *bear* (falling) markets. A *bull market* results when investors are optimistic about the overall economy and purchase stocks. A *bear market* develops when investors are more pessimistic and sell stocks.

Business Risk

Successful investment in common stock, preferred stock and bonds depends on the issuer's financial condition. For example, if the company issuing stock is well-managed and its product line is flourishing, it should pay dividends and its stock becomes more valuable. If the business operates at a loss, it may eventually file for bankruptcy and the stock becomes worthless. The best way to protect against business failure risk is to carefully research the company before investing in its stock.

■ THE RISK PYRAMID

Financial planners recommend holding a *portfolio,* a collection of assets, to spread risk. Adequate diversification reduces the amount of risk associated with individual investments. By holding a number of different investments, the effect of one or more securities failing is minimized and the possibility of successful investing is enhanced.

Planners often recommend a systematic "pyramid" approach to investing for retirement. As shown in Ill. 6.1, investments range from relatively low-risk, low-return to high-risk, high-return. Investments at the bottom of the risk pyramid offer safety, low return and liquidity. Liquidity is the ability to convert financial resources into cash with ease. These investments—savings accounts, life insurance and certificates of deposit—form the base of any sound investment plan. Investments shown higher on the pyramid offer more risk and higher potential return.

Very conservative investors prefer investments such as savings accounts and traditional life insurance products. Less conservative investors will add stock, bonds and mutual funds to their investment portfolio. Real estate or collector's items may be appealing to those with the time and special expertise needed to manage these investments. Commodities or options may be attractive to more speculative investors.

Let's look at each section of the risk pyramid in terms of the investment's risk, return and liquidity.

ILL. 6.1 ■ The Risk Pyramid

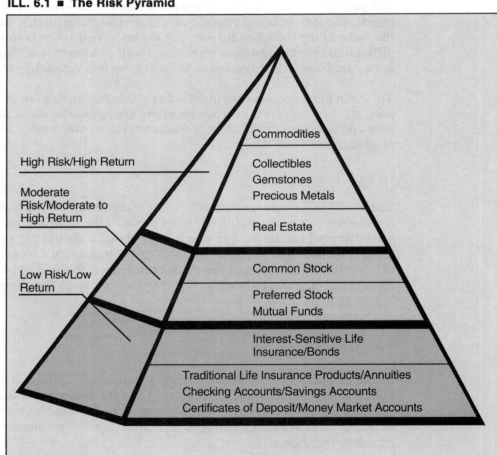

▪ LOW RISK/LOW TO MODERATE RETURN

At the base of the pyramid are conservative investments whose features include low risk, low to moderate return and liquidity. Retirement plans should begin with a solid base consisting of cash, insurance and other low-risk investments.

Traditional Life Insurance and Annuities

As you learned in Chapter 5, *traditional life insurance products*—notably whole life and interest-sensitive policies—are the core of any investment plan. Traditionally, the growth potential is relatively small but insurance offers both savings and protection in the event of a premature death. A variety of product options are available that are relatively risk free and liquid.

For someone approaching retirement, deferred annuities are a sound investment. During the accumulation period, taxes on the investment build-up of earnings are deferred. Although not particularly liquid during the early years, an annuity is completely liquid after its surrender change period expires. This investment offers safety and a moderate return.

Checking and Savings Accounts

Traditional savings vehicles—checking and savings accounts—are highly liquid and almost risk free because they are often insured by the federal government. Because of the low risk, the return is also low. Most planners recommend that some money should be set aside in these accounts for monthly expenses and an emergency fund. After such a fund is established, additional funds can be made available for investment.

Money Market Deposit Accounts

Banks and other financial institutions also offer *money market deposit accounts,* a combination of savings and checking accounts. A sound savings base can be built with these accounts. They offer unregulated money market rates, require a minimum deposit and permit only limited withdrawals so funds in the account cannot easily be depleted. Funds are federally insured (within certain limits) and may be accessed through automated teller machines (ATMs).

Certificates of Deposit

The *certificate of deposit* (CD) was designed with safety of principal in mind. They are federally insured, redeemable debt obligations issued by banks and other depository institutions. Money is effectively frozen and must be left in the account for a specified period of time or interest earned will be forfeited. In return for this longer commitment, higher rates of interest are available.

Money Market Mutual Funds

Money market mutual funds, sponsored by nonbank financial institutions, offer small investors attractive yields on short-term highly liquid securities. These funds pool the resources of many investors to purchase short-term securities issued by the U.S Treasury, large commercial banks and financially strong corporations. Although not federally insured, these investments are usually safe.

Bonds

A *bond* is a debt obligation (usually long-term) in which the borrower promises to pay a set coupon rate until the issue matures, at which time the principal is repaid. These investments include corporate bonds, U.S. savings bonds, Treasury bonds and so on. Bonds are fairly illiquid and are normally purchased for modest interest income.

Corporate bonds are offered to raise money for a company's growth. Usually sold in $1,000 units, corporate bonds carry varying degrees of risk and interest. Typically investors receive a fixed interest payment twice a year. (We will cover bonds in more detail later in the chapter.)

■ MODERATE RISK/MODERATE TO HIGH RETURN

The middle section of the risk pyramid consists of investments that are purchased for growth, income or speculation. Depending on the stock selected, there is modest risk/modest return to high risk and potentially high return. For example, an investor may choose *blue chip stock* (safe and conservative), *income stock* (usually utility stock that pays higher than average dividends) or *cyclical stock* (speculative stock that follows business cycles).

Preferred Stock

Any stock represents a share of corporate ownership. *Preferred stocks* are shares whose indicated dividends and liquidation values must be paid before common shareholders receive any dividends or liquidation payments. The risk and income levels range from moderate to high, depending on whether income, growth or speculative stocks are selected.

In general, stock is only moderately liquid because investors may not be able to sell stock when they want at the price they want. When stock prices are falling, an investor may have to take a loss by selling below the original purchase price.

Mutual Funds

A *mutual fund* is a pooled investment in which professional managers buy and sell assets with the income, gains and losses accruing to individual owners. Mutual funds are diversified so an occasional loss in one security is often offset by gains in other securities. Mutual funds range from long-term, conservative investments to highly speculative investments. They may be either load (with a sales fee) or no-load (with no sales fee) funds. In either case, the fund stands ready to buy back its shares at their net asset value.

Common Stock

Common stock represents proportional ownership of an incorporated enterprise. Stockholders share both the possibility of a company's gain or its loss. Common stockholders are the residual claimants for earnings and assets after all holders of debt and preferred stock have received their contractual payments. More information about investing in stocks, bonds and mutual funds is presented later in this chapter.

■ HIGH RISK/HIGH RETURN

The top of the risk pyramid includes speculative investments that might return large profits in short periods of time. However, there are no guarantees a profit will be made and, in fact, there is a real danger that there will be no gain and the principal may be lost. In general, high risk investments are not appropriate for retirement planning since the risk of losing everything usually outweighs the potential return.

Real Estate

Land is a limited resource so real estate is often considered a good investment. The term *real estate* includes raw acreage, vacation property, second homes and apartment or office buildings, not all of which are wise investments. Although it can be profitable for seasoned investors, investment property can create problems for the beginner. The value of the property may decrease because of changing economic conditions. Mortgage interest may or may not be tax deductible. Because managing rental property is time consuming and difficult, a professional property manager may be needed. When the investor wishes to sell, the real estate market may be soft and the selling price may fluctuate widely, depending on economic conditions.

Precious Metals, Gemstones and Collectibles

This category on the risk pyramid includes gold, silver and other precious metals; gemstones; and such collectibles as stamps, coins, fine art and antiques. Assets listed in this section are tangible items that have substance and can be seen and touched. These items are acquired not only for their financial gain but for their intrinsic value. The value of the asset is relative and based, in part, on the tastes of the viewer.

Precious metals, gemstones and collectibles generally produce no income until they are sold. Such assets involve all of the risk inherent in traditional investments plus they are highly illiquid, very speculative and subject to fraud risk. Because of the high risk, these investments are not recommended for retirement planning. Investors interested in these speculative investments should deal with only reputable dealers and investment firms.

Commodities

Investors can make relatively large profits in the commodities market. *Commodities* are a select group of items—cotton, silver, corn, pork bellies and many others—traded on one of the commodity exchanges. Commodity contracts are traded either *spot* (for immediate delivery) or in the *futures market* (for delivery at a prescribed future date).

Trading is quite risky and requires substantial expertise, time and financial resources. The commodity's performance depends on weather conditions, government intervention, consumer attitudes and a variety of other factors. Generally, commodities are not recommended as retirement investments because the potential for loss is great, they pay no interest and tax advantages are limited.

■ A CLOSER LOOK AT STOCKS, BONDS AND MUTUAL FUNDS

Most of your clients will invest in low-risk/low-return to moderate-risk/moderate-return investments. Because your clients will commonly choose stocks, bonds and/or mutual funds, you should be familiar with these investment vehicles as a means to enhance retirement income. In the following sections, we will discuss the features, advantages and disadvantages of each investment.

Equity Investments: Common and Preferred Stock

As stated earlier, stocks are a security representing ownership interest in a company. Corporations issue units or *shares* of common and preferred stock to raise *equity capital* in order to grow and expand. Both types of stock provide dividend income, appreciation of value and possible stock splits.

A *dividend* is a dollar amount that a company pays its stockholders quarterly and represents a portion of the corporation's earnings. Although the corporation's board is under no legal obligation to pay dividends, most board members like to keep stockholders happy by declaring dividends in the form of cash or additional stock.

Changing economic conditions cause the value of the stock to rise or *appreciate in value.* If the market value of the stock increases, the stockholder may continue to hold the stock or sell it at the higher price. The difference between the purchase price and selling price represents profit.

Investors can also increase earnings and profits through stock splits. By declaring a *stock split,* a company increases the number of shares of outstanding stock by exchanging a specified number of new shares for each outstanding share of stock. For example, in a 2-for-1 stock split, two new shares of stock are exchanged for each old share. Stock splits are used when a company, believing the price of its stock is too high for many consumers, wants to enhance the stock's trading appeal by lowering its market price.

Advantages of Common Stock Ownership

Millions of people invest in common stock because they enable investors to participate in the profits of a firm. Regardless of fluctuations in the market, stocks usually provide an attractive, competitive return over the long run. Therefore, common stocks can be the basis of a long-term wealth accumulation plan.

Stocks can also provide a steady stream of retirement income from the dividends they provide.

In addition, common stock ownership carries three primary rights or privileges:

1. *Residual claim to income.* All funds not paid out to other classes of securities automatically belong to the common stockholder; the firm may then choose to pay these residual funds out in dividends or reinvest them for the benefit of common stockholders.

2. *Voting privileges.* Because common stockholders are the ultimate owners of the firm, they are accorded the right to vote in the election of the board of directors and on all other major issues.

3. *Preemptive right to purchase new securities.* Through a procedure called a rights offering, common stockholders can purchase new shares somewhat below current market price.

Advantages of Preferred Stock Ownership

Most corporations that issue preferred stock do so to achieve a balance in their capital structure. It is a means of expanding the capital base of the firm without diluting the common stock ownership position or incurring contractual debt obligations.

Preferred stock has the following advantages:

- *Cumulative dividends.* If preferred stock dividends are not paid in any one year, they accumulate and must be paid in total before common stockholders can receive dividends.

- *Conversion feature.* Some preferred stock may be convertible into "X" number of common shares.

- *Call feature.* Some preferred stock is callable—that is the corporation may call in the security prior to maturity over *par,* the face value or principal value of the bond.

- *Cash dividends.* An investor in preferred stock receives cash dividends before common stockholders are paid. This is especially important when a corporation is experiencing financial problems and cannot pay dividends to both common and preferred stockholders.

Disadvantages of Stock Ownership

Stocks are subject to several types of risk that can affect their earnings and dividends, price appreciation and rate of return. For example, foreign competition can affect a company's sales and profits and cause the value of its stock to fall. Because the performance of a stock is subject to outside forces, it may be difficult to determine the true value of a stock. Preferred stock is especially susceptible to inflation and high interest rates.

ILL. 6.2 ■ Features of Alternative Security Issues

	Common Stock	Preferred Stock	Bonds
1. Ownership and control of the firm	Belongs to common stockholders through voting right and residual claim to income	Limited rights may include a participation feature	Limited rights under default in interest payments
2. Obligation to provide return	None	Must receive before common stockholder	Contractual obligation
3. Claim to assets in bankruptcy	Lowest claim of any security holder	Bondholders and creditors must be satisfied first	Highest claim
4. Risk-return trade-off	Higher risk, higher return	Moderate risk, moderate return (Dollar amount of dividend is known before stock purchase)	Lowest risk, moderate return
5. Tax status of payment to recipient	Taxable as ordinary income, in most cases	Same as common stock	Fully taxable (with some exceptions)

Bonds

Bonds are competitive investments that have the potential for attractive returns. Many corporations and state, local and federal governments issue bonds to finance their operations. In general, bonds are safer than common stocks and usually pay a higher annual income. They are especially appealing to retired investors or pension funds that must plan for the retirement of its participants. Unlike stocks whose return varies based on market conditions, bonds provide a fixed return if they are held to maturity.

As we've defined previously, a bond is a negotiable, long-term debt instrument that carries certain obligations on the part of the issuer. Bondholders have no ownership in the organization that issues the bond. In essence, bondholders are lending money to the issuer in return for its promise to return that money (with interest) at some point in the future.

The bond agreement specifies such basic terms as:

- *Par value (face value)*—the initial value of the bond. Most corporate bonds are traded in $1,000 units.

- *Coupon rate*—the actual interest rate on the bond, usually payable in semiannual installments. To the extent that the interest rates in the market go above or below the coupon rate after the bond is issued, the market price of the bond will change from the par value.

- *Maturity date*—the final date on which repayment of the bond principal is due.

All bonds fall into two major classes—secured or unsecured debt. Bonds may be secured or collateralized by a lien on a specific asset such as equipment or other real property. *Mortgage bonds* are issued by corporations and secured by mortgages on properties owned by the issuing corporations. The bond itself is secured by a pledge of real property.

A number of organizations issue debt that is not secured by a specific claim to assets. These *debentures* are bonds secured solely by the issuing organization's promise to repay the principal and pay interest, according to the schedule specified in the bond. Available vehicles include:

- *Treasury bonds*—issued to fund the needs of the U.S. government and backed by the full faith and credit of the U.S. government;

- *Agency bonds*—issued by organizations of the U.S. government such as the Resolution Funding Corporation (RTC) or the Tennessee Valley Authority (TVA);

- *Municipal bonds*—issued by state, county, city and other political subdivisions (most of these bonds are tax-exempt—no federal income tax on interest income);

- *Corporate bonds*—the basic long-term debt instrument for most large U.S. corporations; and

- *Institutional bonds*—marketed in $1,000 denominations by private, non-profit institutions such as hospitals and churches.

The method of repayment for bond issues may not necessarily call for a lump-sum disbursement at the maturity date. Although a bond may be retired in that way, bonds are more commonly retired in a number of other ways.

- *Serial payments.* The bonds are paid off in installments over the life of the issue.

- *Sinking fund provision.* Semiannual or annual contributions are made by the corporation into a fund administered by a trustee for the purpose of debt retirement. The trustee uses the proceeds in the market to purchase bonds from willing sellers. If no sellers are available, a lottery system is used to select current bondholders and then force a sale from these outstanding bondholders.

- *Conversion.* Debt may be converted into common stock, but there may be penalties for this conversion.

- *Call feature.* A call provision allows the corporation to "call in" or force in the debt issue prior to maturity.

The corporation will pay a premium over par value to redeem the debt. This option may be used when interest rates on new securities are considerably lower than on previously issued debt.

Advantages of Investing in Bonds

Investors purchase bonds for interest income, possible increases in value and repayment at maturity. The interest and principal payment are set by contract and must be met regardless of the economic position of the issuing organization. Bond rises will fluctuate as the overall interest rates in the economy change. If overall interest rates rise, the market value of the bond will fall. Conversely, if interest rates fall, the market value of the bond will rise.

Disadvantages of Investing in Bonds

There are two major sources of risk that bond investors face: default risk and interest rate risk. *Default risk* is the risk that a debt security's contractual interest or principal will not be paid when due. *Interest rate risk* is the risk that a rise in

ILL. 6.3 ■ Description of Bond Ratings

Standard & Poor's	Moody's	Description
	Bank Grade (Investment Grade) Bonds	
AAA, AA, A	Aaa, Aa, A	High-grade to medium-grade investment bonds. Capacity to repay principal and interest judged very high (AAA, Aaa) to slightly susceptible to adverse economic conditions (A, A).
BBB	Baa	Adequate capacity to repay principal and interest. Slightly speculative.
	Speculative or Noninvestment Grade Bonds	
BB	Ba	Speculative. Significant changes that the issuer could miss an interest payment.
B	B	Issuer has missed one or more interest or principal payments.
CCC, CC, C	Caa, Ca, C	Highly speculative to poor-quality issues that are in danger of default. C ratings mean no interest is being paid on the bond at this time.
Default or D	Default or D	Issuer is in default. Payment of interest or principal is in arrears.

interest rates will take place, thereby reducing the market value of fixed income securities.

Mutual Funds

You will recall that a mutual fund is an investment alternative for individuals who pool their money to buy stocks, bonds, CDs and other securities selected by professional managers working for investment firms. Mutual funds offer diversification which provides a degree of safety for the investors.

Mutual funds allow investors to choose from a wide variety of risk, liquidity and tax-treatment alternatives. A diversified portfolio may contain only low-risk or speculative stocks or bonds, tax-exempt securities, short-term highly liquid securities or a combination of these investment vehicles.

In general, investors may purchase mutual funds for:

- *capital appreciation*—accumulate wealth to build up investment capital through long-term growth;

- *high rates of return*—aggressive growth funds or so-called performance funds can provide large profits from capital gains; or

- *current income*—funds that high-grade common stock can provide a steady stream of income through dividends.

Advantages of Mutual Funds

In addition to a professionally managed and well-diversified portfolio, mutual funds also offer a variety of services that may be appealing to investors. In most cases, investors can reinvest the fund's dividends in additional shares of the fund, withdraw money from one fund and invest it in another or switch funds into IRA accounts. Many funds can be acquired with limited capital and additional shares can be purchased in small amounts.

Disadvantages of Mutual Funds

A major disadvantage of a mutual fund is its market risk. In addition, some mutual funds may be fairly expensive to acquire because of sizable commission (or "load") charges. There is also an annual management fee for the professional services provided. Finally, the fund's performance reflects the performance of the market in general and may be substantially less than expected.

■ INVESTMENT OBJECTIVES

Millions of Americans will invest in some or all of the items listed on the risk pyramid. The investments they select should be determined by their objectives. Investors whose savings goals are short-term will put funds into investments that are easy to liquidate and whose liquidation would cause no adverse tax consequences. When people are saving for the future, however, they may chose to invest in order to take advantage of growth opportunities in some higher-risk, higher-return investments.

Although most investors would like to earn the highest possible return, many people are *risk averse* and prefer to avoid risky situations. They may take an occasional risk if they feel the potential return is worth it. For example, these people may be comfortable betting $1 in a state lottery with a potential return of $20 million. In general, however, they avoid higher risk investments and are willing to accept lower returns. These investors often invest their funds in bank savings accounts, CDs and other virtually risk-free investments.

Other people, however, are *risk seekers* who expect to earn a higher return for taking part in riskier investments. Their aggressive investment strategies might include purchasing precious metals, gems or commodities. In general, these investors are willing to sacrifice some safety to achieve greater returns. It is this mix of risk-averse and risk-eager investors that allows the market to function effectively.

Investment decisions must be based on several factors, including safety, expected income, liquidity and growth potential. Let's look at how each factor affects investment decisions.

The Safety Factor

Safety in an investment means a minimal risk of loss. When determining whether to invest in something, individuals must determine how much risk they are willing to assume. They should ask a very basic question: "Can I afford to lose this money?"

During the retirement years and just prior to them, the major objective of most people is to preserve the value of the investments or savings they already have. Therefore, these people prefer safe investments—savings accounts, municipal bonds and preferred stock. Speculative stocks, commodities, options and collectibles are just a few of the investments often considered too risky.

The Income Factor

The second factor investors consider is the amount of income or return generated by the investment. The amount of return is usually dependent on the degree of risk the investor wishes to assume. Safe investments, such as CDs, will yield predictable income while riskier investments, such as mutual funds, will yield less predictable results.

If your clients are supplementing Social Security and an employer-sponsored retirement plan, they may seek investments with the highest current yield. As we have seen, these investments will include money instruments, long-term bonds, preferred stocks, rental real estate or utility common stock. However, if their income needs are met by other sources, they should probably choose investments that maximize their total returns. These investments include common stocks and investment real estate.

The Liquidity Factor

The third factor investors consider is *liquidity,* or the ease with which an asset can be converted into cash. Investments range from cash (the most liquid) to real estate and collectibles (the least liquid because of market conditions or economic reasons).

During the retirement years, liquidity is quite important because budgets are geared for expenses. Clients who are retired will need available cash for emergencies and, therefore, may be interested in more liquid investments. During their working years, clients may earmark some of their funds for investments but they could also use those funds for emergencies.

After retirement, savings accounts, money-market funds and short-term government obligations are safe choices. They may lack high yields, but they are highly liquid. Although stocks, real estate and bonds are also good investments and may be sold quickly, your client may be unable to regain the amount of money originally invested.

The Growth Potential Factor

There is inherent risk in any investment that grows and increases in value. As we've stated, in general, the greater and faster the *growth,* the higher the risk, and each investor must decide how much risk is acceptable in relation to potential return.

Investors may purchase stocks issued by certain corporations to provide capital for their future growth and expansion. Those interested in growth stocks should study the market, diversify and take advantage of opportunities open to them. In general, investors who purchase growth stocks forego immediate cash dividends for greater dollar value in the future. As the corporation grows and prospers, the dollar value of the investor's stock increases.

Substantial growth opportunities are also afforded by some mutual funds and real estate investments. More speculative investments—commodities and options—emphasize more immediate returns rather than continued growth. Precious metals and collectibles offer even less predictable growth potentials.

■ SUMMARY

Financial security in retirement depends on the adequacy of your clients' financial resources. Even if their actual retirement date is 30 or more years in the future, it is never too early to begin a retirement plan for them. Part of that plan will include capital accumulation and investment planning for their investment fund. As an insurance professional, you should begin each plan with a strong insurance base. Then you can suggest a variety of investment alternatives to provide your clients with needed income during their retirement years.

In addition to Social Security benefits and personal investments, your clients will probably also have an employer-sponsored retirement plan. We will discuss the third leg of the retirement income stool—employer-sponsored retirement plans—in Chapters 7 and 8.

■ CHAPTER 6 QUESTIONS FOR REVIEW

1. A technique for reducing risk by spreading investment dollars among different investments or types of investments is called

    a. denomination.
    b. pyramiding.
    c. diversification.
    d. guaranteed allocation.

2. Which of the following is/are advantages of investing in mutual funds?

    I. Professional management
    II. Increased diversification

    a. I only
    b. II only
    c. Both I and II
    d. Neither I nor II

3. A common stock's returns are affected by a number of factors including all of the following, EXCEPT:

    a. inflation risk.
    b. market risk.
    c. interest rate risk.
    d. default risk.

4. Bonds secured by the issuing organization's promise to repay the principal and interest are called

    a. mortgage bonds.
    b. debentures.
    c. negotiable instruments.
    d. secured debt.

5. Some risk is involved in most investments; in general, the greater the risk,

    a. the greater the potential return.
    b. the smaller the potential return.
    c. the more expensive the investment.
    d. the more likely the investment is to fail.

Corporate
Qualified Plans

I n addition to Social Security and personal savings, many people rely on an employer-sponsored retirement plan as a source of retirement funds. Typically, employers implement plans that are "qualified" under the Internal Revenue Code, which must satisfy a number of stringent compliance requirements imposed by various federal agencies, to provide future retirement income for their employees.

In this chapter and the next, we will discuss tax qualified plans—the third "leg" of the retirement income stool. We will begin with an overview of qualified plans, including their tax advantages and eligibility and vesting rules. Finally, we will compare and contrast defined contribution and defined benefit plans.

■ ■ ■ ■ ■

■ AN OVERVIEW OF QUALIFIED PLANS

In 1974, the passage of the *Employee Retirement Income Security Act (ERISA)* introduced new standards for employer-sponsored retirement plans, including guidelines for employee coverage, funding and contributions. When a retirement plan meets all of the government's strict requirements, it becomes a qualified plan. A *qualified plan* is a tax-deferred arrangement established by an employer to provide retirement benefits for employees. This means the employee pays no taxes on the amounts contributed by the employer on his or her behalf or on funds accruing in his or her account until the benefits of the retirement fund are distributed to the employee.

When employers make contributions to such plans, they receive certain tax deductions and other tax benefits. In addition, employers benefit because such plans often boost employee morale, increase the length of employment and enhance company loyalty. Employees benefit from a qualified plan because it offers a build up of tax-deferred savings which, if undistributed, provides income at retirement or upon termination of employment.

To obtain their tax advantages, qualified plans must meet specific I.R.C. requirements. Employers may seek a ruling in advance from the IRS to determine whether a proposed plan meets these requirements. In general, these requirements mandate that a qualified plan must:

- be established by the employer for the exclusive benefit of employees and their beneficiaries;

- be permanent in nature;

- be in writing and communicated to all current employees;

- be financed or funded by the employer, the employees or both;

- provide contributions and benefits that are not discriminatory under ERISA or I.R.C. provisions;

- comply with contribution and benefit guidelines; and

- comply with regulations affecting minimum participation, coverage, separation from the sponsor's general assets, vesting, funding, disclosure and more.

The purpose of these requirements is to assure that qualified plans do not discriminate in favor of highly compensated employees and that they are operated in a financially sound manner.

■ TAX ADVANTAGES ASSOCIATED WITH QUALIFIED PLANS

The trade-off to the sponsoring employer for accepting heavy compliance and reporting responsibility is the availability of several tax advantages that go along with qualified plans. With a qualified plan, an employer can provide benefits to employees under conditions that minimize current tax exposure for both parties.

The tax advantages of a qualified plan include:

- The employer's contribution is generally deductible in the year it is made, assuming that the contribution is made no later than the date on which the employer's income tax—including extensions—is filed.

- Expenses incurred to establish and maintain the qualified plan are considered to be deductible business expenses to the sponsoring employer.

- The employer's contribution to the plan on behalf of the employee is not included in the employee's current income. Earnings or gains from investments held in qualified plans accumulate tax free until they are actually distributed to plan participants. (This includes earnings attributable to employee contributions.)

- Some dramatic tax advantages for retirement distributions such as five-year averaging or ten-year averaging may be available.

- A beneficiary of a participant may receive up to $5,000 in death benefits free from income tax liability, subject to certain restrictions.

■ TYPES OF QUALIFIED PLANS

Since ERISA, all qualified plans fall into one of two categories: defined contribution or defined benefit plans. Plans that shelter otherwise taxable income without promises of specific future benefits are called *defined contribution plans*. Under these plans, the employer's contribution rate is defined. Plans that promise specific retirement benefits are termed *defined benefit plans*. Under these plans, the employee's retirement benefit is defined. Before covering specific plan provisions, it is important to understand the basic distinctions between these two approaches.

Defined Contribution Plans

The most popular type of qualified plan is the defined contribution plan. These plans provide for an individual account for each participant and for benefits based solely on the amount contributed to his or her account and its earnings. Consequently, the amount of future benefits that the participant will actually receive is not currently known; those benefits will ultimately depend on contributions, plus any income, expenses, gains, losses and forfeitures of accounts of other participants. In addition, the length of the employee's participation and the employee's retirement age will also affect the amount of future benefits to which he or she will be entitled.

The most common types of defined contribution plans include money purchase plans, target benefit plans, profit-sharing plans, stock bonus plans, 401(k) plans, employee stock ownership plans (ESOPs) and thrift or savings plans. We will cover each of these plans in more detail later in this chapter.

Defined Benefit Plans

The other type of qualified plan, which is generally considered to be more complex and costly to administer, is the defined benefit plan. This plan promises a specific retirement benefit to its participants, typically utilizing a formula to determine an employee's benefit. Because the benefits are predetermined, the employer becomes legally liable for contributions based on the actuarially determined amounts needed to fund the benefit amount over time. No matter what is actually earned on the underlying assets, the employer must pay the promised benefit to the employee.

For example, defined benefit plans may approach benefit amounts as a "replacement" percentage of the participant's compensation while employed. Since compensation, even from the same employer, changes over the years, the income which the retirement benefit seeks to replace or partially replace can be an average of the compensation paid over an employee's total career. For example, the plan could be based on 2 percent of the participant's monthly compensation. If the average compensation is $25,000 a year, the plan will pay $500 a month at retirement (.02 × 12 months × $25,000 = $6,000 ÷ 12 = $500 a month). Or a defined benefit plan may adopt a final-pay provision under which only the highest years of compensation are averaged to calculate the compensation which is to be replaced during retirement. Many plans use the highest five years of compensation during the ten-year period immediately prior to retirement. Thus, the expression "high-five" has a unique meaning in the pension administration world.

The specific plan provisions of both defined contribution and defined benefit plans will be discussed in more detail later in this chapter.

■ ELIGIBILITY RULES FOR QUALIFIED PLANS

Qualified plans must cover all current employees who meet minimum age and service requirements. In general, an employee is eligible to participate in the plan if he or she is:

- age 21 or older and

- has completed one year of service.

In some cases, a plan may reduce or eliminate the age requirement and the one-year service rule can be extended to two years if the plan provides for complete vesting upon two years of service.

Leased Employees

Some companies "lease" rather than hire employees. Such workers include temporary help from an employment agency or full-time workers who are employed for a particular service but are not hired as employees. If the leasing company has a qualified plan, it may have to cover these leased workers and treat them as regular employees for the purposes of the plan.

Excluded Employees

Some employees may be excluded from participation in a qualified plan. These employees include:

- employees under age 21;

- employees who have worked less than one year;

- part-time and seasonal employees who work less than 1,000 hours annually;

- union employees; and

- nonresident aliens who have no U.S. income.

■ VESTING RULES FOR QUALIFIED PLANS

Vesting is a term used to describe a participant's rights to contributions made by the employer on his or her behalf. (The participant is always considered to be 100 percent vested in amounts attributable to his or her own contributions.) The sponsoring employer may select either of two approaches to minimum vesting standards. Employers can normally choose five-year cliff vesting or three-to-seven year gradual vesting. (An employer can also choose to vest participants more quickly and, thus, more liberally than mandated minimum vesting standards.)

Cliff Vesting

The first approach is five-year *cliff vesting* under which the participant is 100 percent vested in the employer's contributions after completion of five years of service with the sponsoring employer. There is no entitlement to employer contributions prior to the completion of the five years. In other words, if the employee leaves the company before the fifth year, all the benefits attributed to the employer's contributions are forfeited.

Gradual Vesting

The second approach, *gradual or graded vesting,* gives the participating employee rights to the sponsor's contribution in stages over the participant's third through seventh year of service with the employer. The normal vesting percentages under gradual vesting are as follows:

Completed Years of Service	Percentage Vested
1	0%
2	0
3	20
4	40
5	60
6	80
7	100

Accelerated Vesting

Accelerated vesting schedules are used for top-heavy plans. A plan will be classified as *top heavy* if "the present value of the cumulative accrued benefits for key employees exceeds 60 percent of the present value of the plan for all employees." A *key employee* is one who falls into any of the categories below during the current year or any of the past four years:

- 5 percent ownership of the company;

- compensation exceeding defined contribution dollar limit and representing one of ten largest ownership interests;

- more than 1 percent ownership of company and compensation exceeding $150,000; or

> • an officer of the company and compensation exceeding 50 percent of the defined benefit dollar limit.

A top-heavy plan utilizing cliff vesting must provide 100 percent vesting for all employees after the completion of three years of service. A top-heavy plan using gradual vesting must follow the minimum vesting schedule below (or be more liberal):

Completed Years of Service	Percentage Vested
1	0%
2	20
3	40
4	60
5	80
6	100

■ COVERAGE REQUIREMENTS FOR QUALIFIED PLANS

Government regulations prohibit discrimination in favor of *highly compensated employees*. A highly compensated employee is defined as a participant who meets any one of the following five criteria:

1. 5 percent ownership of the company during current or preceding plan year;

2. received annual compensation from the employer in excess of $75,000 (indexed annually);

3. received annual compensation from the employer of $50,000 or more (indexed annually) and was among the "top paid" group during previous 12-month period;

4. officer of company and received compensation exceeding 50 percent of the defined benefit dollar limit (50% × $115,641 in 1993) during the preceding plan year; or

5. meets one of the above compensation criteria *and* is one of the 100 highest paid employees during the current plan year.

In order to satisfy government requirements, all qualified plans must satisfy at least one of the following nondiscrimination tests:

- the percentage test;

- the ratio test; or

- the average benefits test.

The Percentage Test

To satisfy the percentage test, at least 70 percent of the *eligible* non-highly compensated employees must be covered under the plan.

Example:

Assume a company has 100 employees, but only 60 employees satisfy the minimum age and service requirements and 10 of these are union members. Of the 50 employees *eligible* to participate in the qualified plan, 10 are highly compensated. Therefore, to satisfy the percentage test, at least 28 (40 × .70) non-highly compensated employees must be covered by the plan.

The Ratio Test

If the plan does not meet the percentage test, it may pass the ratio test. This test compares the ratio of highly compensated employees to non-highly compensated employees. The percentage of non-highly compensated employees covered by the plan must be at least 70 percent of the percentage of highly compensated employees currently eligible to be covered by the plan.

Example:

Assume a company has ten highly compensated employees who all participate in the plan. The company has an additional 40 employees who are eligible to participate.

Number of highly compensated employees covered:	10
Number of non-highly compensated employees eligible to participate:	40
Number of non-highly compensated employees (out of 40 eligible) who must participate:	.70 × 40 = 28

Average Benefits Test

If a plan fails the percentage or ratio test, the *average benefits test* must be used. To pass this test, the average benefit provided to non-highly compensated employees must be at least 70 percent of that paid to highly compensated employees.

To apply this test, determine the number of highly compensated vs. non-highly compensated employees. Then the *employer-provided benefit* (employer contributions or benefits) is calculated as a percentage of each employee's total compensation. For example, a contribution may constitute 10 or 20 percent of the employee's total compensation. Then the benefit provided to non-highly compensated employees must equal at least 70 percent of that provided to highly compensated employees.

Example:

Assume a company has 50 employees, 10 of whom are highly compensated. The average benefit for the highly compensated employees is 20 percent of their compensation. The non-highly compensated employees must have an average benefit equal to at least 14 percent of their compensation (.70 × .20) to meet this test.

The 50/40 Test

After a plan has passed one of the nondiscrimination tests described above, the company must maintain the plan to benefit the lesser of:

- 50 employees or

- 40 percent or more of all eligible employees.

To determine the minimum number of employees who must benefit from the plan, first determine the number of *eligible* employees. (Employees who do not meet age or service requirements or who are union members or nonresident aliens may be excluded.) Multiply the number of total eligible employees by .40. (This number should not be greater than 50 for this test to be applicable.) To satisfy the 50/40 test, the number of employees who are *actually* participating in the plan must be equal to or greater than the number of employees who must benefit from the plan.

Example:
Assume a company has 80 employees. Of that number, ten failed to meet the age and service requirements, leaving 70 eligible employees. To satisfy the 50/40 test, at least 28 of the employees (.40 × 70) must be covered by the plan.

■ INTEGRATION WITH SOCIAL SECURITY

As you learned in Chapter 4, Social Security provides monthly benefits for retired individuals who have worked for a minimum period of time. Social Security may work in conjunction with a qualified plan through a process called *integration* to provide benefits. Integration permits the employer to take credit for contributions made toward an employee's Social Security benefits. If the combined benefits of the employer-sponsored retirement plan and Social Security are nondiscriminatory in favor of highly compensated employees, the plan integrates properly.

Because Social Security weights benefits toward the lower-paid individual, the employer can adjust this factor by weighting its plan benefits in favor of higher-paid employees. Integration provides a means to give highly paid employees a larger portion of plan benefits or contributions without being discriminatory. Defined benefit plans are integrated less frequently—partly because these plans are not intended to maximize owner-employee tax shelters nor minimize expenses for other employees. Conversely, the defined contribution plan often is integrated because it is intended to maximize owner-employee tax shelters and minimize non-highly compensated employee expenses.

Social Security integration rules are an important planning tool for retirement planners. Integration is a logical extension of "needs selling" because Social Security will partially supplement efforts to provide a satisfactory income replacement level at retirement. However, integration rules are fairly complex and may be confusing. These rules must be thoroughly understood by the planner before any discussion takes place with a prospect.

■ DEFINED CONTRIBUTION PLANS: HOW THEY WORK

As explained earlier, defined contribution plans are based on contributions made by the employer and the earnings they generate. In a defined contribution plan, the amount of retirement benefit that will be available is not known until retirement actually begins. The rate of return earned on the invested assets of a defined contribution plan directly impacts the employee's ultimate retirement benefit. Obviously, greater investment earnings will produce larger retirement benefits. And if greater yields are applied to larger contributions, the retirement benefit will be greater.

The age of an employee participating in a defined contribution plan also affects the amount that will be available to produce retirement income. It is clear that defined contribution plans favor younger participants because the lower the employee's age when he or she becomes eligible to participate, the longer will be the time frame over which assets allocated to the employee may accumulate and earn interest. Younger eligibility translates into a greater number of initial contributions. And, younger eligibility combined with sufficient length of participation in the plan will provide such a participant with a large amount of forfeitures. *Forfeitures* are employer contributions left in the plan by employees who leave the sponsoring employer before becoming fully or partially vested. The forfeited amounts are simply left in the plan and proportionally distributed to the remaining employees.

Most qualified employers favor the defined contribution plan for at least four reasons:

1. These plans are relatively easy to understand because they work like other investment scenarios. Money is invested and the end result depends on how well the investments do.

2. Investment risk is borne by the participating employee who, in more and more plans, has input into how his or her account funds are invested.

3. These plans are subject to less stringent funding and compliance requirements than their defined benefit counterparts.

4. Plan sponsors may choose from several types of qualified defined contribution plans to meet the specific needs of the employer and its participating employees.

Types and Limitations of Defined Contribution Plans

In most defined contribution plans each participant has an account to which annual additions are made. Annual additions may come from any one of three sources, which include:

1. the employer's annual contribution;

2. the employee's contribution (if any); and

3. nonvested forfeitures allocated to the participant's account.

The maximum annual addition, from all sources, that may be made to an employee's account in a defined contribution plan is the lesser of $30,000 (known as the *Code Section 415 limit*) or 25 percent of the employee's compensation. Any excess contributions must be removed from the plan or its tax-qualified status will be jeopardized.

Contributions may be made to several types of defined contribution plans. These plans generally provide that the employer will regularly contribute a certain amount to the plan for each employee.

Money Purchase Plans

Money purchase plans often appeal to medium-sized and larger businesses. Employers can make bigger contributions and receive bigger deductions than are available with a profit-sharing plan. However, in order to take advantage of the extra contributions and deductibility, an employer must make a commitment to fixed contributions.

A money purchase plan is a popular type of qualified plan in which the employer's contributions are pre-established either in terms of dollars or, more commonly, fixed percentages of up to 25 percent of employee compensation. Contributions may also be based on a "point" or unit formula allocating a specified dollar amount or percentage of salary to be contributed for each year of a participant's service with the employer. The employer *must* make annual fixed contributions in accordance with the plan's documents; they cannot be related to the employer's profits.

Profit-Sharing Plans

A *profit-sharing plan* is a type of defined contribution plan for sharing company profits with employees. A profit-sharing plan is often the qualified plan of choice by employers whose cash flow has little history or is erratic. An employer is not required to make an annual contribution to a profit-sharing plan. If earnings are poor, or the employer has a pressing need for funds, a year's contribution may be skipped. However, the law mandates that contributions to profit-sharing plans be "recurring and substantial."

Employees do not make contributions to profit-sharing plans—employees earn wages, not profits. Typically, contributions are allocated to individual employee-participants as a percentage of their salaries.

401(k) Plans

In recent years, 401(k) plans have achieved great popularity and acceptance. A *401(k) plan* refers to a cash or deferred arrangement (CODA) that can operate as *part* of certain types of defined contribution plans, including profit-sharing plans (most commonly), stock bonus plans, thrift plans or money purchase plans established prior to the enactment of ERISA (1978). Newer money purchase plans may not have 401(k) provisions.

ILL. 7.1 ■

Age-Weighted Profit-Sharing Plans

The past few years have seen the development of a number of new product offerings designed for the qualified plan market. One such product is the *age-weighted profit-sharing plan*. These plans have particular appeal for small to medium-sized closely held businesses, which generally have one or more older owner/stockholders.

Traditionally profit-sharing plans use compensation as the basis for allocating participants' shares of contributions, forfeitures and earnings. Participants with equal compensation are given equal allocations. The result, however, is often more favorable for younger employees, who have more years to accumulate those allocations.

For example, assume that Carl, age 55, and Lucy, age 35, both earn the same salary and are given a 6 percent pay allocation to ABC, Inc.'s profit-sharing plan this year. The value of this allocation will be significantly less for Carl at his retirement in ten years than it will be for Lucy at her retirement in 30 years.

Age-weighted plans attempt to overcome this disparity by providing participants with equal benefits at retirement, as opposed to making equal contributions during participation. This means that the plan takes into account not only a participant's compensation but his or her age as well. If ABC, Inc. were to adopt an age-weighted plan, it would allocate more of the current year's contribution to Carl than to Lucy in order to provide equal benefits to both at retirement. In fact, all the older employees at ABC, Inc.—a group that happens to include its owners and key executives—would receive a substantially larger share of this year's contribution.

Age-weighted plans are the result of new IRS regulations that allow defined contribution plans to be tested on projected benefits as well as contributions, for purposes of meeting the nondiscrimination rules. Using an assumed interest rate, each participant's allocation is projected to retirement age, then converted into a benefit. This benefit is then tested against the general nondiscrimination rules for defined benefit plans.

Thus, by combining the simplicity and flexibility of traditional profit-sharing plans with the benefits-oriented approach of defined benefit plans, the age-weighted plan has many advantages that would appeal to older corporate business owners and executives.

With a *cash or deferred arrangement*, an employee may elect either to take a part of his or her salary in cash—with an immediate tax liability—or defer the salary by having it shunted into a 401(k) account. The maximum amount that an employee can defer into the plan, known as the *elective contribution*, is indexed for inflation (this amount was $8,994 in 1993). Any elective deferral by the employee is currently federally tax deductible to the employer just as if it had been paid out in wages. Like wages, the amounts deferred are subject to Social Security (FICA) taxation and federal unemployment (FUTA) tax.

Most 401(k) plans are salary reduction plans under which an employee chooses to reduce his or her salary by a given percentage in advance of earning the wages. Any elective contribution is not currently taxable income to the participant and is 100 percent vested from the time it is made. The plan may require that a certain percentage be deferred as a condition of participation, but most plans avoid this requirement because it might lead to discriminatory contributions favoring the highly paid. Many employers provide matching contributions that are "pegged" to the employee's elective deferral percentage or amount. For example, an employer might contribute $1 for every $2 the employee defers, up to a specified maximum. When an employer offers a matching contribution, lower-paid employees have increased incentive to participate in the plan. This can do much to prevent potential discrimination disqualification of the plan. The government also has special and strict nondiscrimination requirements that apply to all 401(k)s.

Distributions from 401(k) plans may qualify for five-year or ten-year forward averaging for employees who satisfy the criteria for these elections. Distributions from 401(k) plans are available on account of retirement, death, disability, termination of employment or financial hardship caused by "immediate and heavy financial needs" (instances where the participant has no other resources to meet the pressing financial need). Financial hardship withdrawals, which are limited to the amount of the financial need, do not escape current taxation and are subject to the 10 percent penalty for premature withdrawals.

A 401(k) plan may allow for loans, though certain procedures must be established so that the loan will not be treated as a taxable distribution. These rules—which apply generally to all qualified plans—are explained on page 133.

Thrift and Savings Plans

Thrift and savings plans are qualified plans that have a structure similar to profit-sharing plans with 401(k) provisions. However, thrift plans incorporate after-tax employee contributions rather than the before-tax salary reductions used under 401(k)s. Employee participation is voluntary and the participant chooses the amount of his or her contribution within the plan's guidelines. The employee may generally choose investment options from a "menu" of investments available through the plan. Employers may provide full or, more commonly, partial, matching contributions. "In-service" distributions, which occur while the participant is still employed, are permitted under some plans, but may generate IRS exposure on amounts exceeding the participant's cost basis. Most plans offer withdrawal provisions only after a minimum of two years of participation.

Thrift and savings plans must satisfy many of the requirements generally associated with qualified plans. These include maximum age and service eligibility requirements, vesting standards, nondiscrimination rules and use of a trustee to oversee plan assets.

Generally, forfeitures under thrift and savings plans are used to reduce the employer's upcoming contributions. However, thrift and savings plans may reallocate forfeitures among continuing participants on a percentage of payroll ratio.

Employee Stock Ownership Plans and Stock Bonus Plans

Employee stock ownership plans (ESOPs) and stock bonus plans are similar to profit-sharing plans in many ways. Annual employer contributions are not required, future account balances are not guaranteed and forfeitures may be reallocated.

Under *ESOPs,* the employer contributes company stock to a participant's account. Both the employer and employee benefit. An employer who sponsors an ESOP or a stock bonus plan delivers employer securities to the plan trustee—not cash. Cash can be preserved for other business uses including expansion. Under most circumstances, there is no limit on the amount of employer securities that can be held by the plan. However, employer contributions are limited to 25 percent of the covered payroll. Employees benefit because they own shares in the company for which they work. As a rule, increased corporate profits translate into increased revenue or appreciation for stockholders. Employees covered under an employer stock program usually experience increased pride and productivity.

Distributions to participants may be made in the form of cash, which is immediately taxable. More commonly, distribution is made in the form of stock and taxation occurs when the stock is ultimately sold by the retired participant. For terminated participants, tax exposure occurs when the stock is distributed to the terminated participant based on the employer's cost basis. If the former participant chooses to hold the stock in anticipation of further appreciation, the appreciation will not be taxable until the stock is sold and a capital gain is realized. If the employer securities are not tradable on a stock exchange, the employee must have the right to have the securities repurchased by the employer. This required feature is known as a *put option.* The employee "puts" the securities up for sale to the sponsoring employer, who must redeem them.

Target Benefit Plans

A target benefit plan is a hybrid arrangement that seeks to utilize the best features of both the defined contribution and defined benefit approaches to tax-advantaged retirement planning. Although the combined approach is sometimes difficult to understand, the availability of larger contributions (without corresponding guaranteed future benefits) makes a target benefit plan attractive to employers.

Although a target benefit pension plan is technically classified as a defined contribution plan, it shares many characteristics with defined benefit plans. The lump sum necessary at an employee's normal retirement age is established for each participant. The employer's contribution is based on this future value, the time remaining until the employee's normal retirement age according to the plan instrument and the assumed rate of return.

Like defined benefit plans, target plans implement a benefit formula to determine the employer's annual contribution. However, the "targeted" benefit is not guaranteed. Once the amount of the annual employer contribution needed to support the estimated benefit has been determined, the employer's contributions remain largely fixed. Most target benefit plans are designed with a provision that helps to maintain the stability of the employer's cash outflow corresponding with annual contributions to the plan. Such a provision has excess earnings or losses allocated to each participant's account. In traditional defined benefit plans, variances from expected returns become the sponsoring employer's concern because benefits are, indeed, guaranteed.

Under a target benefit pension plan, it is the participating employee who is directly impacted by the rate of return earned on plan assets. The ultimate benefit that plan participants will receive will be directly affected by investment performance on the plan's assets. Most target benefit plans invest wholly or partially in such vehicles as variable annuities or mutual funds. Interestingly, when the rate of a target plan's actual investment performance exceeds the rate (element) used in the actuarial calculations originally applied to determine the "targeted benefit," the true benefit that the employee receives can be greater than the target amount. Like their defined benefit cousins, a target benefit plan tends to favor older employees more than a defined contribution plan.

■ DEFINED BENEFIT PLANS: HOW THEY WORK

Defined benefit plans have two features that distinguish them from defined contribution plans:

1. The participant employee is guaranteed an amount of pension benefit at retirement.

2. The plan does not face a $30,000 (or 25 percent) limit on annual contributions to an employee's account.

A *defined benefit plan* is a retirement plan under which benefits are determined in advance while contributions vary. The benefit may be designed as a specific dollar amount or, more often, as a specific percentage of wages to be "replaced" at retirement.

The amount of contributions an employer makes under a defined benefit plan is generally determined by a formula and ultimately by actuarial calculation. The plan administrator, often with the help of an actuary, factors a number of significant variables and calculates the amount that the employer should contribute periodically (generally monthly or yearly) so adequate dollars will be available to distribute the promised benefits when each employee reaches retirement age.

The amount of contribution that the employer is permitted to deduct is substantially different under a defined benefit plan than under a defined contribution plan. Under a defined contribution plan the maximum contribution that the plan-sponsoring employer may contribute—and deduct—is limited to the lesser of 25 percent of the employee's compensation or $30,000. With a defined benefit plan, the maximum benefit that an employer may deduct is the amount necessary to fund the plan benefits that have been determined under the terms of the plan document. In fact, the contribution *must* be sufficient to fund those benefits assuming it is to be invested over the expected time until the employee retires.

Generally, a defined benefit plan is more cumbersome and costly to administer than a defined contribution plan. Annual contributions have to be calculated each time they are made. Actuaries must be engaged periodically to certify the accuracy of the contribution amounts. But, for an employer whose objective is to maximize retirement funding contributions for the owner and key employees, especially older ones, the financial and administrative trade-offs may well be worth the extra trouble. In order to understand how a defined benefit plan really works, it is necessary to look at how benefits are determined and how predicted earnings compounded over time can be used to determine a reasonably correct annual funding contribution.

Determining Benefits Under a Defined Benefit Plan

Defined benefit plans are designed to "replace" a percentage of preretirement earnings during the postretirement years. However, there is some question among plans as to just how "earnings" are defined. Two working definitions of "earnings," both of which include an average of the employee's compensation over an established period of time, are used in determining benefits in defined benefit plans.

1. The *career average method* averages a worker's earnings over his or her employment with the company. Because of inflation and potential salary raises for long-term employees, the career average method may leave substantial gaps in preretirement income replacement during the retirement years. (Some plans do make adjustments for inflation.)

2. The *final average method* typically factors the retirement benefit by calculating an average of earnings over the final ten, five, or three years of employment prior to retirement. This method will provide the retired employee with a larger pension because an average of a retiree's final, and generally highest, years of pay produces a higher number than will an average of compensation throughout the years of a worker's employment.

As stated earlier, virtually all defined benefit plans will use one of four formulas to calculate future annual retirement benefits.

1. The *flat amount formula* determines benefits according to a specified amount. For example, all employees will receive $600 per month. Generally, employees covered under a flat amount benefit formula, who earned the same compensation, receive the same retirement benefit. However, a plan document may include a provision that reduces the flat amount of an employee's benefit if his or her service is less than a certain time period (often ten years) specified in the document.

2. The *flat percentage of earnings formula* provides benefits based on a stated percentage of the employee's preretirement average compensation. Length of service does *not* come into play in this formula. An example of this formula would be a defined benefit plan that provides a benefit of 50 percent of preretirement pay. The final average method of defining "earnings" is generally used with this formula to address inflation.

3. The *flat amount per year of service formula* provides a retirement benefit in the form of an established dollar amount for each year of employment covered under the plan. This formula is commonly used by union pension plans. Federal tax laws define a year of service as 1,000 hours worked in a 12-month consecutive period. For example, a flat amount per year of service formula plan that offers a benefit of $30.00 per month for each year of participation or "covered service" for a worker with 30 years of participation under the plan would provide a monthly pension of $900.

4. The *percentage of earnings per year of service formula* provides a percentage "unit" of compensation for each year of participation in the plan. If each unit is 3 percent, a covered worker with 25 years of service will have a benefit of 75 percent of compensation. Both career average and final average methods are used under this system that tends to favor younger workers who have the potential for many years of future service.

Limits on Annual Benefits

The government has set limits on the amount of retirement benefit allowed under a defined benefit plan at the normal retirement age, generally 65, and younger. The intent of this IRS rule is to restrict highly compensated employees from reaping "abusive" benefits under this type of qualified plan.

The maximum annual retirement benefit that is permitted at age 65 is the lesser of an annually indexed dollar amount ($115,641 in 1993) or 100 percent of the employee's average pay over the highest three ("high-three") years of preretirement earnings. When retirement begins prior to an employee's attainment of age 65, the law requires that this maximum amount be reduced by a "reasonable" rate of interest which may not be less than 5 percent. Conversely, when retirement begins after age 65, the benefit is to be adjusted (upward) using a "reasonable" interest rate that may be no greater than 5 percent.

Determining Contributions in a Defined Benefit Plan

The ultimate cost of benefits under a defined benefit plan will be affected by the actual experience of the plan, taking into account such events as employee turnover, true investment earnings and the ages of participating employees.

A rate of return or interest must be assumed to determine the amount of employer's annual funding responsibility. A high interest rate assumption translates into a smaller funding contribution because it is anticipated that earnings on contributions will provide a significant percentage of the dollars needed to provide a full retirement benefit under the terms of the plan instrument. However, if plan assets fail to earn at least the assumed return the employer will still have an obligation to provide the promised benefit and must make up for the shortfall when the employee retires. If a low rate of return on plan assets is assumed, larger contributions will be required of the employer to make up for lower earnings.

Employee turnover also affects contributions made to a defined benefit plan. The *turnover rate* expresses the statistical probability of the severance of employment for a given group of employees. Employee age has the greatest impact on turnover rates—younger workers change jobs more often. Turnover rate is also affected by sickness (morbidity) and death (mortality) within a work force.

A high turnover rate means that only a small proportion of employees will actually be around to receive benefits at retirement. This translates into lower required funding contributions because forfeitures under a defined benefit plan are generally used to reduce the employer's subsequent contributions.

Accounting for Variances from Assumptions

What happens if investment income, mortality and morbidity, administration expenses, turnover and other actuarial variables differ from what the plan administrator or actuarial consultant estimated? The dollar amount accumulated in the plan may be less or actually more than the actual retirement benefits to be paid.

To maintain control, a plan uses a prototype *funding standard account.* The funding standard account shows hypothetical account balances that would exist as if the plan's true experience reflected all the actuarial assumptions. If a difference appears between the actuarial predictions and the actual plan performance, the plan trustee is required to correct any inadequacy by calling for increased employer contributions. If a surplus shows, the plan trustee can instruct the sponsor to reduce upcoming periodic contributions.

Government rules require a defined benefit plan sponsor to periodically engage the services of an actuary to oversee the computation of contributions. The annual contributions must be adequate, but not excessive. The plan's actuary must implement a formal, government-approved method for establishing a sponsoring employer's annual actuarial costs.

Overfunding

Because of investment gains, some corporations may terminate their defined benefit plans and apply the overfunded amount to company operations or a dividend to shareholders. In this case, a nondeductible 50 percent penalty tax is imposed on excess plan assets that revert to the employer-plan sponsor.

■ SUMMARY

In this chapter, we discussed the basics of qualified plans and focused on specific types of plans used primarily by corporate employers. In the next chapter, we'll continue our discussion of tax-qualified plans, with a look at IRAs, Keoghs, simplified employee pension plans (SEPs) and tax-deferred annuities (TDAs).

■ CHAPTER 7 QUESTIONS FOR REVIEW

1. Employer contributions to a qualified plan are deductible by

   a. the employer.
   b. the employee.
   c. both the employer and the employee.
   d. neither the employer nor the employee.

2. By integrating a plan with Social Security, an employer can

   a. decrease benefits for highly compensated employees.
   b. increase benefits for highly compensated employees.
   c. deduct benefits for rank-and-file employees.
   d. exclude benefits for rank-and-file employees.

3. If employer contributions and earnings amount to $6,000, an employee who is 40 percent vested is entitled to

   a. $6,000.
   b. $3,600.
   c. $2,400.
   d. $0.

4. As a general rule, employees may participate in a qualified plan if they are

   a. age 21 or older.
   b. union members.
   c. seasonal employees.
   d. under age 26.

5. A company has 20 employees and maintains a qualified plan. Only 14 of the employees are eligible to participate in the plan and four of them are highly compensated. If all of the highly compensated employees are covered, how many of the remaining employees must be covered to satisfy the percentage test?

   a. 10
   b. 8
   c. 7
   d. 5

8
Individual Retirement Plans

As you learned in Chapter 7, employers are often responsible for sponsoring a retirement plan and providing at least part of the funds needed for the employee's retirement. However, these programs may not always address the needs of certain employers or those individuals who are not covered by a retirement plan in their workplace.

In this chapter, we will describe four retirement plan alternatives: individual retirement accounts (IRAs), Keogh plans, simplified employee pension plans (SEPs) and tax-sheltered annuities (TSAs). We will explore what they are, the rules under which they operate and many of the tax advantages associated with each retirement plan.

■ ■ ■ ■ ■

■ INDIVIDUAL RETIREMENT ACCOUNTS (IRAs)

Although the government provides a minimal level of retirement income through the Social Security system, it is clear that benefits from this system must be supplemented from other sources if a person is to maintain a comfortable standard of living after retirement. In 1974, legislation was signed to allow qualified individuals to provide retirement savings for themselves through *The Employee Income Security Act of 1974 (ERISA)*. This legislation was passed to encourage retirement savings by persons who were not actively participating in qualified pension, profit-sharing or Keogh plans. ERISA, and its subsequent amendments, expanded the tax shelters for many persons through the establishment of individual retirement accounts or IRAs.

An *IRA* is a program available to all individuals as a personal retirement savings plan. IRAs were designed to encourage individuals to save for their own retirement by allowing for tax-deferred accumulation of the retirement funds and, in some cases, tax deductibility of contributions made to the plan. Depending on their particular situation, individuals may also be able to make contributions on behalf of their spouses.

Basically, there are two types of IRAs: individual retirement accounts and individual retirement annuities. *Individual retirement accounts* are established with qualified custodians or trustees, such as banks, savings and loans or credit unions. Some trustees charge a small annual fee, typically ranging from $25 to $50 for their management services. Allowable investments for individual retirement accounts provided by these trustees include stocks, bonds, CDs, mutual funds, government securities and a variety of other investments.

Individual retirement annuities are annuities issued by an insurance company in compliance with certain standards and guidelines. For example, the annual premium for any individual cannot exceed the IRA contribution limit (discussed shortly) and no individual retirement annuity can require fixed premiums.

In making a decision about where to invest their money, individuals should know that, because each annual contribution is independent of any other, changes can be made in the investment of IRA funds. It is possible, therefore, that a person could have several different investments as a result of the separate individual annual deposits being placed in different accounts. Under certain circumstances it is also possible to roll IRA funds from one investment into another.

Although the prevailing IRS rules that govern IRAs have been on the books since 1986, much confusion remains as to who can establish an IRA, the amount that can be contributed each year and exactly how much of that contribution is deductible. Let's begin by discussing who is eligible to establish and contribute to an IRA. Then we will discuss the maximum allowable contributions to IRAs and the deductibility from taxable income of those contributions.

Eligibility for IRAs

Anyone who is under the age of 701/2 and who receives compensation can establish and contribute to an IRA. For the purposes of determining IRA eligibility,

ILL. 8.1 ■ Excluded Investments for IRAs

Certain investments are *not* permitted for IRAs:

* commodity futures contracts (although units of commodity limited partnerships are permitted);

* tangible personal property;

* investments in collectibles (art, antiques, gemstones); and

* gold and silver coins minted outside the U.S.

"compensation" includes wages, salaries, tips, bonuses, professional fees and alimony received under a divorce or separation agreement.

There are three exceptions to the age 701/2 restriction:

1. *Spousal IRA contributions.* If the participant is working and is older than 701/2, he or she may contribute up to the permitted limits for a spouse who is under age 701/2.

2. *SEP contributions.* Employers that participate in SEPs are required under the Technical Corrections Act of 1979 to make simplified employee pension plan (SEP) contributions for all eligible employees, regardless of age.

3. *Rollover contributions.* Employees who receive a distribution from an employer's qualified plan or IRA can reinvest all or any portion of the funds in an IRA.

Participants over the age of 701/2 must begin to take at least minimum withdrawals from their IRA or SEP accounts.

Maximum Contributions

The amount that may be contributed to an IRA will vary depending on the individual's marital status and earned income. Participants may make the following maximum annual contributions:

- *Single wage earner*—100 percent of compensation (or taxable alimony) or $2,000, whichever is less;

- *Married working couple*—100 percent of compensation or $2,000 per person, whichever is less. Unfortunately, many taxpayers don't realize that they may contribute less than $2,000 to an IRA.

- *Married couple with only one working spouse*—100 percent of the working spouse's compensation or $2,250, whichever is less. Under the *spousal IRA,* each nonworking spouse may maintain an IRA and the contribution amount may be divided between the individual accounts in any manner the couple wishes. However, not more than $2,000 can be contributed to the account of either spouse.

- *Divorced individual, receiving taxable alimony*—100 percent of his or her taxable alimony or $2,000, whichever is less. A divorced, nonworking taxpayer may contribute to an IRA up to, but not including, the year in which he or she attains age 701/2.

Deductibility of IRA Contributions

The deductibility of IRA contributions has been a subject of confusion ever since 1986 when significant changes affecting IRA deductions were put into effect. Prior to that time, any contributions an individual made to an IRA (within the contribution limits) were tax deductible. Today, the ability to deduct IRA contributions is determined by the participant's:

- status as an active participant in a qualified plan;

- tax filing status (single; married, filing jointly; married, filing separately); and

- adjusted gross income.

Each of these factors will help to determine whether an IRA contribution is fully deductible, partially deductible or nondeductible. Let's begin with the definition of an active participant.

Active Participant

An *active participant* is an employee who:

- has not been excluded from a defined benefit plan in the current taxable year;

- had an allocation made to his or her account in a profit-sharing plan or stock bonus plan during the current taxable year; or

- was entitled to (but didn't necessarily receive) contributions or reallocated forfeitures to an employer-operated money purchase (percentage of wage-determined contribution) pension plan.

An active participant's spouse who files jointly is also considered to be an active participant (regardless of whether the spouse participates in his or her own employer-maintained retirement plan). An employee who participates in a qualified pension, profit-sharing or stock bonus plan, including Keogh plans, 401(k) plans and simplified employee pension plans (SEPs), or a retirement plan for government employees, is also an active participant.

Filing Status

For the purposes of IRA deductibility, the three main categories for federal income tax filing status are:

1. *single*—for never married, divorced or legally separated individuals;

2. *married, filing jointly*—for a husband and wife filing one return for their combined income; or

3. *married, filing separately*—for a married couple filing separate tax returns.

Adjusted Gross Income

Adjusted gross income (AGI) is compensation, interest and investments income and Social Security benefits reduced by certain adjustments, such as alimony, contributions to Keoghs and early withdrawals penalties. IRA contributions are *not* subtracted in calculating AGI.

With these explanations of active participant, filing status and AGI in mind, let's look at the rules governing the deductibility of IRA contributions.

Nondeductible IRA Contributions

An IRA contribution is *nondeductible* from taxable income if the taxpayer is an active participant in a qualified plan and is:

- single, with AGI greater than $35,000;

- married, filing jointly, with an AGI greater than $50,000; or

- married, filing separately, with an AGI greater than $10,000 for the covered individual.

It should be emphasized that such active participants may still make IRA contributions, up to the prescribed limits, but they may *not* deduct those contributions. Even though their contributions may not be tax deductible, IRAs may still be an important part of a retirement plan for your clients.

Fully Deductible IRA Contributions

The *full deduction,* up to the allowable dollar limits, is available to a taxpayer who is *not* an active participant in an employer-sponsored retirement plan. The full deduction may also be taken by a person who is an active participant and is:

- single, with an AGI of $25,000 or less;

- married, filing jointly, with a combined AGI of $40,000 or less; or

- married, filing separately, with an AGI of $0.

Partially Deductible IRA Contributions

Taxpayers who are active participants in a qualified plan may claim a *partial deduction* if they are:

- single, with an AGI between $25,000 and $35,000;

- married, filing jointly, with a combined AGI of between $40,000 and $50,000; or

- married, filing separately, with an AGI of $0 to $10,000.

It often takes a little number crunching to determine the partial amount of an IRA contribution that a taxpayer can deduct. The deductible portion of the IRA contribution is calculated by reducing the regular $2,000 IRA limit (or $2,250 spousal limit) as follows:

- single—reduce by $20 for every $100 of AGI between $25,000 and $35,000;

- married, filing jointly—reduce by $20 for every $100 of AGI ($22.50 of every $100 of AGI for a spousal IRA) between $40,000 and $50,000; or

- married, filing separately—reduce by $20 for each $100 of AGI between $0 and $10,000.

For the purpose of illustration, we have provided deductibility problems and calculations for three different situations.

Example: Single Taxpayer

Charles Walker, single, is an active participant in a qualified plan. His AGI is $33,000 (or $8,000 in excess of the $25,000 full deduction limit). The deductible dollar limitation for Charles is calculated by reducing the regular $2,000 IRA limit by $20 for every $100 of the $8,000 excess ($8,000/$100 × $20) or $1,600. Therefore, he may deduct up to $400 of his $2,000 IRA contribution.

Example: Married, Filing Jointly

Barry and Bernice Goren both work and file their taxes jointly. Bernice is an active participant in her employer-sponsored plan; Barry is not. Their AGI is $45,000 (or $5,000 in excess of $40,000). The deductibility limit for Barry and Bernice is $2,000 less ($5,000/$100 × $20), or $1,000. Each spouse may deduct $1,000 of his or her $2,000 contribution to an IRA.

Example: Married, Filing Jointly, Spousal IRA

Mike Hope and his unemployed wife, Bonnie, file a joint return. Mike is an active participant in his company's qualified plan. Their AGI is $47,000 (or $7,000 in excess of $40,000). Because of Mike's active participation, the $2,250 limitation is reduced by $1,575 ($7,000/$100 × $22.50) and becomes $675. The $675 deduction may be allocated between the two IRA accounts.

Distributions from IRAs

Because IRAs are intended for retirement purposes, there are restrictions that discourage participants from withdrawing their IRA funds prior to a certain age. By the same token, in order to prevent IRA participants from perpetually sheltering their accounts from taxation, there are rules mandating when distributions must begin.

An IRA participant between age 591/2 and 701/2 may take an allowable *distribution,* or withdrawal, at any time and for any amount that the account balance will support. Any distribution that is attributable to contributions that were deductible—including the earnings on those contributions—is taxed as ordinary income, reportable for the year in which it was constructively received. There is no tax liability on the distribution of any nondeductible contributions, but any earnings from those contributions will be subject to ordinary income tax upon distribution. The IRS, under Code Section 72 annuity rules, has provisions that govern the split between taxable income and return of nondeductible contributions for distributions from IRAs.

With few exceptions, a payout from an IRA that is made before the account owner reaches age 591/2 is considered a premature distribution and subject to reportability, taxation and a 10 percent penalty in the year received. Borrowing from an IRA or pledging the account as collateral for a loan is also considered a premature distribution.

There are exceptions to the 10 percent penalty for withdrawals from IRAs occurring before the owner's having attained age 591/2. These are:

- death of the owner prior to age 591/2;

- permanent disability of the owner triggering the withdrawal; and

- distribution of the account's value—at any age—in substantially equal payments, made at least annually, over the lifetime of the account owner or the account owner and his or her spouse.

Distributions from IRAs must begin by the required beginning date—April 1 of the year following the year in which the taxpayer attains age 701/2, whether the owner is retired or still working. If the owner does not take a lump-sum distribution by this date, he or she must take *minimum annual distributions*. These annuity-type withdrawals must be the lesser of the account value or (typically) the account value divided by the life expectancy (according to IRS tables found in Publication 590) of the owner or the owner and his or her beneficiary.

If the owner dies on or after the required beginning date, any amount remaining in the IRA must be distributed to the beneficiary at least as fast as under the distribution method that the owner was using at the time of his or her death.

If the owner dies *before* the required beginning date and he or she has named a beneficiary for the account, the account's value must begin to be distributed within one year of the owner's death and may be distributed as slowly as over the beneficiary's life expectancy. The balance remaining in an IRA at the owner's death is included in the owner's gross estate for determining federal estate tax liability. If the beneficiary is the account owner's spouse, payments can be deferred until the later of December 31 of the year following the year in which the owner died or December 31 of the year in which the deceased owner would have attained age 701/2. If the IRA does not specify a beneficiary, payments must be fully distributed no later than December 31 of the fifth anniversary year of the owner's death.

ILL. 8.2 ■ IRA Tax-Free Accumulation

If an individual invests $2,000 each year in an IRA, interest earnings accumulate tax free and do not increase the individual's gross income until the savings are withdrawn. There is a sizable benefit to contributing the maximum annual amount since compounding of interest can dramatically increase savings over a long period of time.

The following chart shows how the balance of an IRA increases with consistent contributions and tax-free accumulation (assumed interest rate of 6 percent).

Current Age	Total Deposited by Age 65 ($2,000 per year)	IRA Value at Age 65
30	$70,000	$236,242
35	60,000	167,604
40	50,000	116,312
45	40,000	77,992
50	30,000	49,346
55	20,000	27,944
60	10,000	11,950

All distributions from IRAs (attributable to earnings and deductible contributions) are taxable at ordinary income tax rates to the recipient. Although beneficiaries often wish to defer distributions as long as possible to avoid the corresponding income tax liability, attempts to avoid the mandatory minimum distribution are met by a staggering 50 percent *excess accumulation tax* levied on the shortfall from the required distribution amount. (The IRS usually waives this tax when the distribution underpayment was due to a legitimate error and the taxpayer has tried to correct the error by taking the required distribution.)

In addition to minimum distributions, the IRS also has parameters for the maximum distributions from IRAs. Any year's distribution exceeding $150,000 is subject to a 15 percent penalty tax. This penalty tax also applies to SEP-IRAs, qualified plans and tax-sheltered annuities.

■ KEOGH PLANS

Self-employed people are also able to take a deduction from their adjusted gross income for funds contributed to a Code Section 401(a) qualified retirement plan. These plans, though no different from those discussed in the previous chapter, are often referred to as *Keogh* or "HR-10" plans, the name and designation of the bill which first permitted self-employed individuals to establish and participate in a tax-qualified plan.

Keogh plans provide that self-employed individuals are to be treated for qualified retirement purposes as "employees" of their particular enterprise. Such people would include a sole proprietor who owns an unincorporated business or an individual professional—a physician, an attorney, a dentist—who is the sole owner of an unincorporated professional practice. In addition to having an ownership interest, the individual must also be actively involved in the operations of the business.

Eligibility

Since a qualified plan must be established by an employer for the benefit of its employees, the law confers the status of both "employer" and "employee" to those who are self-employed, for purposes of establishing and maintaining a qualified plan. For example, the owner of a small unincorporated business is also an employee of that business. As an employer, he or she can deduct the contributions made to the qualified plan, provided the contribution meets all qualification requirements. As an employee, he or she is taxed neither on the contributions made on his or her behalf nor on the investment gains in the plan fund.

Even though the owner may be the only employee, the plan must provide for the eventual inclusion of additional employees at a later date. If the self-employed person has employees, they must be included in the plan, subject to permissible age and length-of-service limitations.

Active partners are also considered to be self-employed and eligible to participate in a Keogh plan on a tax-favored basis. However, limited partners who do not contribute any personal services to the company are not considered self-employed and may not participate.

A self-employed person's spouse *must* participate in the plan if he or she is a bona fide employee and meets the same tests applied to other employees. However, an employer-employee relationship is not formed by simply filing a joint income tax return.

Earned Income and Compensation

Earned income and compensation have a direct bearing on the allowable contribution that can be made to a Keogh plan. *Earned income* can be defined as earnings attributed to personal services that constitute a meaningful income-producing factor for the business. As noted, net income received by a limited partner who does not provide personal services to a business will not be considered earned income for Keogh contribution purposes. For self-employed individuals, *compensation* is defined as earnings from self-employment. It is a self-insured's compensation that will determine allowable contributions.

As a general rule, deductions for contributions to a profit-sharing plan cannot exceed 15 percent of compensation paid during the year. For a money-purchase plan, the ceiling is 25 percent. These 15 and 25 percent limits are applied to self-employment income after the contribution amount and the self-employment tax deduction are subtracted from earned income. Because the self-employment tax deduction must also be subtracted, earned income for Keogh purposes is reduced and the maximum allowable contribution is correspondingly reduced.

Plan Overview

As far as plan design and qualification, there is no distinction between plans established for Keogh purposes and those described in Chapter 7. Self-employed individuals may select a defined contribution, a defined benefit or a profit-sharing plan approach. The steps involved then are determined by the funding medium used under the type of plan to be installed. For example, a plan investing wholly in annuity contracts may be established without either a trust or a custodial account, but those requiring greater investment latitude should be administered by a bank or other competent entity as trustee.

Prototypes or master plans are normally used to install a Keogh plan, and plans must be in writing before the end of the taxable year for which the deduction is claimed. The plan must provide procedures for establishing a funding policy that complies with ERISA, describe procedures for operating and administering the plan, detail procedures for amending the plan and specify how and when payments to and distributions from the plan will be made.

■ SIMPLIFIED EMPLOYEE PENSION PLANS (SEPs)

Simplified employee pension plans (SEPs) were created as an outgrowth of two other programs: IRAs and Keogh plans. SEPs were introduced by the Revenue Act of 1978 to encourage employers to provide retirement benefits for their employees. With a SEP, employers can establish a retirement plan without much of the paperwork and administrative burdens of qualified plans or profit-sharing plans.

Basically, a SEP is a plan that entails individual retirement accounts (IRAs) established and maintained solely by employees, but to which the employer can contribute. In other words, an employee can treat the plan as a regular IRA and make deductible or nondeductible contributions to it (under general IRA rules) while contributions can also be made by the employer on behalf of the employee. (Note that the ''employee'' may be a self-employed individual.) Thus, the plan provides the benefits of deductible contributions, tax-deferred earnings and no current taxation to plan participants on contributions made on their behalf. Many employers—large and small, corporate and noncorporate—prefer a SEP plan over a qualified pension or profit-sharing plan because administration, operation and installation are much more simple and contributions can be more flexible.

Advantages of a Simplified Employee Pension Plan

To encourage retirement savings, SEPs have several distinct advantages for both the employer and employee. The advantages to the employer include:

- ease of plan creation and operation;

- establishment of a specialized retirement plan that will help to attract and retain employees;

- increased productivity due to reduced employee turnover and reduced recruiting and training costs; and

- attractive tax advantages because SEP contributions can be deducted as an "ordinary and necessary" business expense.

For the employee, SEP contributions or employee deferrals are excluded from gross income for income tax purposes and are tax-deferred until the savings are withdrawn. Also, plan participants have the ability to select the contribution level and investment options that best meet their budgets and retirement goals.

Participation Requirements

For every year a contribution is made under a SEP agreement, employees must satisfy *minimum participation requirements*. Although the employer may choose less restrictive requirements, the employee is usually expected to meet three criteria to participate in the plan. The employee must:

- be age 21 or older;

- have worked for the employer during at least three of the past five years; and

- receive at least an indexed dollar amount of compensation for the year ($385 in 1993).

Employees who have not met these eligibility rules may be excluded from the SEP. In addition, the law also allows the exclusion of union employees and non-resident aliens who have no U.S. income.

Contribution Limitations

A SEP is similar to a profit-sharing plan because the employer does not have to make a contribution to the plan each year. The law also limits the amount an employer may contribute to the IRAs of eligible employees under a SEP arrangement. Employer contributions are limited to the lesser of:

- 15 percent of an employee's annual compensation; or

- $30,000 per year.

An employee for whom an employer contributes under a SEP may also make contributions to the SEP-IRA subject to the usual rules regarding contributions by an individual to an IRA.

Distributions from SEPs

As with all qualified retirement plans, distributions from SEPs are expected to take place on or after a participant's retirement. The tax rules regarding allowable, premature and excess accumulation distributions from a SEP are the same as the rules that apply to IRA distributions.

Salary Reduction SEPs (SARSEPs)

An alternative to the simplified employee pension is one that allows individual employees to elect to have employer contributions directed into the SEP or received in cash. These *salary reduction SEPs* can be established by employers that had no more than 25 employees who were eligible to participate in the plan during the prior year. Elective deferrals are subject to the same limit as are 401(k) plans ($8,994 in 1993). This election is available only if at least half of the employees eligible to participate choose to have amounts contributed to the SEP and the deferral percentage for highly compensated employees is in keeping with I.R.C. guidelines.

■ TAX-SHELTERED ANNUITIES (TSAs)

A *tax-sheltered annuity (TSA)* plan is a retirement vehicle to meet the needs of employees of certain nonprofit, charitable, educational and religious organizations. These plans are permitted under Code Sections 403(b) and 501(c). In creating special tax breaks for these entities, Congress provided some favorable incentives for nonprofit organizations to establish retirement programs for their employees. Contributions to a TSA are excluded from a participant's gross income and his or her earnings in a TSA accumulate tax free until distribution. To insure that TSAs are used for long-term savings for retirement, TSAs (like IRAs and other retirement plans) are subject to penalties if the savings are withdrawn before the participant retires.

Eligibility Requirements for TSAs

Tax-sheltered annuities are qualified plans and, as such, have minimum requirements. One of the requirements is the type of employer that can establish a TSA. To be eligible, an employer must qualify as a public educational institution, a tax-exempt 501(c)(3) organization or a church organization. Eligible entities include:

- elementary and secondary schools (public and private);

- colleges and universities (public and private);

- zoos and museums;

- research and scientific foundations;

- private hospitals and medical schools; and

- churches and religious organizations.

Some nonprofit employers, such as fraternal orders, credit unions and chambers of commerce, are *not* eligible to establish TSAs for their employees.

The TSA plan must satisfy certain eligibility requirements, which include:

- The annuity must be purchased by the employer and must be nonforfeitable.

- There may be only one salary reduction agreement per eligible employee per year.

- The TSA must be nontransferable and may not be sold, assigned or pledged as security for a loan, except to the issuer of the annuity contract funding vehicle.

- The premium amount (which translates into contributions to the plan) must fall within certain guidelines.

The two types of funding vehicles which are permissible for TSAs are annuity contracts—either fixed or variable—and mutual funds. Including life insurance as part of a TSA plan will generate currently taxable income to the plan participant representing part of the premium (the so-called P.S. 58 costs).

Pretax Contributions

A TSA plan may be employee elective, nonelective or a combination of the two. Most plans today are elective, which enable employees to make contributions by means of salary reductions. When the contribution is attributable to a pre-arranged salary reduction, the contribution amount does not constitute reportable income (for federal income tax purposes) to the employee since it is not constructively received. Rather, the amount of the agreed upon elective contribution is shunted into the employee's TSA account. Although not currently federally taxable, any salary reduction amounts are still subject to FICA (Social Security withholding) taxes. However, contributions that come from the sponsoring employer (rather than from an elective salary reduction) are not deemed to be wages and are not subject to FICA taxes.

Limits on Contributions

Subject to Code Section 415 limits and the exclusion allowance (noted below, which operate independently to limit available contributions) the maximum annual salary reduction for an employee under a TSA is $9,500. (This amount is not currently adjusted for annual inflation, but will be adjusted upward when the indexed amount of contributions to a cash or deferred arrangement—such as a 401(k) plan—equals $9,500.) The $9,500 limit applies to contributions from combinations of plans, such as both a TSA and a salary reduction SEP or a 401(k) plan.

Employees are also permitted to make "catch-up" contributions to their TSA accounts. Catch-up contributions permit employees with 15 or more years of service to make up for prior contributions that could have been made under the plan, but were not. The contribution for any single given year may be increased by the smallest of the following catch-up increases:

- $3,000;

- $15,000, reduced by the amounts of any prior catch-up contributions; or

- the excess of $5,000 × the prior years of the employee's service, reduced by the elective deferrals made on behalf of the employee thus far.

Some employees may be entitled to larger contributions under a number of special provisions found in the I.R.C. An employee may elect only one of the special contribution provisions.

One special excludable contribution limit on the amount of contribution that may be made annually to a TSA is the lesser of 25 percent of an employee's compensation or an overall maximum dollar limit of $30,000. Another special excludable contribution limit is the lesser of the Code Section 415 limitation or the lower of:

1. the employee's regularly computed exclusion allowance;

2. $4,000 plus 25 percent of the employee's includable compensation (compensation net of the TSA contribution); or

3. $15,000.

Several special provisions are available to members of the clergy as well as other church and synagogue employees. These provisions operate in addition to the provisions available to other types of 501(c) or tax-exempt employers.

- A clergyperson or church employee may measure years of service in terms of all years that relate to employment with organizations that are part of a particular church. Changing "employers" or parishes does not freeze past service credit.

- If adjusted gross income is less than $17,000, employees may elect an "alternative allowance," the amount of annual includible (net of contribution) compensation or $3,000, whichever is less.

- Employees have a "catch-up" provision allowing them to make annual additions of $10,000 in a single year, up to a $40,000 lifetime maximum.

Withdrawals and Loans

Loans are available with many TSA plans; however, such loans must meet the same requirements that generally apply to loans from qualified plans. These rules are explained on page 133.

Withdrawals of amounts attributed to salary reduction contributions made after December 31, 1988 from TSAs are permitted only in instances of death, disability, severance, a loan, attainment of age 59 1/2 or financial hardship. Any earnings credited to such salary reduction contributions may not be withdrawn for reasons of financial hardship. The amount of any withdrawals for reasons other than those mentioned will constitute ordinary income that is not only taxable to the participant, but subject to a 10 percent penalty tax as well.

Distributions from TSAs

As with other plans, distributions from TSAs are subject to a 10 percent penalty tax if made before the participant reaches age 591/2. The penalty tax does not apply to distributions made as a result of:

- disability or death;

- a divorce court order;

- a series of substantially equal payments over the life of the participant or the joint lives of a participant and his or her beneficiary;

- a participant's departure from the organization after age 55; or

- certain medical expenses.

Any amount or portion distributed from a TSA that is not attributable to the participant's "basis" (employee's contributions) is taxable at the employee's ordinary income tax rate. An employee's basis may have come from excess contributions that were taxed or premiums on life insurance within the TSA plan that were taxable to the participant in previous years. Generally, distributions attributable to mutual fund shares are taxed as ordinary income. If distribution from the plan takes the form of an annuity and is paid out for reasons other than the death of the participant, special rules apply for taxation. The tax-free portion of the annuity income is spread evenly over the annuitant's life expectancy by the calculation of the exclusion ratio, discussed in Chapter 5, to determine the split between the taxable and nontaxable portions.

For TSAs, the exclusion ratio can be easily calculated using the following formula:

$$\frac{\text{Employee contributions}}{\text{Life expectancy} \times \text{Annual annuity benefit}}$$

To illustrate how to determine the income tax actually owed on periodic annuity payments, assume that a client has contributed $40,000 to an annuity that distributes $4,000 annually. According to the Pension and Annuity Income tables found in IRS Publication 575, the client has a life expectancy of 15 years. The exclusion ratio would be:

$$\frac{\$40,000}{15 \times \$4,000} = .67$$

Based on this calculation, 67 percent of the distribution is excluded from current taxation; 33 percent of the $4,000 or $1,320 is currently taxable. The tax-free portion of the annuity is spread over the annuitant's anticipated lifetime of

15 years. Any undistributed amounts in a decedent/participant's TSA will be includable in his or her gross estate.

■ SUMMARY

An important part of retiring comfortably is selecting an appropriate retirement plan that will provide needed income. As a retirement planner, you will be faced with determining which employer-sponsored or individually sponsored plan best meets your client's needs. You must, therefore, be familiar with how these plans are established; who may participate in the plans; how contributions are made and limited; and how and when distributions may be made.

As previously discussed, distribution of benefits is determined by the provisions of the specific retirement plan. Although distributions have been discussed briefly in Chapters 7 and 8, various retirement distribution alternatives are discussed in greater detail in Chapter 9.

■ CHAPTER 8 QUESTIONS FOR REVIEW

1. All of the following individuals could establish an IRA and make a contribution this year, EXCEPT:

   a. Lowell, age 19, who works part-time delivering pizzas while attending school.
   b. Amy, age 45, who is a participant in her employer's profit-sharing plan.
   c. Randall, age 67, the sole owner of Concept Images, Inc.
   d. Renee, age 52, who volunteers at her local hospital.

2. All of the following individuals would be considered "active participants" when determining IRA deductibility, EXCEPT:

   a. a married employee who has not been excluded from participation in a defined benefit plan in the past year.
   b. a single employee for whom an allocation is made in a profit-sharing plan.
   c. an employee who was entitled to contributions under an employer-sponsored money purchase plan.
   d. a single, self-employed consultant with an adjusted gross income of $59,000.

3. Which of the following correctly identifies an exemption from the 10 percent penalty levied on early withdrawals from IRAs?

   a. Temporary disability of the owner
   b. Withdrawal to pay medical expenses
   c. Death of the owner prior to age 59 1/2
   d. Ten-year forward averaging.

4. The formula used to determine how much of a distribution from a tax-sheltered annuity (TSA) is taxable and how much is not is generally known as a/an

   a. exclusion ratio.
   b. life expectancy table.
   c. bracket offset formula.
   d. alternative exclusion allowance.

5. Employer contributions to a SEP-IRA are tax deductible by

   a. the employer.
   b. the employee.
   c. both the employer and the employee.
   d. neither the employer nor the employee.

9

Retirement Distribution Alternatives

An individual's retirement distribution may be one of the largest sums of money he or she will ever receive. What a person decides to do with this money has a significant impact on the retiree's financial security and that of his or her family. It is natural, therefore, for people to have questions about how they can receive this income during their retirement years.

In this chapter, we will explore many of the issues that impact the retirement distribution decision. As a financial services professional, you should be prepared to discuss the most common distribution options available to your clients and the income tax consequences of these options.

■ ■ ■ ■ ■

■ GENERAL RULES FOR DISTRIBUTIONS

In Chapters 7 and 8, we described a variety of qualified plans available to employers and individuals to provide retirement benefits. The appropriate plan will be determined by the employer's or individual's objectives and circumstances. However, regardless of the plan or plans selected, at some point the retirement savings in a retirement plan are withdrawn. To ensure that a participant uses these funds for retirement, various restrictions apply to the withdrawal of funds from retirement plans.

For an employer-sponsored program, the retirement plan document will specify the earliest age at which an employee may retire and receive full retirement benefits. In most cases, "normal" retirement age is 65, but the plan may permit early retirement. Some plans allow withdrawals from a plan due to separation from the company, but other plans will require these separated employees to leave their retirement savings in the plan until they reach retirement age.

The qualified plan document outlines certain restrictions or guidelines about when *distributions* or withdrawals may take place. Distributions from retirement plans that meet these restrictions and guidelines are called *allowable distributions*. Generally, allowable distributions are permitted at age 65 but may be taken as early as age 591/2, or sooner for specific reasons, such as an early retirement provision in a qualified retirement plan. And, to assure that retirement savings are not kept in a perpetual tax shelter, distributions must begin in a prescribed fashion once a participant reaches age 701/2.

60-Day Rule

When an individual receives a distribution from an employer-sponsored qualified plan, he or she has 60 days from the date the money is received to determine what to do with it. The 60-day period begins when the participant actually receives the distribution from the plan. At this point, the participant may decide to:

- accept a lump-sum distribution, paying taxes and, possibly, a penalty if the distribution is made prior to age 591/2;

- make a tax-free rollover into an IRA or other qualifying plan; or

- receive the benefits in installments.

If the distribution from a qualified plan is received in two or more installments, the employee has 60 days from the final payment or installment in which to make a rollover. For example, if a participant receives a partial distribution on February 1 and the remaining distribution on July 1, the 60-day period begins on July 1, the date of the final payment. If after 60 days the participant has not reinvested the funds in a rollover IRA or annuity, the distribution will be taxed as current income and, if the participant is younger than 591/2, he or she may also have to pay the 10 percent penalty discussed in Chapter 8.

The decision about the best way for the participant to receive a distribution from a retirement account is a complicated one that calls for a high level of expertise in federal income taxation. A financial services professional who is not a

ILL. 9.1 ■

New 20 Percent Withholding Rule

In 1992, Congress passed a controversial withholding requirement for lump-sum distributions made from qualified pension and annuity plans after December 31, 1992. Lump-sum distributions will be subject to a 20 percent withholding tax unless the employee arranges for the distribution to be transferred *directly* to another retirement plan or IRA. Qualified plans must now offer a direct transfer option for all distributions eligible for rollover treatment.

The new withholding requirement reduces investment flexibility since the actual amount distributed to the employee is reduced. Furthermore, although the employee receives the net amount, the gross amount must still be rolled over to completely defer taxation. In other words, the employee must make up the 20 percent difference—even if this means borrowing the money—to prevent paying income tax on the amount not rolled over.

tax expert would be wise to leave specific advice regarding such distributions to the client's accountant or tax attorney. By deferring to tax experts, the agent can ensure the client that his or her needs will be met and can avoid any personal liability exposure. However, it is still important for every retirement planner to have a working knowledge of the mechanics of various retirement plan distributions in order to communicate with other professionals and to be able to recognize a situation in which a potential lump-sum distribution may need to be reallocated.

Before we discuss various retirement distribution options, let's look at some distributions that may occur prior to normal retirement or age 65.

■ PREMATURE DISTRIBUTIONS

You will recall from our discussion in Chapter 8 that IRAs and qualified plans are intended to be long-term retirement savings arrangements, and participants are generally penalized for withdrawing the savings before age 591/2. Such *premature distributions, occurring before a participant attains age 591/2*, are taxable at ordinary income tax rates and generally do not qualify for any type of forward averaging. Premature distributions are also subject to the 10 percent penalty.

However, there are a number of exceptions to the 10 percent penalty tax exposure for IRAs and qualified plans. These exceptions include distributions made:

- to a beneficiary as a result of the participant's death;

- in substantially equal payments over a participant's lifetime or life expectancy (or joint life expectancy);

- to a permanently disabled participant;

- as a result of early retirement between age 55 and 591/2 under a plan's "early retirement" provisions (does not apply to IRAs);

- under a divorce decree (or qualified domestic relations order) (does not apply to IRAs);

- as a result of a plan loan (such loans are not considered ''distributions'');

- to correct an excess contribution;

- to make a rollover to another qualified plan or IRA; or

- as a dividend on stock held by an ESOP.

In addition, 401(k) plans and TSAs with elective deferrals may permit certain types of "hardship" withdrawals, if the provisions are contained in the plan documents. Approved circumstances which may permit a hardship withdrawal include illness, college expenses and eviction or foreclosure prevention. Hardship withdrawals occurring before the participant attains age 591/2 are considered to be "premature" and are subject to taxation as ordinary income as well as the 10 percent penalty.

Postmortem Distributions

If a participant in a qualified plan dies during his or her working years and before retirement distributions begin, the IRS requires that the value of the participant's account be distributed to a beneficiary within five years of the employee's death. The beneficiary must then report the funds received as income. The beneficiary may take the amount in a lump sum or may spread the receipt of funds over five years. However, many individual cases will be eligible for one of a number of *exceptions* to this five-year rule. When the beneficiary is a *surviving spouse,* he or she can:

- withdraw the entire amount within five years;

- use all or part of the distribution to establish a rollover IRA in his or her own name; or

- withdraw the savings periodically using annuity distributions over the beneficiary's life expectancy. Distribution can be deferred only up until the later of December 31 of the year in which the deceased participant would have reached age 701/2 had he or she lived, or December 31 of the year following the year he or she died.

A *non-spousal beneficiary* may withdraw the entire balance from the qualified plan within five years after the participant's death. The beneficiary may also have the distribution spread over his or her life expectancy or joint life expectancy to reduce the distribution's tax consequences. These distributions must begin within one year of the employee participant's death.

A $5,000 death benefit exclusion may also apply to distributions from qualified plans. Although pure life insurance benefits from life insurance maintained in qualified plans is not taxed as income, life insurance proceeds that are part of the cash value are fully taxed under annuity rules.

Disability Distributions

Qualified plan participants who become disabled prior to age 591/2 may receive distributions from a qualified plan. The IRS defines disability as being "unable to engage in any substantial gainful activity by reason of any medically determinable physical or mental impairment which can be expected to result in death or to be of long continued or indefinite duration."

Once disability has been established by a medical report and the submission of evidence to the IRS, the disabled participant may receive distributions from the plan without an early distribution penalty. However, the distributions must be reported as income. If the plan allows nondeductible after-tax employee contributions to be used for disability benefits, the participant's tax liability can be reduced.

Early Retirement

Early retirement is appealing for many people, especially if their qualified plans permit distributions without a premature distribution penalty. If a participant decides to retire prior to the age of 65, the distribution will not be considered premature if the distribution is made under the early retirement provisions of the plan and:

1. the participant is at least age 55; and

2. the participant is separated from the employer's service.

Series of Periodic Payments

A plan participant under the age of 59½ may elect to receive distributions from a qualified plan, but to do so without penalty, the payments must be made at least annually in a series of substantially equal installments over the participant's life expectancy (or joint life expectancy). There are severe penalties if the payment schedule is altered before the participant reaches age 59½ or within five years of the date of the first payment after the age of 59½, whichever is later.

Decrees of Divorce or Separation

If the distribution is a result of a divorce or separation decree, the former spouse may receive a distribution prior to age 59½. The spouse may take the entire distribution and report it as income or roll the entire amount into an IRA.

Loans from Qualified Plans

Qualified pension and profit-sharing plans, 401(k) plans and TDAs may offer loans to participants as long as certain guidelines are followed. Basically, such loans must be adequately secured, bear a reasonable rate of interest, carry a reasonable repayment schedule and be available on a nondiscriminatory basis.

In order that a loan not be deemed a taxable distribution to the plan participant, its term and amount must meet the following requirements:

1. It must be repaid within five years, unless it is to be used to acquire a principal residence.

2. The amount is filled to the lesser of:

   - $50,000 minus the amount, if any, by which the highest outstanding loan balance during the year preceding the loan exceeds the outstanding loan balance on the date of the loan, or
   - one-half of the participant's vested plan benefit or $10,000, whichever is greater.

Any loan that does not meet these requirements will be considered a taxable distribution to the participant. In addition, if the plan provides for spousal benefits, and the participant wants to pledge his or her account as security, the spouse must consent to the loan in writing.

Rollover Contributions

The Employee Retirement Income Security Act of 1974 (ERISA) permitted the tax-free transfer of retirement savings from one plan to another. Employees who are separated from an employer may take their retirement savings from the former employer's qualified plan and roll it over to another retirement plan without any current income or penalty tax consequences. The participants keep funds tax sheltered when savings are shifted from one retirement plan to another or between investments. (Rollovers are discussed in more detail on pages 135–36.)

Most participants will not receive a qualified plan distribution until they retire. At that point, they will have three options for handling a retirement distribution: a lump-sum distribution, a rollover IRA or periodic payments from the plan.

■ LUMP-SUM DISTRIBUTIONS

Depending on the participant's age and other circumstances, he or she may be able to take advantage of special tax treatment in selecting a lump-sum distribution. Under a qualified retirement plan, a *lump-sum distribution* is one in which the full amount of the retirement benefit is credited to the employee in a single tax year. If the plan allows it, a lump-sum distribution may be taken by:

- a retiring or nonretiring employee who has attained age 59 1/2;

- an employee who has separated from the employer's service at any age;

- a self-employed employee *who is permanently disabled;* or

- a designated beneficiary upon the employee's death.

The taxation of lump-sum distributions from qualified retirement plans is extremely complex. Basically, an amount equal to the participant's cost basis—if any—is recovered tax free. This nontaxable basis includes, for example, any nondeductible contributions the participant made and any employer contributions that were taxed to the participant. The balance of the lump sum distribution after subtracting the participant's cost basis is the total taxable amount. The general rule is that participants (age 59 1/2) who receive lump-sum distributions may elect *five-year forward averaging,* which operates to tax the distributions as if they were received each year for five years. Though the tax is payable in the year of distribution, the effect of averaging is more likely to lower the rate than if the distribution were taxed wholly as a lump sum. Taxes are levied in the year of distribution at the rates that apply to single taxpayers. Personal exemptions as well as standard or itemized deductions are not applicable.

A special rule applies to lump sum distributions to participants who were 50 or older on January 1, 1986. These individuals may elect either:

1. five-year forward averaging at current tax rates, or

2. ten-year forward averaging at 1986 tax rates, with any capital gain portion of the distribution (attributed to pre-1974 participation) taxed at 20 percent.

Forward averaging is a once per lifetime election. If a taxpayer elects to use income averaging before age 591/2, he or she will not be permitted to use income averaging after reaching age 591/2.

■ ROLLOVER IRAs

Rollover contributions were created by ERISA to encourage savings programs for retirement and to make provisions for the continuation of qualified savings if participation in a plan is discontinued. When a distribution is rolled over into an IRA, the participant avoids paying taxes now and ensures that the savings will continue to grow tax deferred.

A *rollover IRA* has provisions that allow for an uninterrupted tax deferral for the proceeds of a qualified pension plan received by an employee due to retirement, separation from a company or termination of a pension plan. The funds are "rolled" from one retirement account to another. The transfer of rights from one plan or IRA to another plan or IRA, allows employees to build accumulated and vested retirement savings.

Rollovers can also be used to protect retirement funds from taxation while an employee is waiting to become eligible for a qualified plan. Most qualified plans have certain waiting periods that affect an employee's eligibility. An employee may receive a distribution from a former employer's qualified plan but may not yet be eligible to join a new employer's plan. In these cases, rollover IRAs are used as *conduits* to hold retirement funds until they can be moved to a new qualified plan.

Under a rollover option, the IRS permits the participant to roll over either the entire amount of the lump-sum distribution or any part of it. Only the amounts not rolled over become taxable while the remaining amounts of the IRA continue to grow tax deferred. The participant may not include any after-tax contributions to the IRA that he or she may have made to the qualified plan. If the distribution includes stock, this stock may be kept tax deferred as part of the rollover IRA without the necessity of selling the stock. It is important to remember that any part of the distribution not rolled over will be taxed as current income and may be subject to the 10 percent early withdrawal penalty.

Although traditional IRAs are limited to $2,000 maximum annual contributions, an IRA rollover account is not subject to maximum contribution limitations. Remember, however, the rollover must take place within 60 days from receipt of the distribution. This 60-day period does not include any time during which the amount transferred is "frozen" (i.e., cannot be withdrawn because of bankruptcy or insolvency of the financial institution).

Under most circumstances, rollovers are allowed only once in any 12-month period. After funds constituting a distribution from a qualified plan are "rolled over" into an IRA, five-year forward averaging for those funds is no longer be available. Funds "rolled" from one employer-sponsored qualified retirement plan into another employer-sponsored qualified retirement plan retain their eligibility for forward averaging when they are ultimately distributed to the participant. A rollover into an IRA is permitted if a lump-sum distribution is made from a qualified plan to a surviving spouse. Only spousal beneficiaries may take advantage of survivor rollover provisions.

■ PERIODIC DISTRIBUTIONS

If the employer-sponsored qualified plan allows this option, participants may leave their money in the employer's plan and receive periodic payments. If this option is available, the money remains tax deferred and the participant retains the right to special tax treatment later. When choosing this option, the retiree should determine whether the investments offered in the employer's plan will continue to meet the employee's income needs in the future. He or she should also determine whether the money in the plan can be easily accessed in the future.

Annuities

Many qualified plans provide annuity benefits to retired employees. Unlike life insurance that creates an immediate estate upon the insured's death, an annuity protects against "living too long." Many people will acknowledge that they do not want to outlive the savings they have accumulated for retirement. An annuity guarantees continued payments for a specified number of years or for life, thereby assuring that the insured will not outlive his or her source of income.

If the participant receives a retirement distribution in the form of an annuity, it is taxable under special annuity rules. An *annuity distribution* represents the distribution and perhaps the liquidation of an employee's retirement benefits in periodic payments rather than in one lump sum.

If the employee contributed nothing to the plan during his or her working years, the employee is said to have no cost basis in the plan. Therefore, the total distribution received each year will be included in the employee's gross income. However, if the employee contributed to the plan with after-tax contributions, the employee will be entitled to an exclusion when receiving retirement benefits. The employee may exclude part of each payment from his or her federal income taxes. Thus, each payment is partially taxable and partially excludable.

Exclusion Ratio

In Chapter 5, we discussed how to use an exclusion ratio to determine the taxable and nontaxable portions of annuity benefits. The same concept is applied to qualified plan distributions. When both the employer and employee contribute to a plan, the nondeductible after-tax employee contributions represent a *cost basis* or the amount the employee has contributed toward the cost of retirement benefits. The cost basis also includes insurance costs reported as income. When a participant has a cost basis in the plan, part of each installment distribution has already been taxed. These amounts should not be taxed again.

An exclusion ratio is used to determine which part of the distribution is tax free and which is taxable. This ratio, similar to the one discussed in Chapter 5, is calculated by dividing the amount of the employee's contributions by the total account balance or the present value of the participant's accrued benefits.

$$\frac{\text{Cost basis}}{\text{Total account balance}} = \text{Exclusion ratio}$$

If no tax was paid on the employee contributions, taxes will be paid on the retirement distribution.

■ EXCESS DISTRIBUTIONS

The Tax Reform Act of 1986 placed limits on the amount of retirement savings that can be distributed from a qualified plan in one year. Annual distributions in excess of the stated statutory maximums are subject to a 15 percent penalty in addition to any income taxes imposed. Generally, the penalty is imposed on aggregate distributions from qualified plans, tax-sheltered annuities and IRAs.

In most cases, an *excess distribution* is defined as a distribution (other than a lump-sum distribution) that exceeds $150,000 in one calendar year.* If a lump-sum distribution is taken, the ceiling is five times the annual amount, or $750,000. Amounts in excess of these distributions are subject to a 15 percent penalty.

In some cases, a premature distribution will also represent an excess distribution. The 15 percent penalty is then reduced (or eliminated) by the 10 percent penalty imposed on premature distributions.

Example:
Gaylinn Parks, age 43, received a $800,000 lump-sum distribution from a qualified plan. Because she received a $50,000 excess distribution from the plan ($800,000 − $750,000 ceiling), Gaylinn must pay a $7,500 penalty (.15 × $50,000). The $800,000 distribution she received may be subject to a 10 percent penalty if it constitutes a premature distribution.

---

*Actually, the law states the 15 percent penalty is imposed if aggregate retirement distributions exceed the greater of (1) $150,000 or (2) $112,500, as indexed for inflation. In 1993, the indexed amount was $144,551. Therefore, $150,000 remains the distribution limit until indexing of the base $112,500 produces an amount greater than $150,000.

$800,000 premature distribution
$\times \quad .10$ penalty
$ 80,000 total penalty

$ 7,500 penalty tax for excess $50,000 distribution
$-$ 80,000 penalty tax for premature distribution
$ 0 excess distribution penalty due

In this case, Gaylinn's 15 percent penalty for the excess distribution was offset (and entirely eliminated) by her $80,000 premature distribution penalty.

■ SPOUSAL OPTION ANNUITIES

Most qualified plans must provide a survivorship benefit as a distribution option to married participants. This means the plan makes benefit payments to two people, and at the death of the first, continues payments to the survivor until his or her death. This spousal option is typically accomplished by means of a *qualified joint and survivor annuity*. This periodic arrangement calculates the payout of retirement benefits over two lives, the life of the married participant and his or her spouse. During the participant's lifetime, he or she receives a fixed, periodic payment. After the death of the original plan participant, payments equal to at

ILL. 9.2 ■

Excess Retirement Accumulation

Distributions considered to be *income* from retirement accounts in excess of $150,000 annually are subject to a 15 percent excise tax, which is levied in addition to the ordinary income tax. When a taxpayer dies prior to the distribution of the amount held in qualified retirement accounts, the IRS believes it has been unreasonably denied *income* taxes that would have been applied to the "excess" retirement account proceeds if they had been distributed over the retiree's lifetime.

Calculations for the excess retirement accumulations tax compare the present value of the actual pension account's accumulation, amortized over the decedent's/pensioner's statistical life expectancy at the time of death, against the $150,000 (or a greater indexed amount). Any excess differential between the amortized pension assumption, which, of course, is hypothetical, and the actual accumulation is subject to the 15 percent excise tax. Although this excess retirement accumulation tax is reported on the decedent's federal estate tax return, it is treated as an income tax rather than an estate tax. Therefore, it fails to qualify for any estate tax breaks such as the marital or charitable deduction or the unified credit.

Those with the most retirement savings are penalized under this scenario. When the decedent's spouse is still surviving, the excess retirement income tax can be deferred to become an obligation of the survivor (rather than the decedent). The surviving spouse is entitled to this deferral election because he or she is assumed to be the beneficiary of the retirement accumulation. Any amount the survivor spouse receives from the decedent's retirement account(s) before his or her death will be subject to income taxation and "excess" tax if distribution amounts are "excessive." Sooner or later, the IRS receives its taxes!

least 50 percent of the participant's periodic payment are paid to the survivor until his or her death.

If a qualified plan includes a joint-and-survivor rule, the participant is prevented from leaving his or her surviving spouse without retirement benefits (unless the spouse consents in writing). In addition, any distributions from the plan cannot be hidden from a spouse since both spouses must give their written consent before more than $3,500 is distributed from a qualified plan.

Under many plans, a *qualified preretirement survivor annuity* is also available to a spouse when the plan participant dies before retirement payments begin. Such preretirement annuities operate in the same manner in which postretirement annuities do. Distributions from either arrangement are subject to IRS annuity distribution taxation rules.

As discussed in Chapter 5, the spousal option may not generate enough retirement income for both worker and spouse and its potential benefit is effected only if the worker predeceases the spouse. If the plan participant and his or her spouse waive the benefit in writing as a couple seeking pension maximization via insurance protection, the requirement to provide a survivorship benefit will be waived.

■ REQUIRED DISTRIBUTIONS

In addition to penalizing the participant for early withdrawal of retirement funds, the IRS also penalizes the participant for failing to withdraw retirement savings in a timely manner. Generally, distributions from a qualified plan must begin in the year the participant reaches age 701/2 but may be spread over the participant's life expectancy.

Those retirees who are reluctant to begin minimum distributions should be reminded that the IRS imposes a *50 percent penalty tax* on the difference between the amount that should have been distributed and the amount that was actually distributed. For example, assume a participant should take a minimum distribution of $10,000 but elects to receive only $4,000. The penalty tax for the excess accumulation is calculated as follows:

$$
\begin{array}{rl}
\$10,000 & \text{minimum distribution} \\
-\ 4,000 & \text{amount actually distributed} \\
\hline
\$\ 6,000 & \text{excess accumulation} \\
\times\quad .50 & \text{penalty} \\
\hline
\$\ 3,000 & \text{penalty owing}
\end{array}
$$

As this calculation readily demonstrates, the minimum distribution for each participant must be accurately calculated by the plan administrator and taken by the participant. Failure to properly comply with minimum distribution rules could result in serious penalties for the participant.

ILL. 9.3 ■ Life Expectancy Table for Single Life

Age	Multiples (Life Expectancy)
70	16.0
71	15.3
72	14.6
73	13.9
74	13.2
75	12.5

Calculating Required Distributions

Required distributions can be properly calculated by using the annuity tables provided in the plan contract, which must be based on IRS tables. Payments are based on a participant's life expectancy or joint life expectancy. Two tables, one based on the life expectancy of men and the other on women, were once used for this calculation. Illustration 9.3 shows a section of the unisex IRS table now used to determine single life expectancy.

According to Ill. 9.3, a 73-year-old participant's life expectancy is 13.9 years. To calculate that participant's required minimum distribution amount, divide the life expectancy into the balance of the qualified plan at the end of the preceding tax year (December 31).

Example:
A participant who is 73 years old has a life expectancy of 13.9 years. If the balance in his or her qualified plan was $200,000 on December 31, the minimum distribution for this year is $14,389 (rounded).

The life expectancy can be recalculated each year to extend payments over a longer period of time. However, payments cannot be paid for a period longer than the participant's life expectancy or joint life expectancy. But payments can be accelerated and made over a period that is shorter than a participant's life expectancy.

In some cases, a participant will select a *joint life expectancy* payout in order to reduce the annual distribution and pay less taxes. A lower distribution also allows the savings in the plan to continue their tax-deferred growth. The table in Ill. 9.4 shows a section of the IRS table used to determine joint life expectancy.

In the earlier example, our 73-year-old participant with $200,000 in a qualified plan was required to take a minimum distribution of $14,389 (rounded) in the current year. Assuming this participant has a spouse who is 68 years old, the joint life expectancy payout is only $9,756 (rounded). (The calculation is $200,000 divided by 20.5.) As you can see, when this option is used, a lower required distribution and a longer payout period result.

ILL. 9.4 ■ Life Expectancy Table for Joint Lives

Participant's Age	Beneficiary's Age					
	65	66	67	68	69	70
70	23.1	22.5	22.0	21.5	21.1	20.6
71	22.8	22.2	21.7	21.2	20.7	20.2
72	22.5	21.9	21.3	20.8	20.3	19.8
73	22.2	21.6	21.0	20.5	20.0	19.4
74	22.0	21.4	20.8	20.2	19.6	19.1
75	21.8	21.1	20.5	19.9	19.3	18.8

Penalty Waiver

The IRS is anxious to assure that minimum distributions are taken in a timely manner. However, as we mentioned briefly earlier in this chapter, it does not wish to penalize participants who failed to take minimum distributions due to a "reasonable error." But, the participant must be attempting to correct the error.

The IRS considers that a reasonable error may have occurred if the participant:

- took incorrect advice from a plan administrator or consultant;

- incorrectly calculated the minimum distribution himself or herself; or

- misunderstood how the proper amount was to be calculated.

In cases of reasonable error, the IRS may waive the penalty after the participant completes several steps. The participant must first pay the penalty and then request a waiver. The waiver request is attached to his or her income tax form. If the waiver is granted, the IRS will refund the penalty paid.

■ THE ROLE OF THE LIFE INSURANCE PROFESSIONAL

Because the tax laws affecting the distribution of qualified retirement plans are extensive, discussions about specifics should be delegated to a tax attorney, tax accountant or the plan's benefits specialist.

As a life insurance professional, you should not attempt to be an expert in every aspect of a qualified plan and its distribution alternatives. In general, the most important things for you to remember about retirement distributions are:

- The participant must take some action within 60 days of the date he or she receives the distribution or some tax advantages will be lost.

- The decision about what to do with the distribution will depend on the participant's age and how the money will be used.

- The distribution options include a lump-sum distribution, periodic installment payments or a rollover IRA.

- Funds rolled over into an IRA keep growing, tax deferred until they are withdrawn.

- Distributions are often integrated with Social Security benefits and both must be considered when determining a client's retirement income needs.

As a life insurance professional, you are an important resource of retirement information and advice for your clients. Of course, you can assist your clients in preparing for retirement by offering employer-sponsored retirement plans. But, you also have a number of other products that can assure your clients an adequate retirement income.

You can, for example, offer them an individual retirement annuity (IRA) that provides an annual payment of accumulated benefits to the participant until his or her death. Life insurance is another tax-advantaged way of saving for retirement that also protects the client's family against loss of income from his or her death or provides survivors with money to meet expenses. Individuals use after-tax dollars to purchase a policy. The funds grow with no taxes on the earnings until the benefits are distributed. Meanwhile, they can borrow against the policy's cash value at low interest rates.

Regardless of which retirement plan your client selects, remember that your client looks to you for advice about the "best" plan. Every individual's circumstances will be different, and some will be more complex than others. If you need additional assistance in designing a plan or understanding the tax consequences of a plan, you should always seek specialized help.

■ SUMMARY

In the last few chapters, we concentrated on qualified retirement plans that primarily involve the employer as the initiator of the plans and the provider of the funds needed for the employee's benefit at retirement. These qualified plans provide substantial tax advantages and other benefits to both the employer and the employee. And, when the funds are distributed, they often provide the most important source of income for most people.

In Chapter 10, we will review alternative retirement plans that supplement qualified plans for highly compensated individuals. Unlike qualified plans, these "nonqualified" plans can be used by employers on a selective basis as additional incentives to attract and retain highly trained, key executives.

■ **CHAPTER 9 QUESTIONS FOR REVIEW**

1. In general, allowable distributions from a qualified plan

    a. begin at age 65.
    b. must be made to the participant.
    c. must be greater than $3,500 annually.
    d. begin at age 591/2.

2. When a participant fails to withdraw the required amount from the plan after age 701/2, the law imposes a penalty of

    a. 100 percent.
    b. 50 percent.
    c. 15 percent.
    d. 10 percent.

3. If a plan participant retires prior to age 65, the distribution will NOT be considered premature in all of the following instances, EXCEPT:

    a. The participant is at least 55 years old.
    b. The distribution is made under the early retirement provisions of the plan.
    c. The participant is severed from the company.
    d. The participant elects a lump-sum distribution.

4. The purpose of rollover IRAs is to

    a. allow the tax-free transfer of retirement savings from one plan to another.
    b. limit the amount of tax-deferred retirement savings.
    c. allow employers to contribute to employee's IRAs.
    d. permit government regulation of retirement accounts.

5. Required distributions from qualified plans are calculated by using the

    a. exclusion ratio.
    b. annuity tables.
    c. penalty tax waiver.
    d. cost basis.

10

Nonqualified Executive Benefits

As we have learned, employers implement qualified plans primarily for their tax benefits and their ability to keep and attract employees. However, when it comes to providing special benefits to attract and retain the best executives, employers find themselves facing a dilemma because many federal tax provisions prevent such discrimination.

As you will learn in this chapter, there is a way to provide adequate retirement benefits to highly compensated employees through discretionary employee benefit plans. We will discuss ways in which ancillary benefits can be provided through several plans to meet the needs of key employees.

■ ■ ■ ■ ■

■ AN OVERVIEW OF NONQUALIFIED PLANS

Most employers offer some form of group health, life and long-term disability insurance and formal pension or profit-sharing plans to attract new employees and prevent employee turnover. Many employers are particularly anxious to offer upper-level management additional benefits to reduce employee turnover at that key level. However, because such discriminatory practices could jeopardize the tax-advantaged status of an entire qualified plan, companies must offer alternative benefit plans to key employees and executives.

To provide additional incentives to select employees on a discriminatory basis, employers may offer discretionary benefit plans, or *nonqualified plans*. A plan is called "nonqualified" when it is not eligible for the tax benefits of a pension, profit-sharing or other "qualified" plan. This is not to say that nonqualified plans do not enjoy advantages of their own, but generally, these advantages are not as substantial as those granted to qualified plans. Basically, nonqualified plans are used to:

- attract and retain key employees;

- provide supplemental benefits beyond the existing qualified plan;

- provide a plan in lieu of a qualified plan for selected employees; and/or

- take advantage of provisions in the I.R.C. to the advantage of certain employees.

Let's begin by looking at five of the most commonly used discretionary employee benefit plans: deferred compensation plans, salary continuation plans, split-dollar plans, executive bonus plans and golden parachutes.

■ DEFERRED COMPENSATION PLANS

A *deferred compensation plan* is a contractual arrangement entered into by an employer and a selected employee—typically one who is highly compensated. The employer agrees to pay the employee compensation in the future—usually at retirement—for services the employee renders currently. In this way, it is the employee who "funds" the plan. By reducing his or her current salary, foregoing a raise or bonus or simply deferring a portion of the total compensation package until retirement, the employee lowers his or her current tax liability and supplements retirement savings. Typically, these deferred compensation arrangements also include payment in the event of disability as well as payments to the employee's spouse in the event of the employee's death before or after retirement.

A deferred compensation arrangement has a twofold objective.

1. For the employer, it provides a means to attract or retain the services of the selected employee.

2. For the employee, it is a way to lower his or her current tax liability by deferring compensation until retirement (when he or she may be in a lower tax bracket) and to supplement retirement benefits.

Unfunded vs. Informally Funded vs. Formally Funded Plans

Deferred compensation plans fall into three broad categories: unfunded, informally funded and formally funded. The distinction is important because the tax consequences vary by plan.

With an *unfunded plan,* the employee has only an unsecured contractual right to the benefit payments. No assets are set aside to fund the obligation. In effect, the employee simply becomes a creditor of the employer at the time he or she satisfied the conditions necessary to receive benefits, and the employer finances its obligation on a "pay-as-you-go" basis.

An *informally funded plan* is one in which the employer does set aside and accumulate assets to meet its future obligation; frequently, these assets take the form of life insurance. However, because they are assets of the employer, they are attachable by creditors; the employee does not have a secured right to these funds.

A *formally funded plan* is one in which the employer sets aside special assets, often in an irrevocable trust or escrow account, to meet its future obligation. These assets are shielded from the claims of the employer's general creditors.

From a tax standpoint, there is an important distinction between these types of plans. With an unfunded or informally funded deferred compensation arrangement, the employee is not taxed on the plan's benefits until he or she actually receives them. By the same token, the employer cannot take a deduction for the benefits until they are actually paid out. In contrast, a funded plan will result in the compensation being taxable to the employee, and deductible by the employer, as soon as the employee's rights to the deferred benefits become nonforfeitable, usually when the plan is implemented.

Life Insurance and Deferred Compensation

Deferred compensation plans appeal to highly compensated executives who are faced with the unique problem of too much income today relative to future retirement income needs. Since these plans are actually a "substitute" for currently taxed compensation, they offer a way to achieve a better balance between the employee's present income and future income. If the plan is not funded or is informally funded, the benefits, instead of being paid and taxed today, are received during retirement, when the need for them is more acute and when the employee may be in a lower tax bracket.

Life insurance fits neatly into a deferred compensation plan and is a widely used funding vehicle for these kinds of arrangements. The particular type of policy to recommend depends on the employer's financial situation and the age of the key employee. A life paid-up at 65 policy, for example, could be

ILL. 10.1 ■

The Doctrines of Constructive Receipt and Economic Benefit

Two income tax concepts are particularly pertinent to deferred compensation arrangements. They are known as the "Doctrine of Constructive Receipt" and the "Doctrine of Economic Benefit."

Doctrine of Constructive Receipt. Under our tax laws, income that has not actually been received may be taxed as if it had been received, in those cases where the individual "constructively" received the income. This happens when income is set aside for the individual, credited to an account established for him or her or otherwise made available, without any substantial restrictions on the individual's control over the income. The theory of the constructive receipt doctrine is that a person cannot "turn away" for tax purposes from income he or she has a right to receive.

Doctrine of Economic Benefit. A general rule of tax law is that an individual is deemed to have received income if property has been handled or arranged in such a way that a cash-equivalent benefit has been provided to him or her. With regard to a funded deferred compensation plan, this economic benefit doctrine results in taxation to the employee at the time his or her right to the benefits becomes nonforfeitable or nontransferable. This does not apply to arrangements whereby benefits are payable from assets that can be attached by the employer's general creditors.

recommended. The employer applies for life insurance on the life of the executive and insurance premiums are then paid up to the employee's normal retirement date. The employer is the owner, premium payer and beneficiary of the policy; the employee should have no rights to the policy, currently or after retirement. (Any incidents of ownership attributable to the employee could constitute income and become taxable.)

At retirement, the employer can provide the promised benefits by making payment from current earnings or accumulated surplus or the policy's cash value could be used to make the promised benefit payments. For example, the employer could elect to receive the cash surrender value under a fixed period of years option, the duration matched to the term of its deferred benefits obligation. As the employer receives the payments from the insurer, they are paid over to the employee. In this way, the employee's tax liability is limited to the amount received in the taxable year.

In other instances, the employer may desire to keep the policy intact. If the company has sufficient earnings and profits to pay the promised benefit, the policy can remain undisturbed so that the employer receives the face amount upon the death of the employee. These death proceeds would serve as an income tax-free addition to the company's surplus and, assuming the company has a continuing obligation to the deceased employee's spouse or beneficiary, would offset this liability.

The Market for Deferred Compensation Plans

The motivation to enter into a deferred compensation agreement comes from two directions:

1. *The employer.* The employer has an employee whom it wants to recruit or retain and sees a deferred compensation arrangement as an additional employee benefit to induce that person to come to, or stay with, the organization.

2. *The employee.* The employee is well compensated, but wants future retirement security (and perhaps a current tax break as well) and is willing to defer a portion of his or her current income.

Prospects for deferred compensation plans can be found in tax-paying corporations, partnerships and sole proprietorships as well as in nonprofit organizations such as hospitals, trade associations, service organizations and charitable organizations. The individual covered under the plan may be an employee—an important general manager or engineer or sales manager, for example—or an independent contractor, such as a clinic-associated physician or a manufacturer's representative. In fact, one advantage of deferred compensation over a qualified plan is that it may be used where the relationship is one of principal and independent contractor, as is the case with many professional people and the organizations they serve.

Deferred compensation plans are a good choice for business owners who want a strong incentive for their key employees to stay with the business. Because benefits are received *only* if the employee remains with the company until retirement, they are truly "golden handcuffs." If the employee accepts other employment, the benefits are lost. And, to further prevent movement to the competition, a noncompetition clause can be added to the deferred compensation agreement.

Unfortunately, partners and sole proprietors are not eligible for the tax advantages of deferred compensation plans. To avoid current income tax, the sole proprietor or partner should consider other options for themselves, such as an IRA, Keogh or qualified retirement plan.

■ SALARY CONTINUATION PLANS

Planners often used the terms "deferred compensation" and "salary continuation" synonymously. However, there is one major difference between the two plans: a deferred compensation plan uses the employee's income to provide the promised benefit; a salary continuation plan uses the employer's dollars.

A *salary continuation plan* is an arrangement in which the employer agrees to continue a portion of the executive's salary upon the executive's death, retirement and/or disability. These plans are also referred to as "sick pay plans" or "Code Section 105(d) plans." Salary continuation plans differ from deferred compensation plans because salary continuation payments are made *in addition to,* rather than in lieu of, a current raise or bonus. In this way, a salary continuation plan is funded with the employer's dollars.

Like a deferred compensation arrangement, the salary continuation plan is primarily a fringe benefit used by an employer to help retain key personnel and to encourage performance. But the plan offers other advantages, including:

- The employer's promised future payments are not currently taxable. Furthermore, when the employee does receive the payments at retirement, he or she may be in a lower tax bracket.

- The plan is not subject to the majority of ERISA requirements so it is easier to establish and administer.

- The employer receives an income tax deduction when the benefits are actually paid.

- The employer may be selective in rewarding key personnel.

When life insurance is used as the funding mechanism, two additional benefits apply:

- Policy proceeds are not included in the employee's gross estate.

- When the employee dies, the employer receives death proceeds income tax free to aid in funding other obligations.

Yet another advantage to the employer is its ability to retain the executive through the use of "golden handcuffs" that encourage executives to join the company and make it difficult for competitors to lure them away. In exchange for future benefits, the employee must comply with certain conditions of employment before, and sometimes after, retirement. The conditions are set forth in a written agreement with the employer, and may include the executive's promise to:

- remain with the company for a specified number of years;

- refrain from employment or any other service with a competing company; and

- act as a consultant to the company after retirement.

A salary continuation arrangement enables a company to provide substantial retirement benefits for top management on a selective basis. Although certain minimal reporting procedures must be followed, a salary continuation plan requires no qualification with the IRS.

The Market for Salary Continuation Plans

An excellent candidate for salary continuation plans is the small business owner who relies on a few key employees. The loss of those employees, due to retirement, disability or death, could be a huge financial drain on the company. To solve this problem, employers can set up a salary continuation plan funded by insurance. These plans can be used to replace a percentage of the employee's income after retirement by transferring the long-term financial obligation to a life insurance company.

Salary continuation plans are also excellent choices for publicly held corporations with several levels of management. These plans help both the corporation and its key executives to meet their objectives. In addition, a salary continuation plan may be marketed to private corporations, an S corporation or a nonprofit organization. Such a plan can broaden an employer's retirement options for its key employees and do so in both a cost-effective and benefit-effective manner.

■ TYPES OF DEFERRED COMPENSATION AND SALARY CONTINUATION PLANS

As stated earlier, the key distinction between a salary continuation and a deferred compensation plan is whose dollars are being used to provide the promised benefit. A salary continuation plan uses employer dollars; a deferred compensation plan uses employee dollars.

Both salary continuation plans and deferred compensation plans are commonly structured in one of the following ways—as supplemental employee retirement plans, top hat plans, excess benefit plans or rabbi or secular trusts.

ILL. 10.2 ■

The Advantages of Life Insurance as a Funding Medium

While any form of cash accumulation may be used to build the pool of money to pay promised retirement benefits, life insurance, because of its unique nature, is ideally suited for this role. In fact, permanent cash value life insurance is the medium of choice for companies to informally fund salary continuation and deferred compensation plans. Funding is *informal* when it does not provide any vested or nonforfeitable rights or interest to employees.

Funding a deferred compensation or salary continuation plan with life insurance on an informal basis provides the employer with at least three benefits:

1. The cash values accumulate income tax free and the tax on the growth is deferred until the policy matures.

2. Death proceeds from the policy are received income tax free to the beneficiary (the employer).

3. The benefits are paid as an expense to the corporation which then takes an income tax deduction for the benefits when they are paid at retirement.

Although there are other ways to fund a deferred compensation plan, no other funding vehicle provides this leverage as economically or as practically as life insurance.

When using a life insurance policy to provide benefits, it is important to properly arrange the ownership and beneficiary designations of each policy. In most cases, the employer is the beneficiary, as well as the owner of all incidents of ownership in the policy. The insurance cash values become part of general company assets and the proceeds are payable to the company. The insured has no interest in or rights to the insurance policy, either presently or in retirement.

It must be remembered that the deferred compensation or salary continuation agreement has no direct relation to insurance. In fact, an effective agreement could be carried out whether or not there is life insurance. At retirement, the employer may use the cash value of the policy to meet its retirement benefit promise or draw on its other assets to make the deferred compensation payments. If the policy remains in force, the company may still collect the proceeds upon the employee's death.

From the corporation's point of view, the use of life insurance means that the business will be in a sound financial position when new liabilities are created for amortizing the future cost of paying benefits to a retired employee. And, of course, this means greater peace of mind for the insured executive who realizes that the deferred compensation agreement has set up a substantial future liability in his or her favor.

Supplemental Employee Retirement Plans

To provide salary continuation, employers often establish a nonqualified plan called a *supplemental employee retirement plan (SERP)*. These plans are often funded with life insurance contracts. Typically, a SERP contains the following three provisions:

1. The corporation is the owner and beneficiary of life insurance on the key employee's life.

2. The benefit is based on an unsecured promise. The employee reports no taxable income, nor does the employer receive a tax deduction, until the benefit is received at retirement.

3. The corporation funds the employee's benefit at retirement with policy-holder loans against the cash value of the policy.

A SERP satisfies the employer's objective of bringing retirement benefits up to desired levels in an already existing qualified plan. However, an employer may also use deferred compensation plans, executive bonus plans, or split-dollar plans to accomplish its objectives. (These latter options are discussed later in this chapter.)

Top Hat Plans

Either the employer or the employee may initiate a top hat plan during employment contract negotiations. Under a *top hat plan,* the executive forgoes receipt of currently earned compensation, such as salary or commissions, and directs these funds to be paid out at retirement. A top hat plan is typically set up as a defined contribution plan, with the amount deferred and investment gain credited to an account set up for the executive. The executive's retirement benefit is an aggregate amount of all contributions and earnings.

Excess Benefit Plans

The employer may legally exceed the maximum contribution and benefit limit for qualified plans—the Code Section 415 limits—by establishing an excess benefit plan. An *excess benefit plan* provides additional benefits for executives who will already be receiving the maximum benefit under their employer's qualified plan.

Rabbi Trust and Secular Trusts

Assets intended to provide the promised benefits to executives can be place in irrevocable trusts. The *rabbi trust,* originally developed by and named for a rabbi concerned about his future retirement income, segregates assets in a trust with conditions that the funds be used only for retirement. In the rabbi trust, contributions are made to an irrevocable trust and are not taxed to the employee as current taxable income; the employer receives no tax deduction. To avoid current income taxation, the assets in the trust are left subject to the claims of the employer's general creditors.

A *secular trust* may also be used to fund nonqualified deferred compensation benefits. In a secular trust, all trust assets are currently taxable to the employee because the opportunity for forfeiture of assets is sufficiently reduced by a trust provision to create current income to the employee. Funds are not subject to the claims of general creditors, and the employer is entitled to a tax deduction. Secular trusts are appealing to executives who feel that the income tax rate may

ILL. 10.3 ■ Features and Benefits of a Deferred Compensation or Salary Continuation Plan

How is it executed?	Employer and employee enter into a written agreement under which the employer agrees to pay certain retirement and/or survivor/disability benefits to the employee or heirs. The employer indemnifies its obligation by purchasing life insurance on the employee's life and naming itself as beneficiary.
Who is the participating employee?	The employer has complete freedom to "pick and choose" who and how many of its employees may participate. A different plan can be designed for each select employee.
Does the plan have to comply with ERISA?	There is minimal ERISA compliance required, dealing only with reporting and disclosure rules.
What are the tax implications for the employer?	If the plan is informally funded no current deduction is available; however, benefits are deductible when paid and any insurance death proceeds are received tax free. Formally funded deferred compensation contributions are deductible in the taxable year in which the employee includes an amount attributable to the contribution in gross income.
What are the tax implications for the employee?	If the plan is informally funded, there is no current tax; however, benefits will be taxable as income when they are received. In a formally funded plan, the fair market value of the contribution is included in gross income if the right to the contributions is transferable and not subject to substantial risk of forfeiture.

increase in the future or when it appears that the existing corporation will be merged or sold to unfriendly future owners.

■ SPLIT-DOLLAR PLANS

In addition to salary continuation and deferred compensation plans, employers may also use split-dollar plans as valuable executive benefits. These plans are also a popular way of *financing* executive benefits. The term *split-dollar* refers to cooperation in splitting the death benefit and living benefits of cash value life insurance contracts between the employer and the employee, or any other two individuals. In addition, the premium may also be divided between the parties.

Under a split-dollar plan, the employer provides an executive with the benefit of substantially more life insurance than the employee could otherwise personally buy. One party, usually the employer, is given control of the cash values of the policy while the other party, usually the employee, is given control of the pure protection (i.e., the death benefit).

A split-dollar plan is flexible in its design, amount of its benefits, allocation of benefits and in the period of time over which premiums must be paid. The plan does not require IRS approval and the employer may choose which employees may participate. The plan can also be used in a variety of situations including funding a sole proprietor's or partnership's buy-sell agreement.

The Basic Split-Dollar Plan

The *basic split-dollar plan* splits the right to benefits and the obligation to pay policy premiums between two individuals, usually an employer and an employee. Typically, the employer pays the portion of the premium equal to the annual increase in the policy's cash value. The employee pays the balance of the premium due, either directly or through payroll deduction. Once the annual increase in the cash value proceeds equals or exceeds the annual premium, the employer pays all subsequent premiums.

In most cases, the employer and employee will use the *P.S. 58* or economic benefit approach to share premiums. (P.S. 58 refers to the name of the U.S. government tables or premium rates for individual one-year term life insurance policies.) The employee pays an amount of premium equal to the one-year term cost of his or her insurance protection and the employer pays the balance. Under this method, the employer may increase the employee's salary or give the employee a bonus sufficient to reimburse the employee for his or her required premium contributions. The additional salary or bonus is tax deductible by the employer.

Collateral vs. Endorsement Method

Split-dollar plans are set up using some variation of either the collateral assignment method or the endorsement method. Under the *collateral method,* the employee applies for, owns and is the premium payer on the life insurance contract. The employee also names the beneficiary. In a separate agreement, the employer agrees to lend the employee, at a nominal interest rate, an amount equal to the insurance in the cash value of the policy. In exchange, the employee collaterally assigns the policy to the employer as security for the loans that are repayable upon termination of employment or the earlier death of the employee. The remaining policy proceeds are paid to the beneficiary. The employee receives a taxable economic benefit under split-dollar agreements and must report the value as a taxable amount. Income tax treatment is discussed later in this chapter.

Under the *endorsement method,* the employer applies for and owns the policy. The employee's rights are defined in a separate, written agreement. The employee reimburses the employer for the premium that exceeds the increase in cash value. The employer is named as beneficiary for an amount equal to the cash value, and the excess goes to an additional beneficiary named by the employee. If the plan is terminated, the policy is surrendered to the employer or the employee may purchase the policy for its cash or surrender value.

Major Uses of Split-Dollar Plans

Split-dollar insurance has a variety of potential uses. Among the most common are:

- *Employee Benefits for Key Employees*

  As stated earlier, split-dollar plans are excellent incentive plans that can be used to reward executives with substantial amounts of insurance—usually more than they could personally afford. Such a benefit often results in higher morale and increased company loyalty.

- *Reducing the Cost of Funding Deferred Compensation*

  The cost of funding is reduced because it has not paid the full premium for the life insurance. When the employee dies, the company receives insurance proceeds from the policy to pay a death benefit to the employee's beneficiary. The company retains the cash value of the policy.

- *Funding Buy-Sell Agreements*

  A buy-sell agreement is an arrangement made to allow the continuation of a business after the death of one of the owners. The agreement sets the price at which the sale will be made and forces the owners or the estate to sell and the buyers to purchase the property at this price. Such an agreement is often accompanied by the purchase of life insurance, which provides the funds to complete the transaction.

Income Taxation

The income tax treatment for the employer is different from that of the employee for a split-dollar plan. The employer may not take a deduction for the premiums paid because the employer is directly or indirectly the beneficiary of the life insurance policy proceeds. However, when death benefits are paid, the employer generally receives the proceeds income tax free.

Unlike the employer, the employee is subject to IRS revenue rulings that control the income taxation of split dollar plans. These rulings include:

- *Revenue Ruling 64-328*

  The doctrine of economic benefit applies, meaning that the economic benefit of a split-dollar plan is taxed as ordinary income to the employee. The rule applies when an employee's benefit becomes equivalent to available cash. An arrangement designed merely as an unsecured, unfunded promise of future benefits is clearly not the "equivalent of cash." If the assets used to provide benefits under a nonqualified deferred compensation agreement remain as general assets of the corporation, there is no current tax exposure to the employee.

- *Revenue Ruling 66-110*

  The actual cash value of any dividend used for the employee's benefit is taxable income to the employee. The employee must include the total value of policy dividends used for the employee's benefit when computing the economic benefits of a split-dollar plan to the employee.

- *Revenue Ruling 78-420*

  A third party, such as a spouse, may have ownership of split- dollar policies. This arrangement is useful when an estate plan favors spousal ownership of a policy or when ownership of the policy by a trust is preferred. This ruling provides that the employee who receives the benefit of the third-party arrangement is responsible for the economic benefit of the plan and is deemed to make a gift of the value of that benefit to the owner of the policy.

Reverse Split-Dollar Plans

In some cases, a reverse split-dollar plan is used to allow an employee to receive cash from the employer at the lowest cost to the employee under favorable tax circumstances. A *reverse split-dollar plan* is an arrangement in which the insured is the employee, but the employer does not own the policy. Rather, the policyowner is the employee, a spouse or a trust set up by the employee. The policyowner owns an interest in the policy equal to the greater of its premium contribution or the policy's cash values. The employer pays a portion of the premium equal to the policy's P.S. 58 costs and the employee pays the balance of the premium. The arrangement terminates when the employee is age 65, and the policyowner gains control over the entire policy.

A reverse-split dollar plan acts as "golden handcuffs" or an attractive employee benefit. It also benefits the company because, should an employee die before retirement, the proceeds of the policy are paid to the employer, while an amount equal to the cash values or the premiums paid by the employee are paid to the employee's family or estate.

The Market for Split-Dollar Plans

A split-dollar plan combines the premium-paying ability of a company with the life insurance needs of selected employees. As we've seen, there are many ways to set up ownership, premium payments and distribution of the proceeds. In general, these plans are a way for a business to use the insurance proceeds to recoup its contribution to the plan. For example, a close corporation could use a split-dollar plan to set up an insured buy-sell agreement on a cross-purchase basis. In this case, the business applies for insurance on the lives of the shareholders, pays the premiums and receives its share of the proceeds upon the death of a shareholder. The remaining owners can use the balance to purchase the business from the decedent's family.

■   **EXECUTIVE BONUS PLANS**

Another commonly used discretionary employee benefit plan is called an *executive bonus plan*. This plan meets a number of corporate and executive needs, is relatively simple to establish and is easy to understand. An executive bonus plan, also known as an "insured bonus plan" or a "Code Section 162 plan," is a nonqualified plan that provides benefits to both the employer and the employee.

Basically, an executive bonus plan is a simple life insurance fringe-benefit program in which an employee is given ownership of a policy on his or her life, with the employer paying the premiums, either directly or indirectly through a salary increase to the employee. The employee owns the plan from the very start and has control over the policy's cash values and the beneficiary designation.

An executive bonus plan benefits the employer because it chooses who will participate in the plan and may use the plan to attract, motivate and reward employees. In addition, the plan provides a simple way to buy personal life insurance for key executives (including owners) using tax-deductible business dollars. Finally, the employer can fix the costs of the plan in advance, which helps to assure proper cash management.

The executive also benefits from an executive bonus plan because he or she receives permanent cash value life insurance at a very low personal cost. Though the premium payments made on the executive's behalf are considered a taxable benefit, his or her out-of-pocket cost is only the additional income tax generated on the bonus received. Furthermore, Code Section 162 plans are flexible so options may be selected at later dates to meet the executive's needs. For example, the employee could choose to take the policy's cash value at retirement under a payout option or leave the policy intact for its death benefit. Finally, the executive may feel rewarded by the company for his or her personal efforts.

Executive Bonus Plan Structure

An executive bonus plan, because it is characterized as an employee welfare benefit plan, is exempt from all of the participation, funding and vesting requirements of ERISA. The plan document can be as liberal or as restrictive as the employer desires.

The actual plan design is limited only by the imaginations of the life insurance professional, the attorney and the employer involved in its creation. Although it may be tempting to create a rather formidable document, a simple plan is easier to understand, administrate and amend at some later date.

An executive bonus plan may be funded by any form of permanent cash value life insurance, other than modified endowment contracts (MECs). This class of contracts, once used to provide tax shelters, was defined by the Technical and Miscellaneous Revenue Act of 1988 (TAMRA). Passage of TAMRA ended what some felt was an abusive application of the tax advantages afforded the life insurance transaction. To avoid being labeled a MEC and losing the advantage of tax-free policy loans, a policy's premiums cannot be paid more rapidly than necessary to provide the paid-up death benefits that seven level annual payments can purchase.

Annuity contracts are another popular funding alternative for a Code Section 162 plan. Although they lack the advantage of a preretirement death benefit, they can be issued to any executive, regardless of health. Also, annuity contracts may maximize future additional income when compared with some forms of permanent life insurance.

Income Taxation

An executive bonus plan is an employee welfare benefit plan under ERISA since it provides death benefits as well as other benefits. Code Section 162 sets out three requirements that must be met if an expense is to be deductible for the employer. The expense must be:

1. "ordinary and necessary" in the normal course of business and must be helpful in the business;

2. "paid or incurred" in the year it is deducted; and

3. "payment for services actually rendered" in the course of an employment relationship.

The executive has a single requirement: the amount of the premium payment or the bonus must be included in his or her gross income as "compensation for services." Even if the benefit is something other than cash, if it has a measurable value, it must be included as income.

The Market for Executive Bonus Plans

Executive bonus plans are especially appealing to new or struggling businesses with limited funds. The owner can select both the participants and the amount to be spent on each participant. The company can use tax-deductible business dollars to make modest premium payments to purchase substantial life insurance. Unlike the restrictions and "golden handcuffs" imposed by split-dollar or deferred compensation plans, executive bonus plans are portable. If a covered employee leaves the company, he or she may pick up the premium payment so there is no loss of coverage. This may be appealing to an employee since the employer's premium dollars and policy cash values built up to that point also go with the employee.

■ GOLDEN PARACHUTES

A relatively new addition to executive compensation arrangements are the colorfully named *golden parachutes*. These plans are arrangements for allowing terminated, highly paid executives to maintain relatively affluent lifestyles in exchange for agreeing to leave his or her corporate employ. Such agreements are commonly sought when a corporation is acquired by another corporation.

A golden parachute is characterized by extremely generous benefits to the executive or owner/employee. Such an individual is an officer, shareholder or highly compensated person classified as a "disqualified individual." Parachute distributions are not looked upon with a kind eye by the IRS. In addition to creating a tax liability at current ordinary income tax rates, benefits distributed under golden parachute arrangements will be subject to a 20 percent excise if the value of the distributed benefits exceeds three times (300 percent) the individual's average annual compensation prior to the change in the executive's normal employment. An employer receives no tax deduction for benefits distributed under a golden parachute arrangement.

An executive in receipt of large golden parachute distribution amounts may be in great need of expert financial counseling which could present a service and sales opportunity to the financial services professional. You might, for example, recommend an IRA rollover to minimize taxes on a lump-sum distribution; the principal can then grow tax free until withdrawn.

■ SUMMARY

In today's highly competitive business environment, employers must find a way to recruit and retain productive, loyal employees. The successful life insurance professional knows special perks for officers, executives and other highly compensated employees can be provided with nonqualified plans. Your job and your opportunity is to understand nonqualified plans so that you can help your clients decide which plans best suit their needs.

In addition to concerns about adequate retirement income, many of your clients will be concerned about adequate health care after they retire. In the next chapter, we will discuss health care planning for retirement, including Medicare, Medicaid and long-term health care.

■ CHAPTER 10 QUESTIONS FOR REVIEW

1. Which statement below correctly applies to nonqualified deferred compensation plans?

   a. The employee is 100 percent vested in the full amount of any compensation deferred in the year in which such compensation is earned.
   b. Nonqualified deferred compensation plans may not discriminate in favor of highly compensated employees.
   c. The tax advantage of nonqualified deferred compensation is achieved primarily by postponing the "constructive receipt" of compensation by employees.
   d. Amounts deferred under a nonqualified deferred compensation plan are generally placed into accounts which are specifically allocated to and owned by the employer.

2. All of the following statements regarding nonqualified deferred compensation plans are correct, EXCEPT:

a. A deferred compensation plan is an unsecured promise made by an employer to pay an employee part of his or her compensation in the future.
b. Under a nonqualified deferred compensation plan, an employee can rely on guaranteed future benefits.
c. The employer receives no tax deduction for the amount of the compensation deferred until such amounts are actually distributed.
d. Most deferred compensation plans are unfunded.

3. Which of the following is/are approaches to structuring a deferred compensation plan?

I. Deferred compensation plan
II. Salary continuation plan

a. I only
b. II only
c. Both I and II
d. Neither I nor II

4. Split-dollar plans can be used for funding all of the following, EXCEPT:

a. buy-sell agreements.
b. employee benefits for key employees.
c. deferred compensation.
d. stock investments.

5. A plan in which the employer sets aside special assets, usually in an irrevocable trust or escrow account, to fund an employee's retirement is called a/an

a. unfunded plan.
b. informally funded plan.
c. formally funded plan.
d. nonfunded plan.

11

Health Care and Health Insurance

T he U.S. Census Bureau estimates that by the year 2040, the average 65-year-old can look forward to an additional 20 years of life. This increased life expectancy means both good news and bad news for all of us. First, the good news. With a positive attitude and adequate health care, people eventually expect to live an estimated life span of 115 years. Now, the bad news. For most people, with increasing age comes illness, more frailty and medical costs that may be only partially covered by insurance.

The need for adequate health care coverage translates into an opportunity for a retirement planner specializing in life and health insurance to offer clients both an education and well-chosen insurance products. Your knowledge of what types of policies a client might currently have, and whether those policies are adequate to meet his or her retirement needs, is vital.

In this chapter, you will find a brief discussion of available private and government health care programs, Medicare and Medicaid benefits, Medicare supplement insurance programs and disability income insurance. This overview will assist you in helping your clients understand and choose the best retirement health care options for their needs.

■ ■ ■ ■ ■

■ PRIVATE AND GOVERNMENT HEALTH CARE PROGRAMS

The purpose of health insurance is to reduce the financial burden that individuals face when illness occurs. Your clients will expect you, as an insurance professional, to apply your knowledge of insurance to help them select the proper kind of health protection within their financial boundaries. Whether you work with individuals or groups, you will probably be asked to advise clients about which insurance policies to choose.

After retirement, many people will face chronic health problems and will become dependent on formal or informal caregiving systems. The cost of this care will be paid for in a number of ways. Most of the private insurance coverage in the United States is group coverage related to the past or current employment of a family member. As part of an employment benefit package, employers often purchase group insurance policies to cover employees and their dependents. Group health insurance is offered by private insurance companies, service plans like Blue Cross/Blue Shield, health maintenance organizations (HMOs) or preferred provider organizations (PPOs). In addition to medical benefits, the plans may also offer dental and vision care. Group insurance plans provide about 90 percent of private health insurance with employers paying all or part of the cost.

In many cases, group coverage may be continued after the employee leaves the company. Employees who would have lost their benefits upon termination of employment, divorce or a number of other events are now protected under the law. The Consolidated Omnibus Budget Act of 1986 (COBRA) requires that employers offer terminated employees the option of continuing their group coverage for a set period of time, provided the employee pays the entire cost.

People who are unemployed, self-employed or ineligible under their company's group insurance plan may choose to purchase individual health insurance. Although the individual plans provide a variety of coverages and renewal provisions, they are generally much more expensive than group plans and, of course, must be paid for entirely by the individual.

Individuals who are unable to obtain health insurance from the private sector seek assistance from the government. Through a variety of programs, the government mandates or provides medical expense insurance. Although these programs seldom offer comprehensive medical coverage, they may cover an individual's basic health care needs.

As the retirement market swells, more and more people will look to the government to provide for their basic health care needs. After retirement, most people use Medicare, the federally sponsored health care program, to meet their medical cost. However, Medicare coverage is subject to deductibles, co-payments and limitations that must be satisfied by recipients or their insurance companies. In these few pages, our discussion will focus on Medicare and Medicaid—two of the most commonly used (and least understood) government health care programs.

■ MEDICARE INSURANCE

Medicare is a government insurance program instituted to provide a delivery and payment system of medical and hospital care for people age 65 and over and for individuals with specific disabilities. In addition to providing medical benefits, the program acts as a way to control the costs for these medical services through its system of regulations and procedures. In other words, Medicare attempts to hold down the cost of medical care by limiting the scope of its coverage and its benefit amounts, thus making the consumer and service provider more cost-conscious and less likely to "overuse" the program.

ILL. 11.1 ■ Medicare Coverage

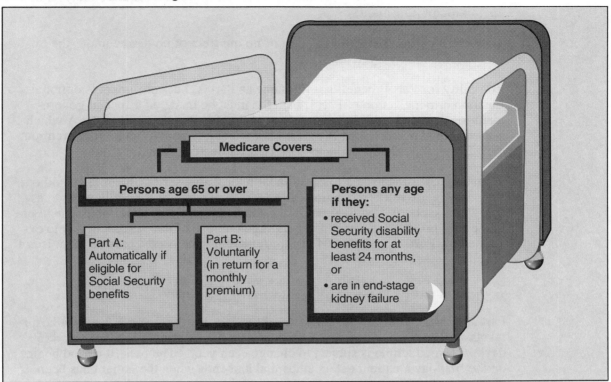

Contrary to popular belief, Medicare does *not* cover all medical expenses. Medicare does not pay for most routine physicals; eye and hearing exams; dental care; self-administered drugs; and many other medical products and services. In addition, some long-term health problems requiring custodial care, like Alzheimer's disease, are not covered. Medicare coverage is also subject to deductibles, co-payments and limitations.

Medicare coverage has two distinct parts, Part A and Part B. Part A provides hospitalization insurance for inpatient hospital care, inpatient care prescribed by a doctor at a skilled nursing facility, home health care and care at a recognized hospice. Part B provides medical insurance for required doctors' services, outpatient services and medical supplies and many services not covered by Part A hospitalization coverage.

Practically everyone age 65 or older, as well as many people classified as disabled, is eligible for Medicare Part A and Medicare Part B. A person is eligible for Part A Medicare benefits if he or she is/was:

- 65 or over and has qualified for Social Security or Railroad Retirement monthly cash benefits;

- entitled to benefits under the Social Security program for 24 months as a disabled worker, disabled widow(er) or as a child age 18 or over who was disabled before age 22;

- diagnosed as having permanent kidney failure and requires dialysis or a kidney transplant; or

- born before 1909 and has few or no quarters of coverage under the Social Security System.

Eligibility for Part B benefits is the same as Part A, but enrollment is optional. Election or nonelection of Part B benefits must be made on a special government form mailed to all individuals qualifying for Part A. Unlike Part A which is available at no cost, Part B coverages require payment of a monthly premium ($36.60 in 1993) that is deducted from Social Security benefits.

Medicare performs its health care function through a series of carefully laid out steps. There are rules, regulations and procedures that must be following to assure that the claim is paid, either to the Medicare recipient as reimbursement or to the care provider as direct payment. The purpose of the next section is to examine how Parts A and B of Medicare function, what is covered and what is not covered.

Medicare Part A: Hospitalization Insurance (HI)

Part A of Medicare pays for all covered services for the first 60 days of a hospital stay except for the deductible amount paid once during a benefit period (60 days). The deductible is subject to change each year.[*] The benefit period begins on the first day a patient enters a hospital and ends when the patient has been discharged for 60 consecutive days. If a patient returns to the hospital a second or third time during a benefit period, the deductible does not have to be paid again. On the other hand, if a patient is released from the hospital and returns 61 days later, Medicare deems that a new benefit period has begun and the deductible must be paid again.

If a hospital stay lasts longer than 60 days during a benefit period, Medicare pays all covered services from the 61st to the 150th day. During this period, however, the patient also must pay a daily amount called a *co-payment*. Like the deductible, the co-payment, which covers part of cost of the service, is subject to change each year. It is calculated on two levels: from the 61st to 90th day of hospitalization, a set daily co-payment is applied; from the 91st to 150th day of hospitalization, another higher daily co-payment is assessed.[†] After 150 days of hospitalization, the Medicare recipient is responsible for *all* hospitalization charges.

Part A covers medical and psychiatric hospital care, skilled nursing facility benefits, home health care and hospice care. Although coverage is fairly comprehensive, there are limitations, deductibles and co-payments for each benefit.

---

*In 1993, the deductible was $676.

†In 1993, the daily co-payment amounts were $169 per day for the 61st to 90th day and $338 per day for the 91st to 150th day.

Hospitalization Benefits

Part A hospitalization benefits cover the following:

1. semi-private room and board;

2. regular nursing services;

3. drugs furnished by the hospital;

4. lab tests, X rays and medical supplies such as dressings, splints and casts;

5. blood transfusions, except for the first three pints, which are paid for by the Medicare recipient;

6. use of appliances such as wheelchairs;

7. use of the operating room, recovery room and special-care units such as intensive care;

8. rehabilitation services such as physical therapy; and

9. care in psychiatric hospitals, with some limitations.

Skilled Nursing Care Facility Benefits

Care at a skilled nursing facility is covered if both the facility and the patient's diagnosis and treatment plan meet Medicare's strict standards. Then Medicare pays for 100 percent of all covered charges for the first 20 days. For the next 80 days, the patient is responsible for a daily copayment.[*] After 100 days, the patient is responsible for all charges.

The benefits are available only after a hospital stay of at least three days; a doctor has certified that skilled nursing is required; and the daily skilled nursing or rehabilitation services are provided by a Medicare-approved facility. Custodial care, offered by most retirement and nursing homes, is not covered. Care is considered custodial when it primarily meets personal needs rather than medical needs or can be provided by individuals without professional training. It includes help in walking, getting in and out of bed, bathing, dressing and taking medicine. Medicare will not pay for this type of care; it pays for skilled nursing care only.

Home Health Care Benefits

Health care benefits for homebound patients are also available under Medicare Part A. Covered services include part-time or intermittent skilled nursing care, physical therapy, medical social services, medical supplies and some rehabilitation equipment. Benefits are paid for by Part A as long as the services are pre-

---

*In 1993, the daily co-payment for skilled nursing facility benefits was $84.50.

scribed by a doctor and care is provided by a Medicare-certified health care agency.

Hospice Care Benefits

A *hospice* is an organization that furnishes a coordinated program of inpatient, outpatient and home care for terminally ill patients. Care includes counseling, control of disease symptoms and pain relief. The full cost of physician and nursing services, medical appliances and supplies is paid for by Medicare.

Terminally ill patients can elect to receive hospice care for an unlimited duration under Part A, but in lieu of other Medicare benefits. Medicare benefits for this care are available for as long as a doctor certifies the care is needed, up to 210 days (though this period could be extended, in some cases). The patient pays 5 percent of the cost of prescription drugs (not to exceed $5 for each prescription) and 5 percent of the cost of respite care (not to exceed five consecutive days or more than the current Part A deductible).

Part A Exclusions

As noted earlier, Medicare does not cover all hospital or medical expenses. Some of the exclusions under Part A of Medicare include:

1. personal convenience items such as television sets, radios and telephones;

2. private duty nurses;

3. private rooms (unless deemed medically necessary);

4. custodial care in a skilled nursing facility; and

5. full-time nursing care, drugs, homemaker services and meals delivered to the patient's home for home health care benefits.

Medicare Part B: Supplementary Medical Insurance

Part B is the medical expense part of Medicare. Part B, or Supplementary Medical Insurance (SMI), is not automatically provided. If an individual elects Part B coverage, he or she must pay a monthly premium for that coverage. Part B covers:

- surgeons' and physicians' fees;

- outpatient services;

- medical lab fees;

- ambulance costs; and

- some outpatient psychiatric care.

In addition to a monthly premium, the recipient must pay an annual deductible before Part B benefits begin.* After the annual deductible is met, Medicare will pay 80 percent of allowable charges for covered medical services and 100 percent of some costs, such as clinical diagnostic lab tests.

The question of what Medicare considers an "allowable charge" continues to create controversy. The amount Medicare will pay depends on the doctor's charge, the medical procedure and the community where the service is provided. Basically, when a doctor's fee is submitted as a claim, a comparison is made between the actual bill, the doctor's customary charge and the prevailing charge in that community for that medical service. After the deductible has been met, Medicare will pay the claim based on the least of those three amounts. In other words, Medicare pays 80 percent of the least of the actual, customary or prevailing charge. Any charges that exceed the allowable charge must be paid by the patient.

Part B Exclusions

Under the medical expense benefit portion of Medicare, the following items and services are excluded:

1. routine physical exams, eye or hearing exams, and related tests;

2. eyeglasses, hearing aids or dental care;

3. services not medically necessary;

4. most immunizations;

5. diagnostic or therapeutic services of a chiropractor, except for conditions detected by an X ray;

6. full-time private nursing care in the home;

7. homemaker services provided by a relative or household member; and

8. most prescription drugs taken at home.

It is clear that the coverage and benefits provided by Medicare are by no means comprehensive or complete. Because of deductible, co-payments and limitations, there are many "gaps" in coverage. Many of the gaps are most obvious in Medicare Part B. The first of these gaps is the annual deductible. The next gap occurs in the difference between the actual fee a doctor charges and the allowable charge that Medicare covers. Any remaining "excess charge" must be paid entirely by the Medicare recipient. The third gap occurs because the recipient must pay a 20 percent co-payment charge of the allowable expense. The most popular way to fill these gaps is with a Medicare supplement or "medigap"

---

*In 1993, the Part B deductible was $100.

policy, sold by insurance companies. We will look at these policies in more detail later in this chapter.

■ MEDICAID

In addition to Medicare, the government offers Medicaid coverage though local welfare departments. *Medicaid* is a joint federal and state health program that provides medical assistance to certain low-income individuals and families. Typically, the services will include inpatient and outpatient services, certain prescription drugs, medical supplies and nursing home care. However, because each state designs its own Medicaid program within federal guidelines, the extent of coverage and the quality of services vary widely from state to state.

Many people are reluctant to apply for Medicaid because it is a form of welfare. It is most often used by people who, because of long-term debilitating illness or insufficient assets, find themselves unable to pay for medical services. The program is generally available to people who are currently receiving Aid to Families with Dependent Children or supplemental Social Security benefits; people who are blind, disabled or elderly and whose income is below a certain level; and people in nursing homes who lack the money to pay for their care. In short, Medicaid provides a bare subsistence of medical care for impoverished people.

Many people over the age of 65, because of increased medical costs, longevity and a decreased income, are turning to Medicaid as a last resort. Under the current system, a person can qualify for Medicaid only when he or she is technically bankrupt. Financial assistance is available only if a person has divested himself or herself of all "nonexempt" assets. These assets include cash over $2,000 (in most states), stocks, bonds, IRAs, Keoghs, CDs, Treasury notes, savings bonds and certain other items, depending on the state involved.

Interestingly, Medicaid does not count certain "exempt" assets in determining eligibility for financial assistance. Although the definition of exempt assets will vary from state to state, the exempt items often include a house used as a primary residence, a car, personal jewelry and term life insurance. Exempt assets are not counted as things of value and do not have to be sold in order to qualify for Medicaid.

When nonexempt, or countable, assets are unavailable to the owner, Medicaid does not consider those items when determining eligibility. Therefore, assets can be protected from Medicaid by transferring them to certain types of joint accounts, by verifying that a person is too incapacitated to access those assets or by holding the assets in a Medicaid qualifying trust.

Medicaid Trusts

A *trust* is a legal device in which one party (the grantor or donor) transfers property to a second party (the trustee) to manage for a third party (the beneficiary). If the donor can change the terms of the trust, the trust is called a *revocable trust*. If the terms may not be altered, it is called an *irrevocable trust*. People may use a Medicaid trust to protect their assets and to qualify for Medicaid benefits. The trust must be irrevocable; the person establishing the trust and the spouse of the Medicaid applicant can have no access to the principal; and neither can be a trustee. Medicaid imposes a 30-month waiting period, and the trust cannot pay for expenses normally paid by Medicaid.

When a transfer of a countable asset is made to a Medicaid trust, it must be done at least 30 months before the day the applicant goes into a nursing home or applies for Medicaid. Unless the transfer is accomplished before then, Medicaid will assume that it was done in order to have Medicaid pay for institutional care and the assets will not be protected.

■ MEDICARE SUPPLEMENT POLICIES

As you can see from our discussion, Medicare leaves many "gaps" in its coverage. With its structure of limited benefit periods, deductibles, co-payments and exclusions, the coverage it provides is limited. To help fill these gaps, commercial insurance companies have developed *Medicare supplement insurance policies,* designed to pick up coverage where Medicare leaves off.

New Requirements for Medicare Supplement Policies

In late 1990, as part of the Omnibus Budget Reconciliation Act, Congress required the National Association of Insurance Commissioners (NAIC) to address the subject of Medicare supplement insurance policies. Specifically, this group's task was to develop a standardized model Medicare supplement policy, which would provide certain "core" benefits, plus as many as nine other supplement policies. These model policies could then be adopted by the states as prototype policies for their insurers. The intent of this law was to reduce the number of Medicare supplement policies that were being offered for sale. It was also intended to help consumers understand Medicare supplement policies (thereby helping them make informed buying decisions) by:

- standardizing coverage and benefits from one policy to the next;

- simplifying the terms used in these policies;

- facilitating policy comparisons; and

- eliminating policy provisions that could be misleading or confusing.

The results of the NAIC's work are ten Medicare standard supplement plans, ranging from the basic "core" policy, with a minimum of supplemental coverage, to policies with increasingly more comprehensive coverage. Following is a brief description of each plan. (See Ill. 11.1.)

Plan A: Core Benefits

The first plan, Medicare Supplement Plan A, is the "core" plan. It includes coverage for:

- Part A coinsurance amounts;

- 365 additional days after Medicare benefits end;

- the Part B coinsurance amount (generally 20 percent of Medicare-approved services); and

- the first three pints of blood each year.

At a minimum, all Medicare supplement policies must contain these "core" benefits. In addition, any company that markets and sells Medicare supplement policies must make available this basic core Plan A as a separate policy.

Plan B

Medicare Supplement Plan B must contain Plan A core benefits, plus coverage for:

- the Medicare Part A deductible.

Plan C

Medicare Supplement Plan C must contain Plan A core benefits, plus coverage for:

- the Medicare Part A deductible;

- medically necessary emergency care in a foreign country;

- the daily co-insurance amount for skilled nursing facility care; and

- the Medicare Part B deductible.

Plan D

Medicare Supplement Plan D must contain Plan A core benefits, plus coverage for:

- the Medicare Part A deductible;

- medically necessary emergency care in a foreign country;

- the daily co-insurance amount for skilled nursing facility care; and

- "at-home recovery," which includes services to provide short-term assistance with activities of daily living for those recovering from an illness or accident.

ILL. 11.2 ■ Medicare Standard Supplement Plans

A	B	C	D	E	F	G	H	I	J
Basic Benefits	Basic Benefits	Basic Benefits	Basic Benefits	Basic Benefits	Basic Benefits	Basic Benefits	Basic Benefits	Basic Benefits	Basic Benefits
		Skilled Nursing Copayment	Skilled Nursing Copayment	Skilled Nursing Copayment	Skilled Nursing Copayment	Skilled Nursing Copayment	Skilled Nursing Copayment	Skilled Nursing Copayment	Skilled Nursing Copayment
	Part A Deductible	Part A Deductible	Part A Deductible	Part A Deductible	Part A Deductible	Part A Deductible	Part A Deductible	Part A Deductible	Part A Deductible
		Part B Deductible			Part B Deductible				Part B Deductible
					Part B Excess (100%)	Part B Excess (80%)		Part B Excess (100%)	Part B Excess (100)%
		Foreign Travel Emergency	Foreign Travel Emergency	Foreign Travel Emergency	Foreign Travel Emergency	Foreign Travel Emergency	Foreign Travel Emergency	Foreign Travel Emergency	Foreign Travel Emergency
			At-Home Recovery			At-Home Recovery		At-Home Recovery	At-Home Recovery
							Basic Drugs ($1,250 Limit)	Basic Drugs ($1,250 Limit)	Extended Drugs ($3,000 Limit)
				Preventive Care					Preventive Care

Plan E

Medicare Supplement Plan E must contain the core benefits of Plan A, plus coverage for:

- the Medicare Part A deductible;

- medically necessary emergency care in a foreign country;

- the daily co-insurance amount for skilled nursing facility care; and

- preventive screening or preventive medical care, such as physicals, tetanus and booster shots, flu vaccines and cholesterol screening.

Plan F

Medicare Supplement Plan F must contain Plan A core benefits, plus coverage for:

- the Medicare Part A deductible;

- medically necessary emergency care in a foreign country;

- the daily co-insurance amount for skilled nursing facility care;

- Medicare Part B deducible; and

- 100 percent of Part B excess charges (i.e., 100 percent coverage for the difference between the actual Medicare Part B charge as billed, subject to Medicare limitations, and the Medicare-approved Part B charge).

Plan G

Medicare Supplement Plan G must include Plan A core benefits, plus provide coverage for:

- the Medicare Part A deductible;

- medically necessary emergency care in a foreign country;

- the daily co-insurance amount for skilled nursing facility care;

- "at-home recovery," as described for Plan D; and

- 80 percent of Part B excess charges (i.e., 80 percent coverage for the difference between the actual Medicare Part B charge as billed and the Medicare-approved charge).

Plan H

Medicare Supplement Plan H must contain Plan A core benefits, plus coverage for:

- the Medicare Part A deductible;

- medically necessary emergency care in a foreign country;

- the daily co-insurance amount for skilled nursing facility care; and

- the "basic" outpatient prescription drug benefit, which provides coverage for 50 percent of outpatient prescription drug charges, after a $250 annual deductible, up to $1,250 a year.

Plan I

Medicare Supplement Plan I must include Plan A core benefits, plus coverage for:

- the Medicare Part A deductible;

- medically necessary emergency care in a foreign country;

- the daily co-insurance amount for skilled nursing facility care;

- "at home recovery" services;

- 100 percent of Part B excess charges; and

- the "basic" prescription drug plan, as described for Plan H.

Plan J

Medicare Supplement Plan J, the most comprehensive of all the plans, must include Plan A core benefits, plus coverage for:

- the Medicare Part A deductible;

- medically necessary emergency care in a foreign country;

- the daily co-insurance amount for skilled nursing facility care;

- "at home recovery" services;

- preventive screening and preventive medical care;

- 100 percent of Medicare Part B excess charges; and

- the "extended" outpatient prescription drug benefit, which provides coverage for 50 percent of outpatient drug charges, after an annual $250 deductible, up to $3,000 a year.

As you can see, no provision of any of these Medicare supplement plans duplicates benefits provided under Medicare—instead, each plan provides *supplemental coverage*. Of course, the more benefits a supplement plan offers, the more expensive it will be. The NAIC recommends that if a state authorizes the sale of only some of these plans, the letter codes of each plan—A, B, C, D, E, F, G, H, I and J—should be preserved. The uniform "naming" system will enable consumers to compare specific policy plans.

■ LONG-TERM CARE INSURANCE

As beneficial as Medicare and Medicare supplement insurance are to the elderly in protecting them against the costs of medical care, there still exists a critical risk that neither of these covers: long-term custodial or nursing home care.

The cost of the extended, day-in, day-out care some older people need can be staggering: as much as $25,000 or $30,000 a year or more for nursing home care and upwards of $1,000 a month—or more—for aides who come to one's home. A study by the U.S. Department of Health and Human Services indicates that people who turned 65 in 1990 face a 40 percent risk of entering a nursing home and about 10 percent will stay there five years or longer.

How can these costs be paid? The solution is *long-term care insurance*.

What Is Long-Term Care?

Long-term care is the broad range of medical and personal services for individuals who need assistance with daily activities for an extended period of time. The need for such on-going assistance is usually a result of a physical or mental impairment brought on by the aging process. Depending on the severity of the impairment, assistance may be given at home, at an adult day care center or in a nursing home.

The responsibility of paying for this kind of care usually falls on those who need the care or their families. Neither Medicare nor Medicare supplement policies are designed to cover long-term, ongoing assisted living. Furthermore, the cost of such care could easily wipe out an individual's lifetime savings. Thus, for many, the solution is long-term care insurance.

What Is Long-Term Care Insurance?

Long-term care insurance is a relatively new type of insurance product. However, more and more insurance companies are beginning to offer this coverage as the need for it grows. It is similar to most insurance plans; the insured pays a premium for specified benefits in the event that he or she requires long-term care, as defined by the policy. Most long-term care policies are "indemnity" plans. This means they pay the insured a fixed dollar amount for each day he or she receives the kind of care the policy covers, regardless of what the care actually costs.

Insurers offer a wide range of indemnity amounts, ranging from, for example, $40 a day to $150 a day for nursing home care. The daily benefit for at-home care is typically half the nursing home benefit. Many policies include an inflation rider or option to purchase additional coverage, enabling the policies to keep pace with increases in long-term care costs.

Long-Term Care Coverages

Currently, there are a variety of long-term care policies on the market, some of which are characterized by innovative coverage concepts. The following is a brief discussion of some typical coverages that may be found in a long-term care policy. Note that the definition of the kind of care provided is a determining factor in where it is administered. It is important to understand the distinctions among the levels of nursing home care as well as the extent and limitations of other kinds of care.

Skilled Nursing Care

This is daily nursing care ordered by a doctor and necessary for certain medical conditions. It can only be performed by, or under the supervision of, skilled medical professionals and is available 24 hours a day. Skilled nursing care is typically administered in nursing homes.

Intermediate Nursing Care

Intermediate nursing care is occasional or rehabilitative care ordered by a doctor. This too can only be performed by skilled medical personnel. Intermediate nursing care is typically provided in nursing homes for stable conditions that require daily, but not 24-hour, supervision.

Custodial Care

Custodial care can be defined as care given to meet daily personal needs, such as bathing, dressing, getting out of bed, etc. It does not require medical training, but it must be given under a doctor's order. Custodial care is usually provided by nursing homes, but can also be given by adult day care centers, respite centers or at home.

Home Health Care

This is care provided in the insured's home, usually on a part-time basis. It can include skilled care (such as nursing, rehabilitative or physical therapy care, ordered by a doctor) or unskilled care (such as help with cooking or cleaning).

Adult Day Care

Adult day care is designed for those who require assistance with various activities of daily living, while their primary caregivers (usually family or friends) are absent. These day-care centers offer skilled medical care in conjunction with social and personal services, but custodial care is usually their primary focus. Some communities have established day-care centers that specifically serve the special needs of those with Alzheimer's disease.

Respite Care

This type of coverage is designed to provide a short rest period for a family caregiver. There are two options: either the insured is moved to a full-time care facility or a substitute care provider moves into the insured's home, for a temporary period, giving the family member a rest from his or her caregiving activities.

Residential Care

A fairly new kind of long-term care coverage, residential care is designed to provide a benefit for elderly individuals who live in a retirement community. Retirement communities are geared to senior citizens' full-time needs, both medical and social, and are often sponsored by religious or nonprofit organizations.

When Do Benefits Begin?

Some of the older long-term care policies required that the insured first be hospitalized before benefits for nursing home care would be paid (or required a prior nursing home or hospital stay before home care benefits were paid).

However, this kind of prior-hospitalization requirement did not account for the fact that many elderly do not need a hospital stay before they need assisted living or custodial care. Consequently, most long-term care policies today base payment of benefits on when the care becomes "medically necessary" (as determined by a doctor) or when the insured becomes unable to function independently. Most policies sold today use this latter requirement.

Determining an insured's inability to function independently requires two assessments: *mental inability* and *physical inability*. Mental inability is measured by *cognitive assessments,* which test an individual's capacity to think, reason and remember; physical inability is measured by *activities of daily living* (known as "ADLs"), such as walking, bathing, dressing, eating, taking medicine and getting in and out of bed.

Within their specified limits, most long-term care policies begin to pay benefits when an insured becomes cognitively impaired and/or when he or she needs ongoing assistance in two, three or more activities of daily living.

Long-Term Care Policy Provisions and Limits

There are a number of long-term care policies on the market today, each characterized by some distinguishing feature or benefit that sets it apart from the rest. However, there are enough similarities to discuss the basic provisions of these policies and their typical limits or exclusions.

Benefit Limits

Almost all long-term care policies set benefit limits, in terms of how long the benefits are paid and/or how much the dollar benefit will be for any one covered care service or combination of services. Maximum dollar amounts and coverage periods vary considerably from policy to policy. In fact, it is not unusual for one policy to include separate maximum coverage periods for nursing home care and home health care. Generally speaking, maximum coverage periods extend anywhere from two to six years. Some policies offer unlimited lifetime coverage.

Age Limits.

Long-term care policies typically set age limits for issue, the average being about age 79. However, some newer policies can be sold to people up through age 89. Many policies set a minimum purchase age, the average being age 50.

Renewability

Most long-term care policies are *guaranteed renewable,* meaning that the insurance company cannot cancel the policy and must renew coverage each year, as long as premiums are paid. A guaranteed renewable policy allows the insurer to raise premiums, but only for entire classes of insureds.

Elimination Periods

An elimination period is the specific time from the beginning of a benefit period during which benefits will not be paid. It is also known as a *deductible period* or *waiting period.* Long-term care elimination periods can range from 0 to 365 days, and many insurers give the insured the option of selecting the deductible period that best serves his or her needs. The longer the elimination period, the lower the premium.

The primary purpose of an elimination period is to control adverse selection and protect the insurer from individuals who may have a preexisting condition (a condition for which the insured received treatment within a certain time period prior to policy issuance). Individuals who have preexisting conditions may find that their policies will not cover any claims arising from that condition for the first 6 or 12 months after policy issue.

Most long-term care policies exclude coverage for drug or alcohol dependency, acts of war, self-inflicted injuries and nonorganic mental conditions. Organic cognitive disorders, such as Alzheimer's disease, senile dementia and Parkinson's disease, are almost always included.

Premiums

The cost for a long-term care policy is based on a number of factors: the insured's age and health, the type and level of benefits provided, the inclusion or absence of a deductible or elimination period and the length of that period, and the options or riders included with the policy. Such options include the right to purchase additional coverage in the future or the inflation-adjustment rider, which automatically increases the policy's coverage to match inflation levels. Generally, the more beneficial the policy's terms are for the insured, the more expensive it will be.

■ DISABILITY INCOME INSURANCE

The odds of facing the problems brought on by disability are not as small as one might think. Most disabilities occur suddenly, and when least expected. In fact, the odds of a person suffering a long-term disability are greater than death at any age prior to 65. In addition, the costs of disability are often greater than the costs resulting from death. When a person becomes disabled, he or she may be unable to set aside adequate funds for his or her retirement. Therefore, attention must be paid to the need for income protection in the case of disability.

Sickness or an accident can impose tremendous burdens on an individual or a family. If a person cannot return to work for a long time after an accident or illness, he or she will need the income protection provided by disability income insurance. Disability income insurance replaces lost income when a person is disabled on a total or partial basis. Payments are made for various lengths of time based on the policy's definition of "disability."

To your prospect, "disability income" and "income replacement" are one and the same: you are providing income if disability occurs, and you are replacing income that has been lost. However, the term "disability income" usually refers to all policies that pay a stated benefit; "income replacement" refers to those in which benefits payable are tied to the actual amount of income lost. As an agent, you must pay close attention to the terms of a particular contract, because neither of these names truly describes the policy's scope.

Most disability income policies provide for both long-term and short-term disability benefits. In addition, they may provide optional coverages such as *cost of living benefits,* under which benefits are adjusted annually to reflect changes in the cost of living. Another optional benefit is for coverage of *rehabilitation* or *relocation.* This benefit covers the cost of retraining, locally or in another geographical location, in order to reenter one's profession or to enter an entirely new profession following a period of disability.

Types of Policies

Disability insurance comes in many forms: individual policies, riders on life insurance policies, group insurance, employers' sick pay plans, governmental plans and union-administered plans. Businesses use disability insurance to protect business owners and key employees, to assure business continuation and to fund buy/sell agreements. Individuals use disability insurance to replace earnings that are lost when a person becomes sick or disabled.

What Is Disability?

When is a person considered disabled? The answer to that question depends on the different definitions given to the term by government plans, Workers' Compensation and/or disability policies. The term "disability" may be broadly or narrowly defined in the policy. A broad definition allows benefits for disabled persons who are unable to perform some or all duties of their chosen occupation. A narrow definition restricts benefits to insureds who cannot work in any gainful employment. In other words, if the person is able to do any type of work, he or she is not considered disabled and is not eligible for benefits.

Disability policies may be grouped by the way in which they define disability and determine benefits based on that definition. In addition, disability benefits may be limited by a narrow definition, as in the case of Social Security, by the policy's definition of "occupation" or by whether a loss of earnings has occurred because of injury or sickness.

Social Security

Social Security is one source of disability income. However, as stated in Chapter 4, Social Security narrowly defines disability as "the inability to engage in any substantial gainful activity by reason of any medically determinable physical or mental impairment which can be expected to result in death or which has lasted or can be expected to last for a continuous period of not less than 12 months." This definition is so restrictive that more than half of the people who apply for disability benefits are denied by Social Security.

Occupation

Because there are physical and, in some cases, mental hazards associated with some occupations, the occupation of the insured is an important factor. Some policies pay benefits if the insured is unable to perform every duty inherent in his or her chosen occupation because of illness or accident. Other policies pay benefits if the insured is unable to perform the principal duties of that chosen occupation. Still others pay benefits only if the insured is unable to perform the duties of any gainful employment.

Income Replacement

Some policies ignore the occupational question and base the eligibility for benefits on whether an insured has suffered a loss of income. Insurance to replace income is important because it keeps the family intact, keeps food on the table and maintains a roof over the family's head. Disability insurance indemnifies the insured for a cessation or reduction of income. The policy ties the benefit payments to a proportion of the actual earnings lost. A full benefit would be paid for total loss of income.

The client's financial position, needs and feelings will determine which disability plan is best. Some plans, like noncancelable coverage, offer more advantages or benefits, but the insured must be able to afford them. However, even if your client has the money to purchase noncancelable coverage, he or she may not be able to obtain it because of rigid health standards.

■ THE ROLE OF THE INSURANCE PROFESSIONAL

As we have seen, health insurance plays an important role in helping people obtain adequate financial protection against heavy medical expenses and lost income due to disability. In spite of the necessity for health insurance, most people do not actively seek out and purchase the protection they need. They generally rely on their employer or the government to provide them with adequate medical protection.

As an insurance professional, you must be able to assess whether a client's disability income needs are adequately addressed by employer or government programs. If additional coverage is needed, you must be able to honestly and intelligently compare products to show how one policy differs from another in coverage, benefits and overall treatment of claims.

■ SUMMARY

Demographic studies clearly show that, as it ages, the postwar generation, will place unprecedented pressure on the health care system. Employers are already paring down on the staggeringly expensive health care benefits traditionally provided in retirement. The retiree can often end up on his or her own when it comes to supporting health care costs. Simply, this means that a retiree must plan on having extra funds to meet uncovered health care expenses. Nowhere is this more apparent than in comparing the many types of Medicare supplement policies. Whether the supplemental coverage is basic or comprehensive, a retiree must understand what will be covered when a claim is made.

In addition to being knowledgeable about health care, those who advise others on the financial aspect of retirement should also become familiar with the importance of estate planning and wealth distribution. In Chapter 12, we will take a closer look at how the life insurance agent fits into the estate planning team.

■ **CHAPTER 11 QUESTIONS FOR REVIEW**

1. Which of these statements regarding Medicare is correct?

   a. Medicare Part B—Supplement Medicare Insurance (SMI) is voluntary.
   b. Under Medicare Part B, coverage for physician's services is unlimited.
   c. Enrollees are billed for premiums on Medicare Part A on a semi-annual basis.
   d. Medicare Part A—Hospital Insurance (HI) carries no deductible.

2. Which of these statements regarding Medicare supplement insurance ("medigap" insurance) is correct?

   a. There are few differences among coverages offered in different Medicare supplemental policies.
   b. Most Medicare supplement insurance is acquired though the Social Security Administration.
   c. There are differences among policies with respect to excess charges, deductibles and limits.
   d. Medigap policies usually duplicate existing Medicare coverage but are considered supplemental policies.

3. All the statements below regarding long-term care insurance policies are correct, EXCEPT:

   a. Better long-term care policies will cover home health care either as a rider or under the basic policy.
   b. The more expensive long-term care policies are likely to provide greater coverage for custodial care.
   c. Long-term care policies that pay benefits on an indemnity basis are generally better than those that pay for costs actually incurred.
   d. Premiums for long-term care insurance are likely to increase by specific age or age bracket.

4. Which of the following terms best describes nursing and rehabilitative services provided by trained medical personnel on a daily basis as ordered by a physician?

   a. Technical nursing care
   b. Skilled nursing care
   c. Intermediate care
   d. Custodial nursing care

5. Which of the following statements about disability income insurance is/are NOT correct?

    I. Disability income insurance is a form of health insurance that can replace lost income when a person is disabled.

    II. If a person can do any type of work, he or she is not considered disabled under a restrictive definition of disability.

    III. The most commonly used source of disability income is Social Security.

        a. I only
        b. II only
        c. III only
        d. I and II only

12

Wealth Distribution

N o retirement plan is complete without addressing what inevitably everyone must plan for: the distribution of property after one's death. Although most people want to make provisions for those who are financially dependent on them at their death, the prospect of selecting an attorney, formulating an estate plan and writing a will can be frightening. And thinking about wealth distribution brings a person face to face with his or her own mortality—something most people prefer not to do.

In this chapter, we will discuss how an estate plan can protect the financial future of one's heirs and beneficiaries. We will focus on estate planning and wealth distribution for individuals, business interests and special situations.

■ ■ ■ ■ ■

■ THE NEED FOR AN ESTATE PLAN

The final chapter in any retirement plan must address how the retiree's property will be transferred or arranged at his or her death. Planning and saving for a family's financial security may accomplish little if assets and property are ultimately consumed by costs or debts or are transferred to the wrong individual. Many people, unfamiliar with the theory and practice of estate transfer, think that the passage of their property at death will be a relatively simple and direct procedure and that assets will be transferred intact and without delay to whomever the estate owner desires.

The fact is, property does not automatically pass from one person to another at death, nor is the process smooth or swift—unless a specific plan or arrangement for transfer has been put into effect. Transfer plans can be simple or intricate, but they must be enacted during the estate owner's life to assure that his or her property will be disposed of at death according to his or her wishes. Furthermore, the disposition of property at death is not a right, but a *privilege* conferred by the state. Each state prescribes the terms and conditions under which property can be transferred, both during life and after death. Consequently, a transfer plan must recognize and conform to these laws.

There are many ways to effect an estate transfer and many tools available to create a plan that meets prescribed law and disposes of property in accordance with the estate owner's wishes. While the full range of estate planning techniques is beyond the scope of this text, we will be discussing a number of important planning tools, including wills, life insurance, property ownership arrangements, trusts, gifting and the marital deduction. But first, let's take a brief look at what happens to an estate upon the death of the owner—a process known as *estate administration*.

■ THE ADMINISTRATION PROCESS

Estate administration—or estate settlement, as it is often called—is the legal process of "wrapping up" a decedent's affairs and disposing of his or her property. The process can be smooth or rocky, depending on the plans the estate owner put into effect during life.

The administration of an estate is governed by state statutes and by *probate courts*. The word "probate" is from the Latin verb "probare," meaning "to prove." When people die, the probate court process settles any questions about the ownership of property and the payment of debts. The probate court exists only to handle the transferral of the death estate to those entitled to it—whether by virtue of their claims as a creditor or as an heir. The entire estate administration is under the court's control until the process has been concluded to the court's satisfaction. Generally speaking, the probate court has three fundamental goals it attempts to achieve during the administration process:

1. conserving estate assets;

2. protecting the rights of the estate's creditors in satisfying their claims; and

3. assuring that heirs and beneficiaries receive their inheritance in accordance with the estate owner's wishes or, in the absence of any documents expressing the owner's wishes, in accordance with state statutes.

The administrative process will vary for every estate and may be more or less complicated, depending on the size and complexity of the estate. In general, the process consists of six steps that interlock and overlap somewhat. Let's briefly look at each of these steps in the estate administration process.

Step One—Appointment of the Personal Representative

The first step of the administrative process is the appointment of the *personal representative* to act on behalf of the estate owner. If the estate owner dies *testate* (having made a valid will), the personal representative may have been nominated in the will. In this case, the representative is referred to as the *executor* of the estate.

ILL. 12.1 ■

The Estate Planning Team

When developing an estate plan, most people will need some expert advice from at least four people: a life insurance agent, an accountant, an attorney and a bank trust officer. These people, working as a team, can analyze a person's affairs and arrange those affairs in a manner that best accomplishes a person's ultimate objectives. Although some overlapping may occur, each individual has a specific job to do.

Life Insurance Agent
As a life insurance professional, you are in a unique position to arouse your clients' interest about the problems of effective estate transfer and to motivate them to take action toward a solution. Since you are already a trained salesperson, you are the logical team member to sell the advantages of estate planning. You can point out the many advantages of proper estate planning and urge your clients to put a plan into effect. For example, life insurance often creates much of the estate value and provides needed estate liquidity.

Accountant
The second member of an estate planning team is an accountant who has specialized knowledge of the estate owner's financial status. The accountant can provide the team with a clear picture of the prospect's finances and needs. In business insurance cases particularly, no one knows a company's financial position better than the accountant who prepares or audits the books. It is the accountant who can reveal bookkeeping or tax problems that may affect the estate plan.

Attorney
Legal questions are involved in most estate planning cases, and legal documents are frequently necessary to make the plans effective and binding. Although all the team members may have some knowledge of the law of wills, trusts and so on, only an attorney may give legal advice and draft the documents. The attorney should be brought into discussions about estate planning as early as possible to prevent any questions of unauthorized practice of law by other team members.

Trust Officer
Bank trust officers or trust companies are trained and experienced in the many phases of law, taxes, investments and business that are necessary to successful trust administration. The trust is essentially an instrument of estate conservation, with certain creative powers and distribution advantages.

Each member of the team operates within their respective guidelines to accomplish the estate owner's objectives—the transfer of property intact to beneficiaries with a minimum tax burden.

If the decedent dies *intestate* (without having executed a will) or if no executor is named in the will, the statutes of his or her state of domicile normally will require the probate court to appoint someone to act as the personal representative of the estate. In this event the person appointed is called an *administrator*.

After the court formally confirms the nomination, the personal representative takes possession of the estate, is responsible for paying debts of, and claims against, the estate and ultimately distributes the estate assets to the heirs and beneficiaries.

Step Two—Notice to Creditors

The second step in the estate administration process is for the personal representative to give notice of his or her appointment. By the same action, notice is given to all creditors to make prompt claim for all money due and owing to them. This is accomplished by a published "Notice to Creditors," a statement that advises that:

- the estate owner has died;

- the person or institution designated in the notice has been appointed the personal representative on behalf of the estate; and

- creditors should make claim for money due and owing to them.

Step Three—Inventory and Appraisal

The personal representative then assembles the assets of the estate, evaluates them, inventories them and files that inventory with the court. This inventory represents evidence of the estate assets and includes personal property, real property, life insurance and any debts and claims on the estate.

The appraisal or valuation of the property, in some states, can be made by the personal representative acting independently. In other states the court must appoint appraisers. In any event, the value as appraised is subject to review by the court and representatives of federal and state tax departments.

Step Four—Interim Administration

After the assets have been valued, the personal representative's real work begins. The fourth step of the administration process involves the sale of estate assets, preservation of assets that are to be passed on, maintenance and operation of a going business, fulfillment of contractual obligations, preparation and filing of tax returns and accounting tasks.

All of these duties require a keen business sense, a basic understanding of tax laws, a deep sense of the fiduciary relationship involved, and, if possible, a close relationship and knowledge of the decedent's family. In all cases, the personal representative must exercise a high degree of care in actions and decisions affecting the estate.

Step Five—Distribution of the Estate

The next step, distribution of a decedent's estate to heirs and beneficiaries, is generally determined by the decedent's will or, if the decedent died intestate, according to the laws of the state. A court decree ordering distribution will not be made until all debts and other charges have been paid. If the representative makes distribution without first obtaining court approval, he or she will be personally liable for the payment of any outstanding lawful claims. Thus the court order of distribution serves to protect the personal representative who makes payment in accordance with its terms. This order and the representative's proof of compliance with its terms entitles the representative to an order discharging him or her from any further liability arising under the appointment.

Step Six—Discharge of Appointment

As noted above, after the personal representative makes distribution to the heirs and beneficiaries, he or she is entitled to an order of discharge. The personal representative files with the court the signed receipts of the various heirs and beneficiaries. At this point, the estate is closed.

Due to the legal requirements the estate administration process (and the estate administrator) must meet, the goals of estate administration—conserving the estate assets and distributing them to creditors, heirs and beneficiaries—can only be met if proper planning was done prior to the estate owner's death. If there was not adequate planning, the estate may face:

- larger than necessary shrinkage factors, including taxes, administration expenses, depreciation and less liquidity—which ultimately reduces the estate to be passed on to beneficiaries; and

- an ultimate distribution that is not in line with the decedent's wishes.

Let's take a closer look at these problems.

■ PITFALLS FACING EFFICIENT ESTATE ADMINISTRATION

One of the primary problems to be faced in transferring property from an estate owner to a beneficiary is *estate shrinkage*. The word "shrinkage" aptly describes what happens to many estates as they are subjected to taxes, administration fees, settlement costs and so on. Additional factors—the erosion of the purchasing power of the dollar due to inflation, fluctuating asset value, lack of liquidity to pay individual estate needs within a few months of death and improper use of settlement options under life insurance contracts—can also cause shrinkage. Lack of provisions for long-term care and costly disability losses due to poor health, too, can cause expected estate values to shrink dramatically. Finally, additional problems are created if the estate owner fails to make a valid will.

Common Estate Shrinkage Factors

As we have seen, the process of transferring a decedent's property to the heirs and beneficiaries must inevitably result in some administration expense that reduces the size of the estate. The extent of this shrinkage depends on the size and complexity of the estate, the nature of the assets and the actual cash spent for administration costs, debts and taxes. For the purposes of our discussion, let's look at three shrinkage factors that can affect even small estates:

1. administration and probate costs;

2. debts and obligations; and

3. state and federal death taxes.

Administration and Probate Costs

The first group of estate shrinkage factors consists of a wide variety of estate obligations or charges that must be met before the estate is closed and the balance is distributed to the heirs and beneficiaries. These liabilities include funeral and administration expenses, including the appraiser's fees for valuing estate property, brokerage fees, attorney's fees, court costs and various other fees.

Administration costs cannot be dismissed lightly. In small estates, for example, the impact of the administration costs often exceeds that of the death taxes and sometimes constitutes the largest single source of estate shrinkage. Although the costs vary by the size and complexity of the plan of distribution, *normal* administration costs can cause an average of 4.3 percent shrinkage in estates over $5 million to an average 4.6 percent shrinkage in estates under $50,000.

Debts and Obligations

Generally speaking, any debt or claim that could have been enforced against the decedent during his or her lifetime is a valid and subsisting claim against his or her estate. Included in the category of "debt" are:

- outstanding bills for recent living expenses;

- pledges to religious institutions; and

- mortgages, leases, installment balances, etc.

Unpaid taxes, income tax payments and general property taxes are also debts against the estate and are sizable current liabilities that may make deep inroads into estate assets. Although some might argue that debt is not a true shrinkage factor, consider that shrinkage is concerned with the costs and expenses that arise as a result of the estate owner's death. Debts unpaid at the decedent's death would have been paid from current income if the decedent had lived. At his or her death, however, they become immediately payable out of estate assets, and are properly considered a major shrinkage factor. In fact, repayment of debt can shrink a $5 million estate by an average of 3.7 percent and a $50,000 estate by an average of 5.8 percent. Again, the situation will vary from case to case.

State and Federal Death Taxes

A *death tax* is a tax on the property transferred or received upon the death of the owner. Death taxes are assessed by both state and federal governments. In many cases, state death taxes will apply even when no federal estate tax is applicable.

State Death Taxes. State taxes charged at death usually include:

- an *inheritance tax,* which is a levy imposed on the share of the estate going to an individual heir or beneficiary;

- an *estate tax,* which is imposed on the estate itself; and

- a *credit estate tax,* which is designed to absorb the credit allowed by the federal estate tax for state death taxes paid.

The impact of these taxes can be significant and must be given careful attention. Most people fail to understand that the average estate is impacted more by state death taxes than by federal taxes.

Federal Estate Tax.   The federal estate tax is imposed on the transfer of property owned by the decedent. It is levied without regard to the share received by different beneficiaries or heirs, excepting the property going to a surviving spouse that qualifies for the marital deduction (discussed later in this chapter) and property passing to charity. It is a tax on the *transfer* of property, measured by the value of that property, but it is not a tax on the property itself.

The federal estate tax is calculated in four steps:

1. determine the gross estate property and its value;

2. subtract the allowable deductions and the personal exemption;

3. apply the appropriate tax rates to the result; and

4. deduct any credits to which the estate is entitled.

The result is the net gross estate. As of early 1993, if the value of the taxable estate, after deductions and exemptions, is below $600,000, no federal estate tax is due.

In protecting the estate (and ultimately the heirs) against as much shrinkage as possible, the estate owner must provide some liquidity or cash. Sources of liquidity to meet these obligations include current assets, borrowed equity in those assets or capital created in the form of life insurance. If cash is not available, then further estate shrinkage occurs through the forced liquidation of valuable estate assets to meet the estate's administration costs, debts and taxes.

No Will or an Invalid Will

In addition to estate shrinkage factors, a second pitfall facing efficient estate administration is the failure of the estate owner to make a valid will. It isn't easy to think about death—so many people avoid the topic and fail to protect their interests and those of their heirs. Almost everyone intends to get organized and make a will someday, yet an estimated seven of ten adults have never made a will. The most common rationalizations you will hear from your clients for not making a will include:

- "I'm not sure of what information will be needed."

- "I've never been married so I don't need a will."

- "My husband (or wife) will get everything anyway."

- "My family knows what I want."

- "I'll be dead; why should I care who gets what?"

Unfortunately, unless an individual's wishes and information about his or her estate are accessible, understandable and legally proper, there may be problems for the beneficiaries and a decedent's intentions may not be carried out.

Concept of Intestacy

One of the best ways to make sure that property one owns reaches the designated heirs is by leaving it to them in a will. Should a person die intestate, each state, through statutes and case law, supplies a ready-made "will" that divides the estate according to each particular state's laws of intestacy. These laws include rigid formulas for dividing property with little or no allowance for a family's special needs.

Although state statutes are designed to be as fair and equitable as possible, *intestate distribution,* or settling an estate with no valid will, is loaded with problems. The deceased's wishes are likely to be ignored and the special needs of survivors and dependents may not be addressed. The consequences of dying without a will include the following:

- *The state will determine both who the heirs are and their share of the estate.* In most states, property will be split among the spouse and children, often with a proportionately larger share going to the children rather than to the surviving spouse.

- *The court will appoint a guardian to care for any minor children.* Failing to provide for a child's care could lead to disaster. The court may choose the least appropriate person to provide for a child's welfare.

- *A court-appointed executor might be costly or insensitive to the estate owner's wishes.* Unless an executor is named in a will to inventory an estate, pay any debts, file income and estate tax returns and distribute personal assets, a judge will appoint a public administrator to complete these tasks. The process could take much longer than necessary with the costs accruing to the estate.

- *Estate settlement may be more costly.* Without a will to guide the disposition of an estate, the process will take longer and, therefore, will be more expensive. Furthermore, a will can direct certain types of transfers that take advantage of specific tax-saving and cost-saving measures, whereas the lack of a will means these measures are lost to the estate.

Fortunately, there are a number of estate planning tools and techniques that can solve or alleviate the problems inherent in intestacy and those associated with estate shrinkage.

ILL. 12.2 ■ Division of Property Under Intestacy Laws

The division of property varies by state, but the laws generally divide the estate as follows:

- Spouse and one child—each receives one-half the estate

- Spouse and two or more children—spouse receives one-third; all children equally divide the remaining two-thirds

- Spouse and parents surviving, no children—spouse receives 50 percent to 75 percent of the estate and parents receive the remainder

- Parents surviving, no spouse or children—parents receive all

- Siblings surviving, no parents, spouse or children—brother(s) and sister(s) receive equal shares

■ ESTATE PLANNING TOOLS AND TECHNIQUES

Contrary to widely held beliefs, many of the methods used to transfer property, such as wills and trusts, are not only for the rich or the elderly. In fact, whatever one's financial position or age, a variety of techniques can be used to transfer property. Regardless of the tools or techniques selected, the fundamental issues that must be addressed are:

- providing the estate with the liquidity it needs;

- arranging for the proper distribution of property to heirs and creditors;

- minimizing estate taxes; and

- reducing the administrative burden on survivors.

Let's look at the most common methods that can be used to accomplish these goals and effect property transfers.

Wills

While there are many tools available to an estate owner in formulating an estate plan, none is as important as the will. A *will* is a legal contract that establishes arrangements for property transfer at and after death. Because a will can be declared invalid for a number of reasons, it should be drawn up by an attorney knowledgeable in estate planning. An improperly written or invalid will may be more costly to the beneficiaries than no will at all. For example, a will that ignores a child who is entitled to part of the estate may be contested and litigation may consume most or all of the estate.

Wills should be reviewed and amended periodically after they are written to reflect changes in a person's financial or personal status. A move to another state, the birth of a child or the death of a spouse are all reasons to amend a will.

Changes are permitted anytime up to the maker's (*testator's*) death through a *codicil,* which is usually a one-page document indicating the desired changes in the existing will.

An estate owner may make a specific *bequest,* leaving a specified item of property to a particular individual. Generally, it is better to leave percentages of the estate rather than a fixed dollar amount to heirs since the assets may shrink or grow over the years. Some items (property held in joint tenancy, life insurance, U.S. savings bonds and pension benefits) cannot be disposed of through a will because a co-owner or beneficiary already exists.

A will is more than the conduit for the transfer of property to specific people or organizations. It can continue specific programs the decedent initiated during life, such as gifts to charity and, if properly prepared, can help protect the estate and beneficiaries from shrinkage caused by inefficient transfers, income and estate taxes and other costs.

Life Insurance

Life insurance can be a valuable estate planning tool. In fact, the primary function of life insurance is to increase the size of an estate—to create, at the insured's death, funds that otherwise would not exist. These funds can be used or arranged as best suits the estate owner: to provide cash or income directly to beneficiaries, to provide liquidity for the estate and prevent liquidation of assets, to fund various trusts employed as tax saving measures and so on. Life insurance can be used as an estate builder, an estate conserver, a funding medium or a self-maturing investment. Like the will, it serves as the cornerstone of an estate plan, providing maximum flexibility and liquidity at the insured's death.

The proper arrangement of life insurance ownership and beneficiary designations for estate planning purposes is very important. If the objective is to provide liquidity for the estate, the simplest and most direct method is to have the proceeds paid directly to the insured's executor or administrator, who has a fiduciary duty to pay the estate settlement expenses. This arrangement is especially advantageous for modest estates in which shrinkage due to administrative costs and debts can be substantial. If the objective is to benefit one or more individuals and they are specifically named as beneficiaries to the insurance, the proceeds will pass to them outside the estate proper, bypassing the probate process, and will be received tax free.

Property Arrangements

How property ownership is arranged is another way an estate owner can coordinate an effective estate plan and transfer. Property has to be held by a single owner or jointly with others. How title is held will determine how it passes from one individual to another. Therefore, it is important to know how property is owned in order to know if a particular owner has the right to distribute all or part of it on either a lifetime or postmortem basis. When property is held under a form of ownership called *joint tenancy with right of survivorship,* it automatically passes to the surviving joint tenant when the first tenant dies, bypassing the probate process. In joint tenancy, each owner has an undivided interest in

ILL. 12.3 ■ Life Insurance and the Gross Estate

If properly arranged, life insurance proceeds paid due to the death of the insured are almost always received by the beneficiary free of income taxes. However, when the issue is the valuation of a decedent's estate for purposes of the estate tax, different rules apply. Life insurance proceeds will be included in the decedent's gross estate if:

- The proceeds are payable to the decedent's estate, either directly or indirectly.

- The decedent possessed any "incidents of ownership" in the policy at death.

- The decedent transferred, within three years of death, a policy on his or her life in which he or she held incidents of ownership.

Incidents of ownership are the rights to exercise any of the privileges of the policy. They include the right to take out a policy loan, to make beneficiary changes, to receive policy dividends, to withdraw cash values, to assign, surrender or pledge the policy and to select or revoke a settlement option.

the property, which means that each has an equal right to make use of and enjoy the property. Any individuals, not just spouses, can be joint tenants.

Joint tenancy does not solve every transfer problem. In some cases, a co-owner can dispose of property without the other co-owner's consent or knowledge. Each co-owner's interest in the property is liable for claims against the other co-owner. And, for estate tax purposes, the IRS has two ways of looking at joint tenancy property. Between spouses only, half of the value of the property owned via a joint tenancy with rights of survivorship is included in the estate of the first to die. For nonspousal joint tenancies, all of the value of the property owned via joint tenancy is included in the estate of the first to die unless documentation can be shown that the first tenant to die only established a fractional interest. Then, only that interest will be included in the estate of the first tenant to die.

Joint tenancy should not be confused with other types of multiple ownership such as tenancy in common or community property. *Tenancy in common* is another form of ownership shared by more than one person, but the arrangements may involve any combination of parties and may be in unequal interests. Furthermore, tenants in common do not have the right of survivorship; the property does not necessarily pass to the other co-tenants at the death. In fact, each separate tenant's interest can be transferred to whomever he or she wishes through a will, the same as individually owned property.

Some states also permit the concept of *community property,* an arrangement between spouses only. Property acquired by either spouse during the marriage is considered to be property of the marriage and each spouse has an equal interest in the property. However, inheritances, gifts and personal injury awards are not classified as community property. One half of the property is included in the estate of the first to die. Thus, each spouse controls the ultimate distribution of his or her half of the community property. Community property arrangements are likely to prevail even when a couple married in a community property state relocates to a noncommunity property state.

Trusts

Depending on the purpose for which they are set up, trusts can be used to safeguard an estate, to manage an individual's money if he or she becomes ill, to keep survivors out of probate court and many other reasons. You will recall from Chapter 11 that *trusts* are arrangements in which the legal title to property is conveyed by one party, the *grantor,* to another, the *trustee,* for the benefit of a third party, the *beneficiary.* The trustee has a legal obligation to manage the trust in the best interest of the beneficiary.

It has been said that the primary advantage of a trust is to separate the *benefits* of property ownership from the *burdens* of property ownership. The full responsibility for managing trust property is upon the trustee. In addition, trusts can offer the following benefits:

- support and care of dependent children;

- estate and income tax savings available with irrevocable trusts;

- experienced investment and property management by a trustee;

- protection of assets in the event the grantor becomes incapacitated;

- protection against beneficiaries who might be or later become spendthrifts; and

- avoidance of probate with respect to the property placed in the trusts.

Trusts can be established to take effect during the grantor's life (an *inter vivos* or living trust) or through a will to become operative at the grantor's death (a *testamentary* trust).

Living Trusts

A *living trust* is a method of transferring property while an individual is still living. Property so transferred passes outside the will and avoids the probate process. In many cases, a living trust is preferable to an outright gift of property. With a gift, the grantor or donor has no control over the property after the transaction, whereas a living trust can be arranged so that the grantor retains control, if he or she desires. Living trusts are also attractive when the grantor's holdings are large and he or she no longer wants the burden of managing them.

Living trusts can be established as revocable or irrevocable. As you'll recall from Chapter 11, with a *revocable trust,* the grantor retains control over the trust property and reserves the right to revoke, change or terminate the trust agreement. Though there are no significant tax advantages to these arrangements (the rights retained by the grantor constitute continued ownership), they can offer the grantor a "preview" of how a contemplated testamentary disposition would work and a way to modify the property arrangement if desired. In this way, revocable trusts are completely flexible.

With an *irrevocable trust,* the grantor gives up the right to revoke, change or terminate the trust. Though obviously not as flexible as a revocable trust, an irrevocable trust has the same investment management advantages and can ensure that the property placed in the trust avoids the probate process and its delays. Furthermore, if the grantor completely gives up all control over and rights to the trust property, he or she can achieve income and estate tax savings.

Testamentary Trust

When a trust is specified in a will and becomes operative at death, it is a *testamentary trust.* Because it is part of and dependent on the grantor's will, a testamentary trust has no more effect during the grantor's life than does a will and its existence after the grantor's death is dependent on probate and the enforcement of the will.

A testamentary trust can fulfill a number of estate planning objectives.

- It can be used to eliminate the necessity for guardianships in the case of minor beneficiaries.

- It can create a life income for the older beneficiary such as a spouse, with a gift of the principal to another at the beneficiary's death, thus avoiding successive transfer taxes.

- It can provide for discretion and flexibility with regard to the trustee's power to distribute trust income and principal, which would not be possible with a direct will bequest.

- It can appropriately restrict the use of the trust property by the beneficiary, and it can incorporate spendthrift provisions that protect the property from dissipation by the beneficiary and from absorption by his or her creditors.

- It can assure that the decedent controls the disposition of the remainder interest in the trust at the death of the beneficiary.

Contractual Transfers

In addition to transfers made by ownership and trust arrangements, property may also be transferred by contract. The benefits of life insurance policies, retirement plans and bank accounts may pass outside a will directly to beneficiaries. In some cases, the transfer is accomplished by a *trustee bank account,* which simply allows the funds to be passed to the beneficiary, thereby avoiding probate.

ILL. 12.4 ■

Life Insurance Trusts

For many estates, life insurance represents the single largest asset the estate owner has. Frequently, a life insurance trust is established to ensure that the beneficiary—whether it's an individual or the estate—receives the greatest benefit from the proceeds.

A life insurance trust is designed to receive, hold, invest or administer proceeds of a life insurance policy or policies for the benefit of a policyowner's beneficiary. Typically, these trusts are unfunded, meaning they have no significant principal except the right to receive benefits under a policy at the death of the insured. (The right to receive death benefits is normally considered sufficient for establishing a valid trust.) At the insured's death, the proceeds are paid to the trustee who then administers them for the benefit of the beneficiary. One of the benefits of a life insurance trust is that a trustee may have discretionary powers that a life insurance company cannot accept, with regard to the payment and administration of proceeds.

Life insurance trusts are often established when the insured has a number of policies and coordinating an efficient settlement plan would be difficult. By directing the death proceeds from all the policies to the trust, a single instrument is used to integrate and administer a coordinated plan.

The Marital Deduction

The transfer of property between spouses creates an opportunity to use the marital deduction. The *marital deduction* is an estate tax deduction for property that passes from a decedent to his or her surviving spouse. This deduction is unlimited, meaning that one can give a surviving spouse *any* amount of property, during life or at death, without incurring gift or estate taxes. Using the marital deduction can be a boon or it can be estate tax-planning quicksand.

Many estate owners make full use of the marital deduction, passing all of their property to their surviving spouses at death. However, this can create problems at the death of the surviving spouse, who cannot take advantage of the tax-free marital deduction. This can dramatically shrink the amount or value of the estate when the surviving spouse dies and the estate is ultimately transferred to children or other beneficiaries.

The marital deduction must be carefully integrated with the maximum of each spouse's unified credit to avoid "overqualification" of the marital deduction. The *unified credit* is a credit that may be applied by the estate against any federal tax due. Currently this credit is $192,800, which creates an "exemption equivalent" of $600,000. In other words, the application of the unified credit effectively exempts estates valued at $600,000 or less from any estate tax. Consequently, a husband could transfer up to $600,000 of his estate to his wife without creating any estate tax liability. It is often wise for each spouse to create a trust to hold an amount equal to $600,000 rather than to pass that amount directly to the spouse under the marital deduction. The spouse may use the income from the trust, but the $600,000 will be removed from inclusion in that survivor's gross estate.

For example, assume Claude's adjusted gross estate is $1 million, which he passes to his wife Joan under the marital deduction. Technically, Claude's taxable estate is $1 million, but no estate tax is due because of the marital deduction. However, Claude in effect wasted his $600,000 unified credit exemption because the entire $1 million may be included in Joan's estate at her death. Assuming Joan did not remarry, the estate tax due at her death would be about $153,000.

A better plan for Claude might have been to establish a marital trust of $600,000, which would pay income to Joan for her life, and pass only $400,000 to her directly under the marital deduction. At Claude's death, his taxable estate would be $600,000, the equivalent of the unified credit, and once the credit is applied, the estate tax liability would be zero. As for Joan, she receives income from the $600,000 trust for her life and has only a $400,000 estate at death. The unified credit available to Joan's estate would reduce her estate tax to zero. Her heirs would benefit from a larger estate.

Property qualifying for the marital deduction includes, but is not limited to, outright bequests, qualifying life insurance proceeds, the deceased's share of joint tenancy with rights of survivorship property and property in a marital trust when the spouse has a power of appointment over it.

Gifting

A *gift* is any transfer of property for less than its fair market value. Many estate plans consist of a program of carefully planned lifetime gifts. Such a program allows estate owners to distribute property according to their wishes and also provides a means of reducing their current taxes and the taxes on their estate. For example, a donor may make an annual gift of $10,000 per recipient without incurring a gift tax. As a result of this annual exclusion, a large part of many estates may be transferred tax-free over a donor's lifetime.

A gifting program makes sense for a number of reasons:

- Taking advantage of the annual exclusion can eliminate some gift or estate taxes.

- Because gifts effectively reduce the size of an estate, taxes and administration costs, generally figured as a percentage of the overall estate, will be lower.

- Gifts of income-producing property may shift the current tax liability on the income to another party who is in a lower tax bracket.

- Gifts of appreciated investment property can often permanently reduce or eliminate capital gains tax liability.

- Nonfinancial pluses to a gifting program include providing resources to organizations about which the donor cares or having the pleasure of the seeing the donee's enjoyment of the gifts while the donor is still living.

Gift Tax Exclusion

In order to prevent taxpayers from avoiding tax liability by divesting themselves of their property through gifts, a gift tax is imposed on the donor and measured by the size of the gift. However, the *annual gift tax exclusion* allows an individual to make a nontaxable gift with no strings of up to $10,000 every year to each of any number of donees. The gift can be made to any party or any number of parties, without regard to the parties' relationship. Gifting property using the gift tax exclusion may present opportunities to "lighten" an estate without invading the lifetime transfer allowance afforded by the unified credit.

An exclusion of up to $20,000 is allowed for gifts made jointly to third parties by a married couple. This joint method of gifting is known as *"gift-splitting."* A gift tax form should be filed to document split gifts even though a tax is not levied. Only present interests qualify for the annual gift tax exclusion. Unlimited spouse-to-spouse gifts are permitted if the property would normally qualify for the marital deduction.

Charitable Gifts

Gifts may also be made to bona fide charities with favorable tax consequences. Lifetime gifts, within maximum limitations, will be currently deductible on the federal income tax forms of taxpayers who itemize. Postmortem transfers to qualifying charities remove the value of the transferred property from a decedent's taxable estate. There is no limit on the amount that may be distributed in a postmortem transfer. Several trust arrangements can be made in which principal and/or income pertaining to certain property can be allocated among donees, other beneficiaries and qualifying charities.

■ TRANSFERRING BUSINESS INTERESTS

When a family business is a major asset of an estate, the value of the business may be impaired substantially by the death of the estateholder, who is frequently the key person in the operation of the enterprise. The importance of planning for business continuation after the death of the estate owner cannot be underestimated. In many cases, life insurance can be used either to maintain the business as a going concern or to retain the values of the business interest for the benefit of the estate following the owner's death. Careful planning, combined with the skillful use of life insurance, may preserve the value of the business until it can be sold or passed to beneficiaries without disrupting business operations.

Buy-Sell Agreements

Every business owner should have a buy-sell agreement because many of the problems caused by the death or disability of a owner are resolved by prearranging a sale of the business. A *buy-sell agreement* is a written arrangement utilizing life insurance policy benefits to provide funds for buying out a deceased co-owner's or partner's proportional business interest. With a buy-sell agreement, the decedent's family or other designated party receives the economic value of the decedent's share of the business and the business goes on with the remaining owners. The advantages of a buy-sell agreement include:

- identifying a buyer before the owner's death;

- setting the price in a normal supply-and-demand environment;

- maintaining values for the heirs; and

- arranging for a smooth transition between owners.

The particular type of buy-sell agreement used will depend on many factors, such as the type of business operation involved and the particular disposition made of the interest.

- A *sole proprietor* or single owner may dispose of the business to one or more key employees, or a buy-sell agreement may be used to hand the business over to a family member.

- A *partner* may contract with other partners to sell his or her partnership interest to them at death through a cross-purchase plan or an entity-purchase agreement (discussed later).

- A *close corporation* stockholder may contract with co-shareholders to sell his or her stock to them at death through a cross-purchase agreement, or to contract with the business to purchase his or her stock outright at death.

The cash received by the deceased owner's estate on the sale of a business interest may be used to meet the cash demands made against the estate. The balance of the estate owner's assets may then pass substantially intact to the estate owner's family.

Cross-Purchase Plan

Life insurance can be used for full or partial funding of the purchase of the company. For example, a *cross-purchase plan* is one form of a buy-sell agreement using life insurance to fund the purchase. This plan forces the estate of a deceased owner to sell and a purchaser to buy at a prearranged price.

With a cross-purchase plan, each party to the plan owns a life insurance on the life of the other parties, in an amount equal to his or her share of the purchase price. To illustrate how a cross-purchase buy-sell agreement operates, assume that a manufacturing business has three equal partners: John, Mike and Kathy. They agree that in the event of death, the remaining two partners will purchase the deceased's share of the business. The business is valued at $1.8 million. Here's how this cross-purchase arrangement would be set up:

Owned by John	$300,000 life insurance on Mike	$300,000 life insurance on Kathy
Owned by Mike	$300,000 life insurance on John	$300,000 life insurance on Kathy
Owned by Kathy	$300,000 life insurance on John	$300,000 life insurance on Mike

If any of the three partners dies, the other partners have sufficient funds, provided by the life insurance proceeds, to acquire the deceased partner's share. The acquisition compensates the partner's family for the full value of the decedent's interest in the business. Insurance becomes a reliable means of having ready capital for the purchase, which will take place at a time that is virtually impossible to predict.

The Entity-Purchase Plan

In the *entity-purchase* version of the buy-sell agreement, the business, as a separate entity, owns insurance on the lives of the partners or shareholders, and is itself the beneficiary of the proceeds. At death, the proceeds are paid to the business, which in turn, purchases the deceased's interest from his or her estate. This price is prearranged or per the terms of a prearranged formula. Because the life insurance is not considered a necessary business expense, the premiums are not tax deductible. However, death benefits are not taxable and are used to carry on the firm's operations.

Unlike the cross-purchase agreement that obligates *each partner* to purchase a portion of the deceased partner's interest, an entity-purchase plan allows the *partnership* as an entity to purchase that interest. The advantages of the entity-purchase plan include equalization of premium payments among partners (regardless of age) and the benefit of cash values while the partners are living. These funds may be used for business expansion or emergencies.

■ PLANNING FOR ESTATES INVOLVING SIGNIFICANT OTHERS

As lifestyles change, new relationships must be addressed by estate planners. When your client has a "significant other" or "lifetime companion" rather than a legal spouse, many estate planning techniques traditionally available to married people may not be appropriate or legal.

- The marital deduction, as applied to both gift and transfers, cannot be implemented.

- Joint tenancies established with survivorship rights will be subject to having 100 percent of the asset's value included in the estate of the first to die unless it can be proven that the property was originally purchased by both parties.

The client with a significant other or lifetime companion, whether cohabitating or not, does have a few estate planning opportunities remaining at his or her disposal.

- *Make a witnessed will.* Without a will, it is very likely the significant other will be entirely disinherited. State intestacy laws make no provision for these relationships.

- *Convert the title to property from sole ownership into a tenancy in common.* This reduces the original sole owner's estate and provides the designated co-tenant with property and its corresponding income and/or appreciation.

- *Name the significant other as the beneficiary of the partner's life insurance and retirement accounts.* As lifestyles change, insurer challenges to beneficiary arrangements are becoming more rare.

■ PLANNING FOR INCAPACITY

In addition to concerns about wealth distribution after death, your clients should consider ways to protect their wealth if they become incapable of managing their personal and financial affairs. Although your clients may feel adequately protected by a will, some additional planning is necessary to address loss of mental or physical capacity due to illness or disease.

There are several methods that a person can used to protect assets and to assure that his or her wishes will be carried out. The most common methods used are joint bank accounts, a power of attorney, conservatorship and living wills.

Joint Bank Accounts

A *joint bank account* permits any account owner to withdraw funds. Such an arrangement is useful for people with poor eyesight or arthritis, which can make writing checks or keeping records difficult. When a bank account is held under *joint tenancy,* the assets pass directly to the surviving owner. This arrangement usually avoids probate, but some estate taxes may be due on large amounts.

Power of Attorney

A *power of attorney* is a legal arrangement that allows someone to act on another person's behalf. The provisions of the plan can be limited to paying bills or broadened to cover all finances, including investments. A power of attorney stops being effective when its maker, known as the *principal,* becomes incapacitated.

To be valid, a power of attorney must be witnessed and notarized as required by state law. Because the exercise of power of attorney is not supervised, mismanagement of a person's assets can and does happen.

ILL. 12.5 ■

The Mature market—Opening up a Dialogue

"What type of benefactor would you like to be?"

This can be a interesting question, perhaps even a compelling question, especially for people who have definite ideas on the subject. For those who have yet to identify their particular "type," Jeffery P. Rosenfeld, president of Plan Wise in Bayside, New York, has established a group of categories from which they can choose. He outlined the following "Four Styles of Giving" in *American Demographics,* (May 1992), based on research his company conducted with benefactors between 1985 and 1991.

Harmonizers (44 percent of the benefactors interviewed) focus on the specific needs of their potential beneficiaries or, as Rosenfeld puts it, they "strive for equity in the social sense."

Equalizers (31 percent) want to treat everyone equally and seek to create equal shares of their estates. An interesting element in this category is that equalizers want to safeguard their plans against potential litigation.

Caregivers (14 percent) are responding to a sense of responsibility—usually for children or grandchildren still living at home or under their care. Some focus their bequests on those who have given them care during their final years. Rosenfeld points out that one of their primary concerns is to conserve their dwindling assets.

Distancers (11 percent) want to make bequests to people or organizations outside their families— friends, charities, etc. According to Rosenfeld, people living in retirement communities are 35 percent more likely to make these types of bequests.

When approaching the mature client, ask the simple question, "What category do you think you fit into?" People enjoy this type of self-identification, and informative dialogue can be the result.

Source: Reprinted with permission from LIMRA's *Managers Magazine.*

Unlike a traditional power of attorney which becomes invalid if the person granting the right becomes incompetent, a *durable power of attorney* continues to operate after the incapacity or disability of the principal. Another approach to granting power of attorney is the *springing power of attorney* that activates *only* when the principal becomes incapacitated.

Conservatorship

Those families unable or unwilling to enter into joint bank accounts or power of attorney arrangements may petition the court to appoint a *conservator* or guardian to manage a disabled person's finances and estate. The court determines whether the disabled person is able to make sound decisions and, if not, a conservator is appointed. Once a conservator is appointed, the disabled person has no control over his or her finances.

Living Wills

Individuals may also have concerns about their wishes regarding medical science's ability to extend life for the terminally ill.

The use of a living will, a legal document that specifies whether "extraordinary" medical procedures should be used to prolong a person's life, helps to assure that an individual's desires are respected.

Living wills can specify whether a number of procedures—surgery, pain medication, life support—should be attempted or given when a patient is unable to make decisions about medical care. In states where they are legal, living wills override the wishes of relatives and protect the attending physician against lawsuits.

Although thinking of disability and incapacity is difficult, your clients should be prepared to face the possibility that, at some point, they may be unable to make decisions about their finances and medical care. You can guide them to an attorney who can make the necessary legal arrangements to handle decision-making in the event of incapacity. Your clients then can be assured that their wishes will be respected when important decisions are made.

■ **SUMMARY**

Estate planning consists of both financial and nonfinancial decisions that affect the estate owner's beneficiaries. As such, the estate plan should be carefully arranged to accomplish the estate owner's objectives while reducing as many costs as possible.

As a retirement planner, you can aid your clients in planning for their final wealth distribution. How well they accomplish this distribution depends in part on what you can do to help them prepare for it. With your help, your clients can analyze their current financial situation, make decisions about what they must do to transfer their wealth with minimal cost and maximum benefit and, finally, take action to attain those goals.

■ **CHAPTER 12 QUESTIONS FOR REVIEW**

1. When a person fails to prepare a valid will, the division of his or her property at his or her death is subject to the laws of

   a. shrinkage.
   b. intestacy.
   c. estate administration.
   d. estate transfer.

2. Which of the following is NOT an advantage of providing a will for one's surviving family?

   a. Individual needs are addressed.
   b. One can nominate his or her own executor.
   c. The decedent's spouse and children will not be required to share anything they do not wish to share.
   d. Selected items of property can be distributed to chosen individuals.

3. All of the following are reasons why a buy-sell agreement is beneficial to the estateholder who owns a business, EXCEPT:

   a. The surviving owners have less control of the business.
   b. Family members will enjoy continued economic support.
   c. Family members can control the business operations free of interference.
   d. The value of the business is preserved in liquid cash.

4. The federal estate tax is a tax imposed on the

   a. value of all property owned by a decedent.
   b. heirs of a decedent on the value of the property left to them by a will.
   c. transfer of property to a decedent's heirs at death.
   d. percentage share of a decedent's property left to each heir.

5. The goals of estate administration include all of the following, EXCEPT:

   a. to conserve estate assets.
   b. to protect the rights of creditors.
   c. to evade estate death taxes.
   d. to distribute property to heirs and beneficiaries.

..... Answer Key to Questions for Review

CHAPTER 1

1. b
2. c
3. b
4. d
5. c

CHAPTER 2

1. b
2. b
3. c
4. d
5. a

CHAPTER 3

1. a
2. b
3. b
4. d
5. c

CHAPTER 4

1. b
2. b
3. c
4. d
5. c

CHAPTER 5

1. b
2. d
3. d
4. c
5. c

CHAPTER 6

1. c
2. c
3. d
4. b
5. a

CHAPTER 7

1. a
2. b
3. c
4. a
5. c

CHAPTER 8

1. d
2. d
3. c
4. a
5. a

CHAPTER 9

1. a
2. b
3. d
4. a
5. b

CHAPTER 10

1. c
2. b
3. c
4. d
5. c

CHAPTER 11

1. a
2. c
3. c
4. b
5. c

CHAPTER 12

1. b
2. c
3. a
4. c
5. c